Progress in Metaphysics

THE JANUS LIBRARY

IMMANUEL KANT • What Real Progress Has
Metaphysics Made in
Germany since the Time
of Leibniz and Wolff?

TRANSLATION AND INTRODUCTION BY TED HUMPHREY

ABARIS BOOKS INC. • NEW YORK

Copyright © 1983 by Abaris Books, Inc.
International Standard Book Number 0-913870-56-0
Library of Congress Catalog Card Number 83-71751
First published 1983 by Abaris Books, Inc.
24 West 40th Street, New York, New York 10018
Printed in the United States of America
A Horace MacVaugh Production

To My Parents
Dorothy Place Humphrey
and
Charles B. Humphrey

Acknowledgements

The art of translating Kant's German into English has by now become highly refined; nonetheless, anyone who attempts to make—especially as a first attempt at translating Kant—the initial translation of a late, unfinished work will often be frustrated. Certainly I was. Thus, I most gratefully acknowledge Professor Gordon Treash's contribution to this project. He went completely through my original, completed translation, reworking sentences on almost every page. This is an arduous, utterly thankless task, and I owe him a debt of gratitude for having undertaken it. Of course, he had to begin with my original renderings and I was ultimate arbiter of which of his suggested changes to adopt, so final responsibility for the translation is mine.

The other help and encouragement I have received while working on this project exceeds my ability to recount, and I therefore mention only the highlights. My work was supported by an NEH Young Humanist summer stipend for 1976; in addition, the American Philosophical Society at Philadelphia provided a grant from its Penrose Fund (grant no. 7563) to defray research and manuscript preparation expenses. These grants were invaluable to my work. Several colleagues read and suggested revisions for various portions of the text; in this regard I want especially to thank Denward J. Wilson, J. Richard Creath, and Michael J. White. Professor Lewis White Beck read the entire manuscript and suggested numerous corrections that greatly improved it. Two secretaries have worked on the manuscript, Mrs. Ruth Bardrick, whose patience with my endless drafts and numerous crochets can neither be expressed nor adequately thanked, and Ms. Cathy J. Mullins, who typed the final manuscript. My wife, Janet, supported and encouraged me in this project from its outset. Without her loving care I would never have completed it.

T.H.

Contents

*Page numbers in brackets refer to the Academy edition.

Translator's Introduction

I. *General.* In his Preface to Kant's *What Real Progress Has Metaphysics Made in Germany since the Time of Leibniz and Wolff?*, Friedrich Theodor Rink states that "the occasion for this work is so well known" that he "can be excused from writing about it at length." What may have been true in 1804, when, shortly after Kant's death, the work was first published, is certainly not so now. Today the work is virtually unknown and, except in Max Wundt's, Heinz Heimsoeth's, and Hermann-Jean de Vleeschauwer's writings, has never played a substantial role in interpreting Kant's thought. This is unfortunate because, while the history of the text raises scholarly problems that I will discuss later, the work has a number of virtues: First, the *Progress* is the only synoptic account of the critical philosophy, both its propadeutic and constructive parts, written by Kant himself, and his argument that the critical philosophy included a means for transcending to the supersensuous is especailly noteworthy. Second, we find in this work Kant's most detailed account of his place in the history of philosophy. Third, it contains a concise critical analysis of the Leibnizian system, along with Kant's evaluation of its major failings. This is particularly important for those who approach Kant's thought from the perspective of Anglo-American philosophy, because, by emphasizing Hume's role in Kant's development, it has traditionally failed to ascribe sufficient importance to Leibniz's. Finally, Max Wundt attached special significance to Kant's *Progress* for the interpretation of his metaphysical views, and de Vleeschauwer has called it the "Cinderella" among Kant's writings.[1] Close study and reflection will, I think, bear these opinions out.

Kant wrote the *Progress* in response to a Prize Question first announced by Nicolas de Bequelin at the session on January 24, 1788 of the Royal Academy of Sciences at Berlin. The original date for submitting manuscripts for judgment by the Academy was 1791. However, for some as yet undiscovered reason, the question, which was published in French— *"Quels sont les progrès réel de la*

Translator's Introduction

Métaphysique en Allemagne depuis les temps de Leibnitz et de Wolff? — was not officially announced until 1790, when the date for submitting manuscripts was set at January 1, 1792. Only one manuscript, by Johann Christoph Schwab — an adherent to the Leibnizio-Wolffian School Philosophy and one of the founders, with J.A. Eberhard and J.G. Maass, of the *Philosophisches Magazin*, in which Leibniz's and Wolff's views were defended against the pretensions of Kant's — was received by that date. Consequently, the Academy *again* delayed the submission date, this time to June 1, 1795. By then it had received more than thirty responses, from which it selected three for special recognition. These were by Schwab, who received the prize, and Karl Leonhard Reinhold and Johann Heinrich Abicht, both defenders of Kant's views. All three manuscripts were published by the Academy under the title *Preisschriften über die Frage: Welche Fortschritte hat die Metaphysik seit Leibnitzens und Wolff's Zeiten in Deutschland gemacht?* in 1796 by Friedrich Maurer. A fourth submission by Christian F. Jenisch, another defender of Kant's views, received an honorable mention.

Because never completed, Kant's was not among the manuscripts submitted to the Academy. Just what his attitude toward the prize competition was and why he did not actually complete his essay we do not know. On the one hand, the Academy's question must have been consummately interesting to him because he clearly regarded his philosophy as a distinct advance beyond that of his German predecessors. Furthermore, the question was announced just when he was polemically engaged with adherents of the traditional School philosophy, who were claiming that Kant's views, where true, contained no significant advance over Leibniz's and Wolff's. In response to these claims, found primarily in writings by Eberhard, Maass and Schwab, Kant published in 1790 a strident defense of his views entitled *On a Discovery According to which Any New Critique of Pure Reason Has Been Made Superfluous by an Earlier One*. The Prize question announced by the Academy, then, would seem to have provided Kant a unique opportunity to state his views on the place of his philosophy in German thought and to explain just what advances over the School philosophy it made. But his essay remained uncompleted and unsubmitted.

For whatever reasons, Kant did not begin work on his essay when the Prize question was first announced, nor even immediately after it was officially announced in 1790. The first concrete evidence we have

that he was considering responding to the question dates from 1793, after the date for submission of manuscripts had been postponed for a third time, to June, 1795. Two preliminary reflections that were in all likelihood written in 1793 contain brief outlines and sketches of topics with which Kant deals in the *Progress*.[2] We possess other such unattached reflections, but they are not datable, and therefore we cannot more closely approximate the time that Kant became interested in the Academy's Question. Nor do we know when Kant decided no longer to work on the *Progress*. The work that we have was compiled by Frederich Theodor Rink — a friend and dinner companion to Kant — from three separate incomplete manuscripts that Kant handed over to him in 1800 or 1802. Precisely what the dates of the manuscripts are, why Kant gave up the project, and, finally, what his state of mind was when he turned them over to Rink for publication are mysteries about which we can only speculate.[3] We are thus left with the option of accepting or rejecting Kant's *Progress* solely on the intrinsic merits of its content.

II. *The Text*. The sole text that we possess for the *Progress* is the one that Rink published in April, 1804, two months after Kant's death. The manuscripts from which it was compiled were reported lost by Erich Adikes in 1911, in his preface to the Academy edition of the *Nachlass*.[4] All subsequent efforts have failed to uncover the original. This is unfortunate if only because we have no standard against which to check Rink's editorial intuitions, and we must accept largely on faith the view that he did nothing to the text that would substantially alter its meaning. However, in another context, Traugott Weisskopf has cast considerable doubt on Rink's general character and on his competence as an editor in particular. While Weisskopf does not discuss the *Progress*, his criticisms of Rink's handling of the materials making up both the *Physical Geography* and the *Pedagogy*, both included in volume nine of the Academy edition, certainly provide grounds for not being uncritically accepting of anything in which Rink had a hand, though none of Weisskopf's criticisms of Rink's editorial work can be carried over directly to what we know of his handling of the *Progress*. The fact remains, we have no choice but to accept the text as Rink presented it to us.[5] He does provide some sparse information about (1) how he assembled the text, (2) what specific flaws he found in the manuscripts, and (3) his concern that the friends of critical philosophy not be betrayed by his (Rink's) editing, all contained in his introduction. Inasmuch as the

Translator's Introduction

Progress does not so much extend Kant's earlier published views as it restates and summarizes them, a point toward which my notes to the translation are directed, I think we are justified in using it in our attempt to deepen our understanding of Kant's views.

The only substantial source of complaint that we can have to Rink's editing is the one expressed by de Vleeschauwer, namely, that Rink provides no clues as to the location in the manuscripts of the marginalia found in Supplement III on pages 329-332 of the text. Similarly, the relation to the *Progress* of the reflections on loose sheets that are generally associated with it also remains a matter of speculation. In "La Composition du Preisschrift d'Immanuel Kant sur les progrés de la mètaphysique," de Vleeschauwer attempts to identify the original textual location of each of the marginalia in Supplement III.[6] He justifies this by arguing that Rink's designation of them as marginalia implies that they are intrinsically related to the text. On the other hand, de Vleeschauwer argues that we can regard the reflections on loose sheets only as *Vorarbeiten*, preparatory jottings, that have no intrinsic relation to the actual text.[7] This view seems correct, especially inasmuch as we can infer that since Rink did not include them in his supplements to the text, they were not among the manuscript materials that Kant turned over to him. The loose sheet reflections that take up topics that Kant discusses in the *Progress* stand in the same relation to it as do those that consider topics dealt with in other works to those works. The *Progress*'s incompleteness does not alter this fact.

Rink's edited text is compiled from three manuscripts that Rink states Kant gave him. Specifically, the text we have derives from the three manuscripts as follows:

1. Pages 259-286, beginning with Kant's "Introduction" and inclusive of but ending with "The First Stage of Metaphysics in the Period and Country under consideration," are taken from manuscript 1.

2. Pages 286-311, beginning with "Metaphysics: The Second Stage" and ending with the "Overview," are taken from manuscript 2.

3. Supplement No. I, pages 315-326, contains a more polished opening for the *Progress*, one written from a more conceptual

point of view; it is an alternate version of the material found on pages 259-271.

4. Supplement No. II, pages 326-329, is a version of the material on pages 286-292, and is the final part of manuscript 1.

5. Pages 329-332 contain marginalia to manuscript 2, according to de Vleeschauwer.

The fundamental textual oddities are asterisks that Rink tells us mark lacunae in the manuscripts. These occur on pages 276, 277, 280, 290 and 292. The breaks in the train and development of thought are immediately apparent on pages 276 and 297. The asterisks on page 280 come at the end of a passage, so one cannot determine whether the passage is conceptually incomplete or whether it could just have been expanded. The same indeterminacy arises on pages 290 and 292, although there the asterisks seem to mark places where the argument could have been expanded for clarity's sake. The asterisks seem to have been inserted by Rink, not Kant.

The text that I have used for the translation, and the one facing it, is the one published by the Preussischen Akademie der Wissenschaften and edited by Gerhard Lehmann, namely, Immanuel Kant über die von der König. Akademie der Wissenschaften zu Berlin fur das Jahr 1791 ausgesetzte Preisfrage: *Welches sind die wirklichen Fortschritte, die die Metaphysik seit Leibnitzens und Wolff's zeiten in Deutschland gemacht hat?* in *Kant's gesammelte Schriften,* hrsg. Preussischen Akademie der Wissenschaften (28 vols.; Berlin: Walter de Gruyter and Co., 1902-.), vol. XX, pp. 253-351. In addition, I consulted Rink's original edition of the work — same title as in the Akademie edition, hrsg. D. Friedrich Theodor Rink, (Königsberg: Goebbles und Unzer, 1804- and the French translation by Louis Guillermit — Immanuel Kant, *Les Progrès de la métaphysique en Allemagne depuis le Temps de Leibniz et de Wolff,* 2nd. ed., (Paris: Librairie Philosophique, J. Vrin, 1973).

In translating specific terms that recur throughout Kant's critical corpus and thereby assume specific technical roles I have followed the translations given them by the translators cited at the beginning of the endnotes. I did this so that readers could move among the English translations without consulting the German.

Translator's Introduction

III. *The Place of the Progress in the Kantian Corpus.* Kant's *Progress* is everywhere flawed by rhetorical and conceptual incompleteness. Furthermore, the fact that Kant did not see the work through the press himself, leaving this job to Rink, probably without even reviewing the state of the manuscripts before releasing them, casts the work's usefulness into question. Nonetheless, one cannot help concluding that the *Progress* is an important work in the critical corpus. In it, even in its present state, Kant does two things: First, because it pertains to the nature of the Academy's Prize Question, he provides an account of the historical and conceptual relations in which he understands the critical philosophy to stand to the thought of Leibniz and Wolff, especially the former. Second, Kant goes beyond characterizing the critical philosophy as a propaedeutic to metaphysics and sets out a "practical-dogmatic" transition to metaphysics as its culmination. As Max Wundt and H.-J. de Vleeschauwer note, this is a significant new step.[8]

These features of the *Progress* allow it to be contrasted with *On a Discovery According to which Any New Critique of Pure Reason Has Been Made Superfluous by an Earlier One,* which Kant published in 1790. This work, which de Vleeschauwer characterizes as deriving from the "same epoque and the same inspiration"[9] as the *Progress,* is marked by a strident polemicism that often interferes with Kant's presentation of his views. Moreover, it is directed more at the Wolffian views of Eberhard than at Leibniz, which diminishes its value. For while Eberhard's views are certainly the product of his adherence to and development of the Leibnizio-Wolfffian School philosophy, they remain Eberhard's views and therefore cannot lay claim to the same degree of importance as Leibniz's, or Wolff's for that matter. Nor can a refutation of them, even by Kant, claim the same level of significance as a refutation of Leibniz's views. Kant's *Discovery* leaves one with the impression that he could, when necessary, be an effective polemicist. But it did not come naturally to him.

Even though occasioned by the Academy's Prize Question, which de Vleeschauwer suspects of having partially been a product of Eberhard's assault on Kant's views[10]—a fact that, if true, Kant must have been aware of—the *Progress* received its fundamental inspiration from the conceptual core of Kant's own thought. This is why, despite the general similarities of their focus, namely, the critical philosophy's relationship to Leibniz's and Wolff's thought, the *Progress* is far more positive than the *Discovery*, charged with Kant's

16

own conception of the nature of metaphysics and of the way in which the critical philosophy is consummated by fulfilling that conception. The negative portion of the *Progress*, its criticisms of Leibniz's doctrines of the indiscernibility of conceptual identicals, of sufficient reason, of pre-established harmony and of monadology, are not just a product of Kant's specific doctrinal disagreements with them. They also derive from Kant's perception that they cannot actually fulfill the end that pure reason has in view, however vaguely, when it engages in metaphysics. The focus of Kant's *Progress* is to instruct the reader concerning (1) the essence of metaphysics with regard to its unique intention as a field of human investigation, (2) an account of the origins, elements and limits of human knowledge as set out in the *Critique of Pure Reason*, (3) the reasons why previous attempts, especially Leibniz's and Wolff's, in attaining metaphysics' specific, unique end have failed and (4) the nature of critical philosophy's attempt at attaining pure reason's ends in pursuing metaphysics.

These goals roughly correspond to the *Progress's* major divisions as set out below:

Translator's Introduction

Each of these major topics is discussed in the next section.

IV. *The Progress's Doctrines*.

A. *Metaphysics*. Metaphysics receives a general characterization in three different passages in the manuscripts constituting the *Progress*. In each Kant states that two features distinguish it from all other forms of investigation, namely, its systematic unity and its concern with the non-sensuous. In fact, these go in tandem. Regarding the first, he maintains that metaphysics exists "almost always only as an idea," and that "its essence and ultimate intention...is to be a perfect whole: either nothing or everything." (8)[11] Metaphysics differs from the empirical sciences, which suffer from an intrinsic lack of completeness that derives from their reliance on empirical data, even though, like metaphysics, they contain a pure rational component. The fundamental difference between metaphysics and the natural sciences on this count, then, is that while the latter may contain an inner core of coherent a priori theory, they must seek empirical facts in furthering knowledge. But searching for such data is inconsistent with the very concept of "metaphysics," which connotes knowledge that is independent of the physical or sensuous.

Metaphysical knowledge must derive from pure reason alone and its content is therefore determined by reason's nature and limits. Thus, the possibility of metaphysical knowledge "presupposes a critique of the entire capacity of pure reason," (321) in which one thoroughly assesses its capacity not only for a priori knowledge of the sensuous but also for transcending the boundaries of the sensuous. Kant's view that a critique of pure reason is required as a propadeutic to metaphysics is found in his earliest critical writings and, indeed, exists even in his essay of 1763, *Enquiry concerning the clarity of the principles of natural theology and ethics*. This view derives from his conviction that the compulsion to seek metaphysical

knowledge, to do metaphysics, is a "natural disposition" (B22)[12] of human pure reason and that "to a greater or lesser degree all men engage in metaphysics." (259) Kant's convictions regarding these human predilections raise questions not only as to why men feel so compelled to pursue metaphysical knowledge but also what they intend to gain by doing so.

Kant finds answers to these questions in his conception of the structure of human reason. Human reason is a faculty fit for knowledge. Properly speaking, human knowledge is conceptualized intuition, intuition providing content and concepts articulable form. (A51/B75) But all objects of knowledge are conditioned by virtue of the form imposed on them in acts of knowing; they necessarily stand in spatial, temporal and conceptual relations. However, Kant isolates a feature of pure concepts that imposes the requirement that their scope and use receive a deduction or justification, on the one hand, and yet, on the other, makes metaphysical speculation possible (A87/B120-A89/B121): Pure concepts can be employed independently of all sensuous content. Thus freed, reason can pursue the unconditioned through a sequence of inferences from the conditioned, dependent existents that the sensible realm comprises to the conditions or principles that can be regarded as their source of explanation. (A303/B359-A305/B361) In pursuing metaphysical knowledge, then, men seek the unconditioned, which can be found only through a transition from the sensuous to the non-sensuous. In the *Progress* Kant defines metaphysics as the science of making this transition. (259-60) Metaphysics is a possible science because man's faculty for conceptualizing can function independently of his capacity for intuiting. It is a natural and inevitable science because men require completeness in their vision of reality, a completeness that sensible knowledge alone cannot supply. Thus, Kant describes metaphysics as "a whole that, like pure logic, neither calls for nor permits additions." (310)

Kant distinguishes three stages in man's pursuit of a non-sensuous, unconditioned principle of reality. "The first was the stage of dogmatism, the second skepticism, and the third criticism of pure reason. This temporal order is based on the nature of the human capacity for knowledge." (264) Both de Vleeschauwer and Wundt note that these three stages not only occur in the history of metaphysics but also, and perhaps more importantly, are intrinsic to the very nature of metaphysical speculation, inasmuch as it derives.

Translator's Introduction

from the requirements and natural dispositions of human nature.[13] Attributing these stages to metaphysics is not unique to the *Progress*. One finds its history characterized in this way as early as 1781, in the Preface to the first edition of the *Critique of Pure Reason* (Aix-xii), in *On a Discovery*[14] and in *Perpetual Peace*.[15] But two points become clear only in the *Progress*, namely, that the stages are both historically and *conceptually* related and that critical philosophy not only contains a propaedeutic to metaphysics but also has a unique theory of the nature and validity of the transition human reason can make from the sensuous to the non-sensuous.

Dogmatic metaphysicians take their inspiration for seeking metaphysical knowledge from mathematics. Mathematical like metaphysical knowledge is a priori and its certainty appears to be beyond dispute. It would seem natural, then, that if one could appropriate its method for metaphysics, the latter could comprise a body of certain truth. The crucial flaw in this approach to metaphysics is that it rests on a disanalogy. Inasmuch as mathematics consists of synthetic a priori judgments, it certainly resembles the knowledge we pursue in metaphysics; however, its propositions, Kant argues, refer necessarily to space and time as their content. They are thus far sensible, and, in that respect, more like principles in the natural sciences than in metaphysics. The sources of a priority in mathematics are pure concepts and *intuitions*, and their reference to intuition is their source of certainty and indisputability. By contrast, Kant contends that metaphysical truth *cannot* involve any reference whatsoever to (human) intuition, because all human intuition is, for him, sensible. Kant agrees with dogmatists that metaphysics will necessarily comprise a body of certain truth, and, what was denied for different reasons by *all* of his predecessors, that its truths are a priori *and* synthetic. However, because it lacks an intuitive component it cannot have the cognitive significance enjoyed by mathematical truth. The disanalogy between mathematical and metaphysical knowledge rests on the latter's essential failure to refer to the sensible. (261-62)

The dogmatists' theory that the method of transition from the sensuous to the non-sensuous in metaphysics is properly based on an analogy with mathematical method was defective and their attempts at thus making the transition were bound to fail. But they did not fail in any overt and obvious manner; for so long as their systems were internally consistent, they could be defended, if not proven true. Nonetheless, their procedure naturally and inevitably led to skepti-

cism, in which the various systems are opposed to one anther so as to induce an inability to decide among them. The skeptical phase of metaphysics derives from the observation that different metaphysical systems can demonstrate their truth only indirectly, by showing that the opposed system is inconsistent or otherwise inadequate. But since all systems are equally capable of such proof and equally subject to such disproof, all come to be seen as equally subject to doubt. Thus, Kant conceives skepticism as "a demand placed on dogmatic philosophers to justify even the a priori principles underlying the possibility of experience." (263)

In characterizing skepticism as a stand off between competing metaphysical systems that requires resolution before one proceeds in making synthetic knowledge claims a priori, Kant clearly envisioned it as having both an historical and a systematic nature. Skepticism here is not just or perhaps even primarily the pyrrhonian skepticism of Sextus Empiricus or the naturalistic skepticism of Hume, neither of whom gave credence to a positive metaphysics of any sort. Kant's theory of the skeptical standstill isolates a motive for executing a critique of pure reason's powers. In turn, the latter provides grounds for dismissing the dogmatists' view that, like natural science and mathematics, metaphysics is a theoretically dogmatic enterprise and for accepting Kant's contention that it can only be a practical-dogmatic one. In Kant's critical philosophy, the Dialectic, especially the antinomies, in which fundamental theories of the principles of existence are opposed to one another, play a critical and multiple role. First, they are an attempt to show that the major dogmatic metaphysical systems are equipollently opposed. Second, by showing how Kant's theory of the elements and limits of human knowledge both expose and resolve the antinomies, they demonstrate its truth. Third, by showing that we are justified in believing in freedom's reality, even if we cannot know that it exists, they prepare the way for the practical-dogmatic transition to the non-sensible that Kant sees as critical philosophy's unique metaphysical innovation. Before examining this new contribution, we shall briefly explore the *Progress's* account of the nature and limits of human knowledge and its criticisms of Leibniz.

B. *The Critique of Man's Faculties of Knowledge.* In the first major section of the *Progress*, pages 265-280, Kant sketchily recapitulates the theories of judgment, faculties for knowledge, and conditions and limits of synthetic a priori knowledge that he developed in the

Translator's Introduction

Critique of Pure Reason. At the beginning of the section he states that assessing the progress of transcendental philosophy in modern times requires three steps: (1) distinguishing between analytic and synthetic judgments; (2) determining how a priori judgments are possible; (3) determining how it is possible to gain a priori knowledge from synthetic judgments. Unfortunately, he does not systematically follow this outline, and the manuscript is to that extent confusing. However, I will follow the outline in the following brief summary of his theory.

(1) Distinguishing among kinds of judgments is the first and, perhaps, most crucial move in critical philosophy. All of Kant's subsequent views regarding metaphysical knowledge, particularly in regard to its nature, its relation to mathematical and scientific knowledge, and the possibility of man's attaining it, rest on these distinctions. Judgments fall into two broad classes, analytic and synthetic. The first are those whose "predicate only clearly (*explicite*) represents what was thought in the concept of the subject, even though obscurely (*implicite*)." (322) Kant's major concern in the *Progress* is to distinguish his sense of analytic judgment from the Leibnizian-Wolffian doctrine of identical judgments. Identities, he claims, "contribute nothing to the clarification of concepts" and are "called empty." Analytic judgments on the other hand "are *based* on and can be resolved into identities," but they also analyze the component elements of concepts and thereby actually clarify them. Kant's distinction here is fine. He holds that analytic judgments and identities resemble one another in not extending our knowledge; they are not ampliative. They differ because identities do not even clarify concepts, while analytic judgments do. Identities cannot convey information because their subject and predicate concepts actually repeat one another. Analytic judgments convey information because the predicate concept, by being a (partial) analysis of the subject concept, clarifies it.[16]

Synthetic judgments extend knowledge because their predicates "contain something that was not thought in the concept of the subject." (322) While analytic judgments are "strictly universal and absolutely necessary," (323) synthetic ones can either be empirical and therefore contingent or a priori, in which case they, too, are strictly universal. On this scheme knowledge claims divide into three classes, and a fundamental issue is to determine into which one various bodies of knowledge fall. Included among analytic judgments are all

22

judgments properly belonging to that area of metaphysics called ontology, for they merely clarify our a priori concepts (260; 315-16). Synthetic judgments a posteriori, which include all ordinary and scientific judgments based on experience, present no more problems for explaining their possibility than analytic judgments. But synthetic judgments a priori, of which mathematics and the pure theoretical principles of science are examples, require an explanation. This is especially pressing because the metaphysical claims that most interest us, those that will allow us to make a transition from the sensible to the supersensible, must belong to this class. For only synthetic judgments a priori extend knowledge and are independent of experience. The press of the desire for metaphysical knowledge forces us to submit pure reason's capabilities to a critique. As Kant puts it:

> The foregoing problem permits no other solution than this: that before going further we consider the relation to those faculties of man by means of which he is able to extend his knowledge a priori, as well as which faculties constitute in *him* what can be specifically called *his* pure reason. (324)

(2) Kant conceived knowledge in the strict sense, cognition (*die Erkenntnis*), to comprise two components. He writes,

> An object is *given* through an intuition that conforms with a concept; without this it is only a thought. Through intuition alone, without a concept, an object is indeed given, but not thought; through concepts, without corresponding intuition, it is thought, but none is given; in neither case is it cognized. (325; cf. A51/B75)

Determining whether synthetic a priori metaphysical knowledge is possible requires that we examine these fundamental faculties of knowledge.

Intuition is (in man) one of the two complementary ways in which a content can be present to consciousness.[17] It is the presentational mode, by which what is presented is apprehended in its particularity. Intuitions comprise both material and formal elements; the former constitutes their particularizing aspects, while the latter constitutes their shared characteristics, namely space and time. For reasons developed fully only in the *Critique of Pure Reason* (A22/B37-A36/B53), Kant maintains that these are pure forms of intuition, by which he means that they comprise the presentational form of the

relations in which we can apprehend the sensations by means of which we perceive objects. The view that space and time are a priori forms of intuition rests on these considerations: Kant accepted Leibniz's views that only substances and their relations exist, that the existence of relations is contingent upon that of substances, and that relations lack causal efficacy and therefore cannot affect sensibility. But he rejected Leibniz's view that we perceive things as spatially and temporally related solely as a function of their intrinsic properties. The reason for rejecting this view was Kant's discovery of spatial and temporal asymmetries exemplified by incongruent counterparts, which do not allow us to give a complete conceptual analysis of space and time.[18]

When Kant says that space and time are pure forms of intuition, he necessarily denies that we perceive them, i.e., become aware of them through affection of sensibility. Rather they derive from "the natural constitution of a subject capable of representing objects in intuition." (267) They derive from it in the sense that by virtue of our natural constitution for being affected, we organize sensations spatially and temporally. Space and time are subjective in two ways: first, they derive from the knowing subject, not things-in-themselves. Second, so far as we can know they pertain only to humans. Kant admits that space and time are not necessary forms of presentational apprehension; we can conceive of beings who intuit either directly, thus without need of sensation and, therefore, perhaps without the forms of space and time or in accord with some other forms. But *we* cannot intuit in either of those ways. (267) Kant's claims about space and time are thus restricted to humans and their knowledge, to which they apply universally. Because space and time have subjective origins, Kant says that they are transcendentally ideal, but, inasmuch as they are universally present in what man apprehends presentationally, they are nonetheless empirically real. (268) This account of human intuition and its forms adequately explains with respect to one of its sources how synthetic a priori cognition is possible for men.

Kant's account of the pure concepts of the understanding in the *Progress* is terse, a surprising fact if only because no other aspect of the critical philosophy was so difficult for him to develop and express. The *Progress's* presentation falls into two parts: pages 271-73 correspond to their metaphysical deduction and pages 273-76 to their transcendental deduction.

Kant initiates his discussion of a priori concepts with an argument that is very similar to the one in section 15 of the *Critique of Pure Reason* (B129-30). This argument is very general, and seems to have been adopted primarily for that reason, since Kant surely did not want to reproduce the specifics of his deductions. Establishing the single point that representing something in intuition as a complex whole requires that it be composed in understanding is sufficient for Kant's needs.[19] When we are presentationally aware of something we in fact apprehend it as a unity. But because our capacity for intuition is sensible, receptive, it cannot present us with complex unities, for receptivity does not involve agency. It follows that the unity of the multifarious intuition we actually apprehend entails not only the forms of sensibility but also the power or agency in us to combine. By combining we determine the manifold of receptively apprehended intuition, determine in the sense that we comprehend it as an inter-related unity rather than as a field of the merely indefinitely presented, a field in which nothing can be "made out." Now while sensation might come from a unified entity, it cannot have unity *for us* unless we unify it. Furthermore, only if a manifold of intuition is composed by us so as to be a unity can it seem to refer to some other unity that might exist independently of us. The understanding is, at its most rudimentary, the power of composing; consequently, the ability to comprehend the manifold apprehended in intuition as an object entails understanding. And for Kant unity comprises the fundamental concept of an object in general.

"Composedness as such is not a mere intuition," but an a priori concept; it "is a fundamental concept originally in the understanding that is the basis for all concepts of the objects of the senses." (271) Conception is the fundamental agency of knowing subjects as such, and it is the means by which they unify for themselves what they merely receive through sensibility. The primordial pure concept is simply that of unity, which provides the most primitive, undifferentiated concept of an object in general. There are, as functions of this fundamental unity, more specific ones by which we articulate the relations within and among unities, and Kant calls these the pure concepts of the understanding or categories. Kant's view here (271-72) is that the pure concepts of the understanding are irreducible to one another and in that sense are unique specific categories, although they are not severally primitive. They are purely intellectual "forms of thought for the concept of an object in general, no matter what

kind it may be, even if it is non-sensible intuition." (272)[20] Kant goes no further than this in developing his theory of the pure concepts of understanding in the *Progress*, not it seems because he left the manuscript incomplete, but rather because this is the sketch of the fundamental strategy for accounting for the categories as he did in the *Critique of Pure Reason*. The *Progress*'s account reduces the second edition derivation of the categories to its most basic steps.

(3) Having argued that there are some absolutely irreducible intellectual concepts, Kant confronts his central problem: Given these concepts, can men have metaphysical knowledge as traditionally conceived? Can they transcend to knowledge of supersensible being merely in virtue of these concepts? This is the question that forces a justification or deduction of our right to use them in various circumstances.

The section of the *Progress* in which Kant discusses the (transcendental) deduction and schematization of the categories is even more brief in its argumentation than the one on concepts. It proceeds through a sequence of *reductio ad absurdum* arguments to show that the theoretically cognitive use of pure concepts requires that they be used only in relation to intuition. The crucial step in the argument is the distinction between knowing and thinking. Strictly speaking, knowing is theoretical knowledge in which "a concept must be combined in the same representation with an intuition of an object so that the former is represented as containing the latter." (273) Granted this, all human knowledge must be sensible, because all human intuition is. Men have no other source of intuition to which they can apply pure concepts.

Having so restrictively defined knowledge, Kant must deal with the nature of its relation to experience. He begins this discussion when he writes "knowledge of the objects of the senses as such...is experience. Accordingly, our theoretical knowledge never transcends the field of experience." Theoretical knowledge and experience are coextensive, which raises the question of their relative priority, especially in light of the ordinary sense of the term experience, namely, that it is simply an isolated act of perception. Kant's acceptance of this as the commonly accepted sense of the term is clearly indicated by his distinction between the *questio facti* of experience, i.e., the question about what it begins with, and the *questio juris* about experience, i.e., the question about whether all experience derives from these beginnings. (274-75, A1-2; B1-3; A84/B116-A85/B117) If all

experience began and originated in perception, the rudimentary sense of experience, then one would have to admit the "empiricism of transcendental philosophy." (275) But Kant has already demonstrated the a priority of the pure forms of intuition and categories, so empiricism cannot provide an adequate answer to the *questio juris.*

Empiricism's failure underlies Kant's reconceptualization of experience, not only regarding its origins but also regarding the very definition of the term. Conceiving of experience as perception or as a mere collection of perceptions is inadequate; rather experience properly consists of the coherence and regularity that "makes it possible for understanding to apprehend them under universal laws and to discover their unity in accordance with principles." (275) The unity, lawfulness, and coherence of what we experience derive from our ability to know. The essential common feature of the aspects of human knowledge that Kant argues are a priori is that they are all relations. Space and time are contexts of presentational relations and the categories are conceptual relations that can be either applied to intuition or be used independently of it. These relations taken together constitute the most fundamental unity of coherent regularity, and this comprises experience in the normative sense that Kant attaches to that term.

Kant's view, which he shares with Leibniz, is that relations cannot affect sensibility. Beginning with this he developed the theory that the very structure of experience must be transcendentally ideal, even if empirically real. Thus, he concludes that, "These concepts demonstrate their reality in sensible intuition, and in conjunction with intuition they make *experience* possible according to its form, which is given a priori." (276) *The capacity to know is logically prior to experience* in both of the senses that Kant admits for that term.

Having established this relationship between knowledge and experience, Kant argues that we can use pure concepts in two very distinct ways. Concepts can be either schematized or symbolized. In the first instance, "Objective reality is directly attributed (*directe*) to a concept by an intuition corresponding to it." (279) Now this can be done for mathematical concepts and the pure concepts of understanding. That is, Kant maintains that the former are constructed and the latter schematized, i.e., shown to unify specific configurations of time (and space), in pure intuition. Since the schematized use of concepts constitutes the foundation of science, Kant claims that concepts have a theoretically dogmatic use in experience, science and

mathematics. Not only are they a priori, but because we can provide an a priori sensuous content for them, they are objectively valid. Pure intuition provides the foundation for the ampliative transition from the subject to the predicate concept in an a priori synthetic judgment.

In metaphysics we do not deal with a sensible subject matter, and as a consequence intuition, or at least human intuition, cannot provide a basis for making a transition from subject to predicate concept. This means that metaphysical claims simply cannot have the same sort of validity that those in experience, science, and mathematics do. Even if we do not view metaphysics negatively, and Kant surely does not, we must admit that the basis for our assent and thus the nature of the validity we can ascribe to metaphysical propositions must differ from those we give to experiential claims. Rather than a schematized meaning, we give metaphysical concepts a symbolic one, that is, a meaning that is conceived on the basis of an analogy with experiential objects. (280) All reasoning that occurs with respect to metaphysical concepts properly so called rests on analogies, by which they provide those concepts and our reasoning with respect to them with the semblance of content.[21] Thus our assent to metaphysical propositions seems to have the same kind of basis as that to experiential ones. This is simply an illusion that the critique of our faculty of knowledge is intended to expose. In consequence of these results, Kant proceeds to examine specific metaphysical claims.
C. *The Progress's Metaphysical Doctrines.* In section two, pages 281-296, Kant evaluates metaphysical progress in Germany since Leibniz's and Wolff's time. He distinguishes among three conceptually related stages. (1) The first he calls the stage of its "theoretical-dogmatic departure," by which he means the attempt to extend pure rational (i.e., theoretical) knowledge without a critique of human pure reason's capacity for it. This stage is exemplified by Leibniz's views. (2) The second stage is skeptical standstill, which is exemplified by Kant's own doctrine of the antinomies, in which he shows that metaphysics based on theoretically dogmatic principles is doomed to frustration. (3) The final stage is the "practical-dogmatic completion" of metaphysics, which is found in the critical philosophy. Kant's discussion of this stage actually takes up the rest of the manuscript, from page 293 to 311. We will consider them in order.

Translator's Introduction

(1) Kant's criticism of Leibniz focuses on four of his metaphysical principles and doctrines, the principles of the identity of indiscernibles (282) and sufficient reason (282-83), his system of preestablished harmony (283-84), and his monadology (284-85).[22] Kant's essential claim with respect to these Leibnizian doctrines is that they fail to get beyond ontology, i.e., the analysis and clarification of pure concepts. As purely conceptual principles, they are inadequate to provide a sufficient theoretical underpinning for knowledge and therefore they cannot serve as sufficient metaphysical principles of the world as we experience it. Kant constantly points to Leibniz's attempt to provide a wholly conceptual account of reality based on his view that space and time and, therefore, perception involve an essential confusion that can be eliminated by conceptual analysis. This was one of the views that the transcendental aesthetic is supposed to show false. Space and time, as we have seen are *sui generis* representations that cannot be given an adequate conceptual analysis. Instead, they are the pure presentational forms in relationship to which otherwise purely conceptual principles and doctrines take on material meaning that applies to what humans perceive. By Kant's lights, Leibniz must accept the view either that there are two intrinsically distinct worlds, the noumenal and phenomenal, between which there are no common principles, with the consequence that transition from one to the other is impossible, or that only one world actually exists, with the result that the other, the perceptual one in Leibniz's case, is illusory. Leibniz chooses the latter alternative, the one Kant rejects. Kant's differences with Leibniz on these issues are a function of their views concerning space and time. His contention that Leibniz's metaphysical views are the result of having failed adequately to discern the nature of space, time, and perception and their role in human knowledge recurs as a litany throughout this section. A single passage captures its essence: "the lack of any a priori intuition, which was not recognized as a principle, and which Leibniz instead intellectualized, i.e., transformed into nothing more than confused concepts, was the reason that he regarded what he could not represent by means of mere rational concepts as impossible, and set up fundamental principles that cannot stand scrutiny and that do violence to common sense." (281-82; cp. 260, 284ff.) Kant's criticisms of each of the four basic doctrines cited above are a specification of this view, and we will not examine them further.

Translator's Introduction

(2) Just as he finds the *nervus probandi* of Leibniz's metaphysics to be an inadequate theory of space and time, Kant argues that dogmatic metaphysics comes to a halt in a systematic skeptical impasse that also is a consequence of misconceiving the nature of space and time. He represents this impasse as the antinomy of pure reason, in which reason attempts to transcend from objects of experience, the conditioned, to their metaphysically first principle(s), their conditions. The antinomy of pure reason plays an important role in Kant's thought, so much so that he says that the two other crucial doctrines of critical philosophy, those of pure sensuous intuition and freedom, rest on

> the rational concept of the unconditioned in the totality of subordinated conditions, where the illusion that produces an antimony of pure reason by confusion of appearance with things in themselves must be eliminated, and this dialectic itself contains guidance for the transition from the sensible to the supersensible. (311)

The point here is that the antimony of pure reason is *the* crucial connection between Kant's doctrines of pure intuition and freedom. And it is absolutely necessary because it allows him to develop both a doctrine of the experienced world's knowability, hence an acceptable theory of science, and a doctrine of man and God as moral beings.

In the Transcendental Aesthetic Kant formulates and argues for a certain theory of space and time, whose efficacy is finally demonstrated only in providing the key to solving the antinomy of pure reason. What then is the antinomy? It is a set of four pairs of opposed views concerning the unconditioned, i.e., supersensible, origins of the objects of experience, that is, of the world as we know it. These views are all supported by arguments that assume that space and time actually exist, that they and spatial and temporal things are real and, finally, that the principles of knowledge, especially the pure rational ones, e.g., the principle of causality, by which we know them hold for existence as such.

Kant certainly agrees with the dogmatic metaphysicians on two points: first, everything of which we are experientially aware is spatial and temporal; second, the principles of knowledge pertain to, indeed seem especially fitted to, the experiential realm. On this latter point he holds, of course, that the pure rational concepts are principles of knowledge only when they are used in relation to intuition. In experience,

reason sees itself summoned to an unceasing progress towards the unconditioned through a series of subordinated conditions that always and without end are conditioned. For each space and each time can be represented only as a part of a still greater space or time, in which, in order to arrive at the unconditioned, the condition of what is given in each intuition must be sought. (286-87)

The characteristic of space and time that any arbitrarily chosen part of them cannot be totally isolated but is always related to, conditioned by, some greater or smaller portion, leads by itself to the sense of the intrinsic conditionedness of everything spatial and temporal. This conditionedness becomes contingency when conjoined with the concept of causality. Wearing this face, the experiential realm simply cries out for completion — explanation — and the dogmatic metaphysician expects to be able to "proceed from the conditioned objects of possible experience to the unconditioned and, through reason, to expand knowledge through completion of this series." (287)

The metaphysician desires to solve four problems about the unconditioned conditions of the experiential realm. First, is it spatially and temporally infinite or finite? Second, does it comprise a whole that is irreducible to intrinsically simple parts or is it constituted of such simple parts? Kant calls these questions the mathematical antinomies because they seek to determine the homogeneous or mathematically additive parts of the experiential realm. Third, is the world mechanistically determined or are there free causes in it? Fourth, is there, or is there not, a necessary being, either as part of the world or as its cause? Kant calls these questions the dynamic antinomies because they concern heterogeneous causal relations pertaining to the experiential realm. One can easily see that all four concern the ultimate and, Kant contends, unexperienceable, therefore nonsensible, origins of the sensible realm. He further maintains that equally convincing arguments for both views on each of the issues can be formulated. The proponent of a view can show its truth only by a reduction to absurdity of the opposed view. Thus, while both sides of an antinomy are internally coherent and the two together are exhaustive and mutually exclusive, neither is directly confirmable to the exclusion of the other. (326-27) Consequently, "thesis and antithesis reciprocally annihilate one another, without end, and reason

necessarily plunges into the most hopeless skepticism, which must turn out tragically for metaphysics." (287-88)

Kant's solution to this antinomy of pure reason, his dissolution of skepticism, lies in his theories of space and time and of the cognitive use of pure concepts. The theory that space and time are pure forms of intuition resolves the mathematical antinomies merely by denying that we have a basis for believing things in themselves possess those properties by virtue of which we experience the world as intrinsically conditioned. If we cannot attribute space and time to things in themselves, the issue of their conditioned or unconditioned nature cannot arise and therefore does not require resolution. And it makes no sense to question the conditioned nature of an experience that exemplifies spatial and temporal properties simply because the knower so constitutes it.

The theory of pure intuition cannot by itself resolve the dynamic antinomies, because the sense of conditionedness that they seek to determine derives from the principle of sufficient reason, which is conceptual not presentational. Thus, Kant deals with these antinomies by appealing to his theory of the cognitive use of the pure concepts of reason. The principle of sufficient reason has cognitive value only when used to denote a succession in the sequence of perception that follows of necessity in accordance with a rule (A144/B183), that is, only when used in relation to what is or can actually be intuited. It cannot be used to make an *inference* from something experienced to something that cannot be. Thus, its cognitive use must be restricted to the experiential realm, in which everything is, as a matter of fact, conditioned and contingent.

The dynamic antinomies cannot be decided one way or another because doing so would entail an illicit use of the concept of causality or an unjustifiable appeal to freedom. Thus, while it is possible to assert that everything within the experiential realm is causally connected, one cannot make the same kind of causal inference to the ultimate condition(s) of that realm as one can draw between things in it. The ultimate condition(s) can be inferred by using the principle of sufficient reason, but because the condition(s) is (are) not and cannot be present in intuition, that inference has only the form of thought and does not refer to a completely given content. Kant's point here is that the inferences we draw to the ultimate condition(s) look very much like causal inferences, but in fact fail to resemble them in not having an intuitable content. The inferences are therefore *cognitively undecidable.* We cannot cognitively *know* whether everything is

32

mechanistically caused or whether some events are freely caused. Nor can we know whether the world was created by a necessary being or is itself self-caused and eternal.

Kant's solution to the antinomy of pure reason, what he calls its skeptical standstill, is, then, itself skeptical; that is, as the classical pyrrhonian skeptics taught, they are matters about which we cannot and must not make theoretical claims to knowledge, but must instead remain content with theoretical aphasia. Because the space and time of the world as we experience it are pure forms of intuition, we cannot decide between the alternatives of the mathematical antinomies. And because the causal maxim can be used only as a form of thought when we attempt to move from experienced objects to their ultimate conditions, we cannot adjudicate the dynamic antinomies. Kant's confidence in the critical philosophy's doctrines of pure intuition and cognitive knowledge underlies his statement that, "I have therefore found it necessary to deny *knowledge*, in order to make room for *faith*. The dogmatism of metaphysics, that is, the preconception that it is possible to make headway in metaphysics without a previous criticism of pure reason, is the source of all that unbelief, always very dogmatic, which wars against morality." (Bxxx) The positive consequence of the critique of pure reason, then, is a doctrine of faith, and that doctrine constitutes the metaphysics that is a proper part of critical philosophy.

(3) The course of argument by which Kant develops his own metaphysics in the *Progress* is circuitous. He proposes, in accord with what he takes to be the Academy's charge, to constrain his concern to the metaphysics of nature, that is, to the non-sensible so far as it relates to nature. However, because he has shown that one cannot effect a theoretically dogmatic transition to the non-sensible, he will make one that he describes as practically dogmatic. The distinction between these two procedures is best clarified by two passages from the *Critique of Pure Reason*:

> For the purposes of this enquiry, theoretical knowledge may be defined as knowledge of what *is*, practical knowledge as the representation of what ought to be. (A633/B661)

> I divide all apodictic propositions, whether demonstrable or immediately certain, into *dogmata* and *mathemata*. A synthetic proposition directly derived from concepts is a *dogma*; a synthetic proposition, when directly obtained through the construction of concepts, is a *mathemata*. (A736/B764)

Translator's Introduction

The transition will be based solely on concepts, thus dogmatic, and concern only what ought to be, i.e., the highest good, consequently practical. Further, while it will involve concepts that pertain to morals — the concepts of freedom and the highest good — it does not proceed to a metaphysics of morals, but of nature.

Kant's transition begins with the concept of purposiveness (*Zweckmässigkeit*), which is an a priori concept that he says we attribute to objects in nature. It is not a concept that we can schematize and therefore is not a constituent of cognitive awareness. Nonetheless we ascribe it to things we experience and it is thus far a concept immanent in our world. "It is like the concept of the structure of the eyes and ears. But the concept gives no further knowledge of what concerns experience than what Epicurus conceded: That is, after nature formed eyes and ears, we use them to see and hear." (293) The concept of teleological order among experienced things derives from "the fact that we perceive in ourselves a capacity to combine in accordance with ends (*nexus finalis*)." (294) In turn, this ability derives from our sense of personal freedom by which we know ourselves as "intelligible objects." (A547/B575) The argument by which we attribute teleology to nature begins with a particular concept of the supersensible, the concept of freedom. We who see ourselves both as objects of experience and as intelligible objects experience it in ourselves, and it is the necessary condition of our acting in accordance with ends. Finally, because we apprehend objects as exemplifying purposiveness, we infer that it must be attributable to an ultimate cause of nature that itself possesses reason and freedom.

The argument is not theoretical but practical, for

> the concept of freedom remains, appearing as sensibly unconditioned causality... and with the concept of freedom the concept of the ultimate end also remains. Indeed, this is indispensible in moral-practical contexts, even though its objective reality cannot be theoretically guaranteed in a dogmatic fashion...

> This ultimate end of pure practical reason is the highest good, so far as this is possible in the world...

> This object of reason is supersensible; to strive toward it as an ultimate end is duty. There must indubitably be a stage of metaphysics for this transition and for progress in it. This is impossible without a theory, however; for the ultimate end is

not entirely within our power, and we must therefore construct for ourselves a theoretical concept of the source from
which it can arise... Thus, this theory will obtain only in a
practical-dogmatic context, and only in this context can sufficient objective reality of the idea of an ultimate final end be
guaranteed. (294)

The crucial move in this passage is Kant's claim that the transition requires theory because the ultimate end that we envision by attributing
freedom to the objects of experience is "not within our power." It is
not an end that we can bring about even by our most concentrated
and successful free moral effort, but one that must be there as a consequence of the agency of a being infinitely more potent than
ourselves. For us, then, that ultimate end and the agency by which it
exists must be accepted as matters of "what *is*, " not matters of what
"ought to be," since ought, for Kant, implies can. Our awareness of
that end and agency is theoretical, although it occurs in a practical-
dogmatic context.

We find ourselves free moral agents with a sense of the highest
good toward which, in accordance with moral laws, we are obliged to
strive in a world that we must believe is so constituted by God that it
is compatible with our strivings toward that end. Further, we must
believe that there is an immortality commensurate with the task of
bringing the highest good about. Kant says that this is the "analytic"
order, i.e., the order in which we conceive — what Descartes called the
ordo cognoscendi — *of the three notions that constitute metaphysics,
that is, "the supersensible in us, over us,* and *after us."* (295) The synthetic order of these ideas, i.e., the order of their deductive relationship — what Descartes called the *ordo essendi* — is God, freedom and
immortality. Kant's conclusion regarding these fundamental non-
sensible concepts, then, is that they do comprise the natural and
legitimate objects of metaphysical speculation and that there is, given
this theory, a means whereby we can ascend from experience to them.
But the means whereby we transcend the sensible is not theoretical,
though it contains theoretical content; it is practical-dogmatic,
dogmatic in being based solely on concepts and practical insofar as it
envisions an ultimate moral end for the existence of the world, including ourselves.

Kant calls the knowledge of the supersensible arrived at in this way
practical-dogmatic, which is not knowledge of the supersensible as "it

is in itself, but rather only in virtue of how we must think it." (296) We assent to this knowledge as a belief, that is, we hold it as a necessary assumption "because an objective practical rule of conduct that is necessary supports it." (297) This is a belief that Kant says "has in itself a moral worth." (298) Its worth derives from the free commitment of our belief. In and among themselves the concepts of these non-sensible objects, God, freedom and immortality, involve no contradictions, and we are therefore able to entertain the belief that they have independent reality. They gain further sway over us inasmuch as "the idea(s) of them are helpful to the ultimate end of our pure reason." (299) The moral necessity that we feel pertains to acting in accord with laws of freedom can seduce us into attributing independent existence to these objects, even though they only have subjective validity.

Kant's discussion of the individual constituents of the non-sensible, God, freedom and immortality, is free of the metaphysical issues that one normally finds among Cartesians — e.g., Is God a substance, and, if so, what kind? — because he conceives them solely from the perspective of what the sense of freedom demands be placed in their concept. Each contributes to our sense that life has a moral destiny that must be at least partially worked out in this world. Together they make up a system that complements our theoretical image of the world by allowing us to attribute a higher end to it.

The concept of God is the foremost constituent of this system — not God insofar as he might be a necessary being or first cause, properties we attribute to him from a theoretical perspective and which we can never adequately prove or disprove belong to Him — but God as required by our sense of moral purpose. This purpose is the attainment of the highest good possible, which is beyond both our finite theoretical and practical abilities to conceive and bring about. We must ultimately invest both of these in God, who as an infinite being can both know what the highest good is and bring it about. Thus, God is a necessary and, indeed, first constituent of our belief in the moral realm. Kant calls this the moral argument for God's existence, admitting that it has no theoretically dogmatic suasive force, but contending that it is "valid for men as rational beings in general" (306) and sufficient to effect a practical-dogmatic transition to the non-sensible. (305)

The highest good possible, a good "worthy of a Divinity that is a moral creator," (306) namely, the perfection of the world, entails as

its supreme condition "the morality of rational beings," (306) who must be free. Thus, the concept of freedom supports the concept of God. The highest good possible in the world requires that man be an agent who is responsible for bringing about that ultimate end through the free governance of his own actions. However, man cannot adequately conceive that ultimate end of the world and therefore cannot ascribe sole responsibility to himself for bringing it about. He must therefore believe in a teleology of the world through which it attains perfection, a teleology to which free beings are not subject, though their morally right actions accord with it. We cannot apprehend this teleology among objects of experience — they are all subject to mechanical causality — but we can attribute it to them as things in themselves. In this way one is able "to assume that the world is to harmonize with the object of moral teleology, that is, with the ultimate end of all things according to the law of freedom...., which allows us to perceive nature a priori as determined (even independently of this perception). As a moral product, this supreme good challenges man himself to be a creator (so far as it is within his power)...." (307) Man's moral action is a condition of the world's perfection, but the highest end exists only in the harmony of that action with a universe teleologically ordered by a supreme power toward the same end; thus, the ultimate effectiveness of our freedom entails that teleology, even if we cannot adequately conceive the end toward which they mutually aim.

The belief that there is a highest end toward which we are obligated to strive provides a "sufficient reason to assume there to be life after death...., even for eternity." (309) From a moral perspective, then, we are able to assume immortality. Once again, this conception of the supersensible, the existence of a "soul," is not predicated on any metaphysical theory about man's substantial nature, e.g., that he is material or immaterial, but only on the belief that God and man are *essentially* moral, a belief that rests on our original apprehension of our intellectual nature.

Kant's account of the supersensible avoids attributing traditional metaphysical properties to its constituents. Instead, it envisions them as a moral sphere that complements but is not directly inferable from the world of which we are cognitively aware. It constitutes,

a circle, whose boundary turns back itself...beginning theoretically and dogmatically with freedom as the

supersensible but as a faculty known by the moral canon. But it also returns to the same place in its practical-dogmatic intent, that is, to an ultimate end directed towards the advancement of the supreme good in the world, the possibility of which is completed by the ideas of God, immortality and the confidence in the success of this intention, which confidence is dictated by morality itself. Thus these ideas are provided objective but practical reality. (300)

This passage clearly displays the systematic nature of Kant's metaphysics. But the metaphysics derives its nature and claim to validity from Kant's critique of human pure reason. Having isolated and given a theory of theoretical knowledge, he proceeds to show how traditional metaphysics, employing pure concepts in contexts that do not provide the necessary conditions for their theoretical use, is essentially antinomic. Pointing out that traditional metaphysical speculation is necessarily stagnant, he advocated aporia with respect to theoretically dogmatic claims about the non-sensuous. But through our sense of freedom that derives from the demand of the moral law on us, he formulates a practically dogmatic metaphysical theory of the supersensible entities that concerned traditional metaphysics, i.e., God, freedom and immortality. In this connection of ideas we can perceive the systematic nature of the entire critical philosophy, a nature to which he alludes when he writes, "The essence and ultimate intention of metaphysics is to be a perfect whole: either nothing or everything." (259) This is the whole that Kant intended to present in the *Progress*.

Ted Humphrey
Arizona State University

Endnotes

1. Max Wundt, *Kant als Metaphysiker*, Verlag von Ferdinand Enke, Stuttgart, 1924, pp. 375-400. Hermann-Jean de Vleeschauwer, "La Cinderella dans l'oeuvre Kantienne," *Kant-Studien, Akten des 4. Internationalen Kant-Kongress*, Mainz 6-10 April 1974, Teil I (vol. 65, 1974), pp. 297-310.

2. Immanuel Kant, *Kant's gesammelte Schriften*, 28 vols. hrsg. Preussischen Akademie der Wissenschaften zu Berlin, Walter de Gruyter, Berlin, 1901-,VXIII, pp. 640-44, no. 6342, and XX, pp. 335-37, D14. Hereafter cited as A.-A., volume and page.

3. Nonetheless, in his masterly paper entitled "La Cinderella dans l'oeuvre Kantienne," H.-J. de Vleeschauwer has presented a great deal of information concerning the relevant issues regarding the circumstances of Kant's concern with the Academy's Prize Question. Despite his reconstruction of events, etc., the most important issues remain undecided, at least in my mind.

4. A.-A., XIV, p. xii.

5. Lewis White Beck brought Weisskopf's criticisms of Rink to my attention. They are contained in Traugott Weisskopf, *Immanuel Kant und die Padagogik*, (Zurich: EVZ-Verlag (Editio Academica), 1970), pp. 171-183. In his essay "Kant on Education," in *Essays on Kant and Hume*, (New Haven: Yale University Press, 1978), pp. 188-204, Beck summarizes Weisskopf's criticisms of Rink.

6. Hermann-Jean de Vleeschauwer, "La Composition du Preisschrift d'Immanuel Kant sur les progrès de la metaphysique," *Journal of the History of Philosophy*, v. XVII, no. 2 (April, 1979), pp. 170-4.

7. But see ibid., pp. 174-195.

Endnotes

8. *Kant als Metaphysiker*, pp. 386-8 and 398. Hermann-Jean de Vleeschauwer, *La Déduction Transcendentale dans l'Oeuvre de Kant*, 3 vols., Eduard Champion, Paris, 1934-37, v. III, pp. 460-462 and 484-86.

9. "La Cinderella," p. 298.

10. Ibid., pp. 299-300.

11. Numbers in parentheses are page numbers of the Academy edition, facing the translation.

12. The numbers preceded by A and B refer to the first and second editions of the *Critique of Pure Reason* respectively.

13. *La Déduction Transcendentale*, v. III, pp. 478-9; *Kant als Metaphysiker*, pp. 386-7.

14. A.-A., VIII, pp. 226-7.

15. A.-A., VIII, p. 415.

16. Kant's formulation of the analytic-synthetic distinction, including the distinction between analytic judgments and identities was severely criticized by Wolffians, especially J.G. Maass, as resting on psychological not logical grounds. See Henry E. Allison, *The Kant-Eberhard Controversy*, the Johns Hopkins University Press, Baltimore, 1973, pp. 36-45, esp. 42ff.

17. The *Progress* does not contain systematic arguments to justify the doctrine that space and time are pure forms of human intuition. The fundamental elements of this view are merely sketched to the extent necessary to allow Kant to present his general theory of cognition; he refers the reader to the *Critique* for specifics.

18. See "The Historical and Conceptual Relations between Kant's Metaphysics of Space and Philosophy of Geometry," *Journal of the History of Philosophy*, vol. XI, no. 4 (October, 1973), pp. 483-512 for a more complete analysis of Kant's arguments concerning pure intuitions.

19.   de Vleeschauwer argues that Kant's arguments here constitute a concession to J.S. Beck and Fichte regarding idealism and understanding's primacy in human knowledge. (*La Deduction Transcendentale,* v. III, pp. 475ff.) However, these arguments are hardly convincing inasmuch as we find Kant expressing himself in nearly identical terms in 1787, much before he had received Beck's and Fichte's criticisms.

20.   Kant's position regarding the universality and necessity of pure concepts is quite different from the one concerning the forms of intuition. Different knowing agents may receive the matter of intuition under different forms, or none at all, if intuition is non-sensible (267), but the pure concept of an object is the same for all.

21.   See the *Critique of Judgment*, section 59.

22.   This presentation of Leibniz's view roughly corresponds with the one in the *Critique of Pure Reason*, A260/B316-A292/B349, as well as *On A Discovery*, VIII, 190-226.

Bibliography

Allison, Henry. *The Kant-Eberhard Controversy*. Baltimore: The Johns Hopkins University Press, 1973.

Beck, Lewis White. *Early German Philosophy*. Cambridge: Harvard University Press, 1969.

_____. *Essays on Kant and Hume*. New Haven: Yale University Press, 1978.

Humphrey, Ted B. "The Historical and Conceptual Relations between Kant's Metaphysics of Space and Philosophy of Geometry," *Journal of the History of Philosophy* XI (October, 1973): 483-512.

Paulsen, Friedrich. *Immanuel Kant: His Life and Doctrine*, trans. J.E. Creighton and Albert Lefevre. New York: Friedrick Ungar Publishing Co., 1963.

de Vleeschauwer, H.-J. "La Cinderella dans l'Oeuvre Kantienne," *Kant-Studien: Akten des 4. Internationalen Kant-Kongress* Mainz 6-10 April 1974, Teil I. 65 (1974): 297-310.

_____. "La Composition du *Preisschrift* d'Immanuel Kant sur les progrès de la mètaphysique," *Journal of the History of Philosophy*, XVII (April, 1979): 143-196.

_____. *La Déduction Transcendentale dans l'Oeuvre de Kant*, 3 vols. Paris: Eduard Champion, 1934-37.

Weisskopf, Traugott. *Immanuel Kant und die Pädagogik*. Zurich: EVZ-Verlag (Editio Academica), 1978.

Wundt, Max. *Kant als Metaphysiker*. Stuttgart: Ferdinand Enke, 1924.

43

Immanuel Kant

über

die von der Königl. Akademie der Wissenschaften
zu Berlin

für das Jahr 1791

ausgesetzte Preisfrage:

Welches
sind die wirklichen Fortschritte,
die die Metaphysik

seit Leibnitzens und Wolf's Zeiten
in Deutschland gemacht hat?

———

Herausgegeben

von

D. Friedrich Theodor Rink.

———

Königsberg, 1804
bey Goebbels und Unzer.

Immanuel Kant

concerning
the prize question
posed by the Royal Academy of Sciences
in Berlin
for the year 1791

What
Real Progress
Has Metaphysics Made
in Germany
since the Time of Leibniz and Wolff?

———

Edited by

Dr. Friedrich Theodor Rink

Königsberg, 1804
at Goebbels & Unzer

Die Veranlaſſung dieſer Schrift liegt am Tage, ich kann mich deſſen
alſo überheben, hier weitläuftiger davon zu reden. Die Preißfrage, von
der ſie handelt, machte, als ſie bekannt wurde, mit Recht einiges Aufſehen.
Drey verdiente Männer, die Herren Schwab, Reinhold und Abicht,
5 trugen den Preis davon, und ihre hierher gehörigen Aufſätze ſind bereits
ſeit dem Jahre 1796 in den Händen des Publicums. Wie ſie meiſtens, ein
jeder ſeinen eigenen Gang, bey der Unterſuchung einſchlugen: ſo iſt auch
Kant ſeinen eigenthümlichen, und zwar den verſchiedenſten Weg gegangen,
den einzigen indeſſen, von dem ſich vorausſehen ließ, daß, wenn er dieſe
10 Preißfrage zum Gegenſtande ſeiner Beantwortung nehmen ſollte, er ihn
wählen würde.

Drey Handſchriften dieſes Aufſatzes ſind vorhanden, aber keine derſelben, was zu bedauern iſt, vollſtändig. Aus der einen war ich daher genöthigt, die erſte Hälfte dieſer Schrift, bis zum Ende des erſten Stadiums,
15 herzunehmen; die andere lieferte mir die letzte Hälfte, vom Anfange des
zweiten Stadiums bis zum Ende des Aufſatzes. Da jede Handſchrift eine
andre Bearbeitung des gegebenen Stoffes, und zwar mit kleinen Ab-
weichungen enthält: ſo kann es nicht fehlen, daß nicht hin und wieder
ein gewiſſer Mangel an Einheit und Zuſammenſtimmung in der Behand-
20 lung fühlbar werden ſollte, der ſich unter dieſen Umſtänden indeſſen
unmöglich ganz beſeitigen ließ. Die dritte Abſchrift iſt in gewiſſer Weiſe
die vollendetſte, enthält aber nur den erſten Anfang des Ganzen. Sollte
die eben erwähnte Inconvenienz nicht noch größer werden, durch eine
gezwungene Zuſammenſchmelzung mehrerer Bearbeitungen: ſo blieb
25 mir nichts andres übrig, als den Inhalt jener dritten Abſchrift in der
Beylage abdrucken zu laſſen, oder ihn ganz zu unterdrücken. Das letztere
ſchien mir eine zu eigenmächtige Beeinträchtigung der Erwartungen aller
Freunde der kritiſchen Philoſophie, daher ich denn den erſten Ausweg
wählte. Auch giebt die Beylage noch einige Anmerkungen Kant's, die
30 ſich am Rande der Manuſcripte befinden, und den Anfang des zweyten
Stadiums, aus der von mir ſo genannten erſten Handſchrift.

Rink's Preface of 1804

The occasion for this work is so well known that I can be excused from here writing about it at length. The Prize Question with which it deals caused something of a sensation when it was announced, and with good reason. Three deserving men, Schwab, Reinhold, and Abicht, were awarded the prize, and the essays that they wrote have been in the public's hands since 1796.[1] Just as most of them had their own approach to the problem, so Kant embarked upon his unique and very different way. Nonetheless, this is the only one, it may be predicted, he would have taken, had he chosen to make this Prize Question the object of a response.

Three handwritten manuscripts of the essay are extant; regrettably, none is complete. I was therefore compelled to extract the first half of this work—to the end of the first Stage—from the first of them; the second provided the last half—from the beginning of the second Stage to the end of the essay.[2] Since each manuscript contains some treatment of the same materials, with only minor deviations, it could not but happen that now and again a certain lack of unity and coherence in the whole should be noticeable, which, under the circumstances, it was impossible to eliminate. The third manuscript—in certain respects the most polished one—contains only the very beginning of the whole. To avoid aggravating the situation through a forced fusion of several drafts, I had no alternatives other than either to publish the content of the third draft in the appendix or to suppress it completely. The latter course seemed an indefensible betrayal of what all friends of the Critical philosophy might expect, and I therefore chose the former. The appendix also includes several of Kant's remarks located in the margins of the manuscripts, as well as the beginning of the second Stage, taken from what I have called the first manuscript.

Doch selbst in dem, was die beyden erst genannten Handschriften enthalten, giebt es einige Lücken, die Kant wahrscheinlich, wie er das gar oft
that, auf beygelegten, aber verloren gegangenen Zetteln mochte ergänzt
haben; ich habe sie an einigen Stellen durch eingeschobene Sternchen * *
bezeichnet.   5

Soviel glaubte ich über meine Anordnung dieser Papiere sagen zu
müssen, um den Beurtheiler dieser Schrift in den richtigen Gesichtspunkt
zu derselben zu stellen. Sie anzupreisen, oder auch nur ihr Gutes, selbst
in dieser mangelhaften Gestalt, hervorzuheben, dessen bedarf es von meiner
Seite nicht. Hat doch, wie ich soeben erfahre, Kant die große Rolle 10
seines Lebens beendigt. Es läßt sich erwarten, daß nun auch der Groll,
den seine Geistesüberlegenheit hie oder da unschuldiger Weise veranlaßte,
einschlummere, und vollkommnere Unpartheylichkeit gewissenhafter
seine wesentlichen Verdienste würdigen werde.

Zur Jubilate-Messe des Jahres 1804.   15

Rink.

Yet even the first two manuscripts contain several lacunae that Kant may well have completed, as he so often did, on accompanying slips of paper that are now lost.[3] I have designated them at the proper places by inserting asterisks * *.[4]

This is as much I believe I need to say about my organization of these papers in order to place them in the proper perspective for the critic of this work. To praise them or to point out what in them is good, even in this defective state is not required of me. Now, I have just learned that Kant has completed the great role he played in his life. It is to be expected that the animosity his intellectual superiority sometimes innocently occasioned will now die out and that a completer impartiality will more scrupulously evaluate his essential merits.

Jubilation Mass, 1804

Rink

Die Königliche Academie der Wiſſenſchaften verlangt, die Fortſchritte eines Theiles der Philoſophie, in einem Theile des gelehrten Europa, und auch für einen Theil des laufenden Jahrhunderts aufzuzählen.

Das ſcheint eine leicht zu löſende Aufgabe zu ſeyn, denn ſie betrifft 5 nur die Geſchichte, und wie die Fortſchritte der Aſtronomie und Chemie, als empiriſche Wiſſenſchaften, ſchon ihre Geſchichtſchreiber gefunden haben, die aber der mathematiſchen Analyſis, oder der reinen Mechanik, die in demſelben Lande, in derſelben Zeit gemacht worden, die ihrige, wenn man will, auch bald finden werden: ſo ſcheint es mit der Wiſſenſchaft, 10 wovon hier die Rede iſt, eben ſo wenig Schwierigkeit zu haben. —

Aber dieſe Wiſſenſchaft iſt Metaphyſik, und das ändert die Sache ganz und gar. Dies iſt ein uferloſes Meer, in welchem der Fortſchritt keine Spur hinterläßt, und deſſen Horizont kein ſichtbares Ziel enthält, an dem, um wieviel man ſich ihm genähert habe, wahrgenommen werden 15 könnte. — In Anſehung dieſer Wiſſenſchaft, welche ſelbſt faſt immer nur in der Idee geweſen iſt, iſt die vorgelegte Aufgabe ſehr ſchwer, faſt nur an der Möglichkeit der Auflöſung derſelben zu verzweifeln, und, ſollte ſie auch gelingen, ſo vermehrt noch die vorgeſchriebene Bedingung, die Fortſchritte, welche ſie gemacht hat, in einer kurzen Rede vor Augen zu ſtellen, 20 dieſe Schwierigkeit. Denn Metaphyſik iſt ihrem Weſen, und ihrer End-abſicht nach, ein vollendetes Ganze; entweder Nichts, oder Alles. Was zu ihrem Endzweck erforderlich iſt, kann alſo nicht, wie etwa Mathematik oder empiriſche Naturwiſſenſchaft, die ohne Ende immer fortſchreiten, frag-mentariſch abgehandelt werden. — Wir wollen es gleichwohl verſuchen.

25 Die erſte und nothwendigſte Frage iſt wohl: Was die Vernunft eigentlich mit der Metaphyſik will? welchen Endzweck ſie mit ihrer Be-arbeitung vor Augen habe? denn groß, vielleicht der größeſte, ja, alleinige Endzweck, den die Vernunft in ihrer Speculation je beabſichtigen kann, weil alle Menſchen mehr oder weniger daran Theil nehmen, und nicht 30 zu begreifen iſt, warum bey der ſich immer zeigenden Fruchtloſigkeit ihrer Bemühungen in dieſem Felde, es doch umſonſt war, ihnen zuzurufen: ſie ſollten doch endlich einmal aufhören, dieſen Stein des Siſyphus

[Introduction]

The Royal Academy of Sciences desires an accounting of the progress of a part of philosophy in an educated part of Europe and for a part of the present Century.

This task appears to be easily solved because it only concerns history. Just as the progress of the empirical sciences of Astronomy and Chemistry have already found their historians, and as the progress made by mathematical analysis and pure mechanics in the same land during the same period will, when someone desires it, soon find theirs, there appears to be no more difficulty with respect to the science in question.

But this science is metaphysics, and that completely changes matters. This is a boundless sea in which progress leaves no trace and on whose horizon there is no visible destination that allows one to perceive how near one has come to it. In regard to this science, existing almost always only as an idea, the proposed task is so difficult as to make one doubt that it can be completed.[5] And should one succeed, the prescribed condition, that this progress be recorded in a short work, just adds to the difficulty. For the essence and ultimate intention of metaphysics is to be a perfect whole: either nothing or everything.[6] Its ultimate end, therefore, requires that it not be treated piecemeal, as, for example, one might deal with mathematics and empirical science, which always progress without end. Nevertheless, we want to attempt it.

The first and most necessary question is undoubtedly this: Precisely what is reason attempting to do in metaphysics? In cultivating it, what ultimate end does it have in view?[7] It is an important, perhaps the most important, indeed the sole ultimate end that reason can propose for its speculation, since to a greater or lesser degree all men engage in metaphysics.[8] But given the continually manifest fruitlessness of their endeavors in this field, one cannot understand why they are vainly called back to it. Only if reason's interest in metaphysics were not the most deep-seated one it can have would men finally discontinue once and for all rolling this stone of Sisyphus.

51

immer zu wälzen, wäre das Interesse, welches die Vernunft daran nimmt, nicht das innigste, was man haben kann.

Dieser Endzweck, auf den die ganze Metaphysik angelegt ist, ist leicht zu entdecken, und kann in dieser Rücksicht eine Definition derselben begründen: „sie ist die Wissenschaft, von der Erkenntniß des Sinnlichen zu ⁵ der des Übersinnlichen durch die Vernunft fortzuschreiten."

Zu dem Sinnlichen aber zählen wir nicht blos das, dessen Vorstellung im Verhältniß zu den Sinnen, sondern auch zum Verstande betrachtet wird, wenn nur die reinen Begriffe desselben in ihrer Anwendung auf Gegenstände der Sinne, mithin zum Behuf einer möglichen ¹⁰ Erfahrung gedacht werden; also kann das Nichtsinnliche, z. B. der Begriff der Ursache, welcher im Verstande seinen Sitz und Ursprung hat, doch, was die Erkenntniß eines Gegenstandes durch denselben betrifft, noch zum Felde des Sinnlichen, nämlich der Objecte der Sinne gehörig genannt werden. — ¹⁵

Die Ontologie ist diejenige Wissenschaft (als Theil der Metaphysik), welche ein System aller Verstandesbegriffe und Grundsätze, aber nur so fern sie auf Gegenstände gehen, welche den Sinnen gegeben, und also durch Erfahrung belegt werden können, ausmacht. Sie berührt nicht das Übersinnliche, welches doch der Endzweck der Metaphysik ist, gehört ²⁰ also zu dieser nur als Propädeutik, als die Halle, oder der Vorhof der eigentlichen Metaphysik, und wird Transscendental-Philosophie genannt, weil sie die Bedingungen und ersten Elemente aller unserer Erkenntniß a priori enthält.

In ihr ist seit Aristoteles' Zeiten nicht viel Fortschreitens gewesen. ²⁵ Denn sie ist, so wie eine Grammatik die Auflösung einer Sprachform in ihre Elementarregeln, oder die Logik eine solche von der Denkform ist, eine Auflösung der Erkenntniß in die Begriffe, die a priori im Verstand liegen und in der Erfahrung ihren Gebrauch haben; — ein System, dessen mühsamer Bearbeitung man gar wohl überhoben sein kann, wenn ³⁰ man nur die Regeln des richtigen Gebrauchs dieser Begriffe und Grundsätze zum Behuf der Erfahrungserkenntniß beabsichtigt, weil die Erfahrung ihn immer bestätigt oder berichtigt, welches nicht geschieht, wenn man vom Sinnlichen zum Übersinnlichen fortzuschreiten Vorhabens ist, zu welcher Absicht dann freylich die Ausmessung des Verstandesvermögens ³⁵ und seiner Prinzipien mit Ausführlichkeit und Sorgfalt geschehen muß, um zu wissen, von wo an die Vernunft, und mit welchem Stecken und Stabe sie von den Erfahrungsgegenständen zu denen, die es nicht sind, ihren Überschritt wagen könne.

52

Introduction

This ultimate end toward which all of metaphysics aims is easy to discover and can provide the basis for its definition: Metaphysics is the science of advancing by reason from knowledge of the sensible to knowledge of the supersensible.[9]

Among the sensible we include not only those representations that are related to the senses, but also those regarded as [belonging to] understanding, at least insofar as its pure concepts are thought of in their application to the objects of the senses, consequently in relation to a possible *experience*. Thus, the non-sensible, e.g., the concept of cause, whose place and origin is the understanding, can, with respect to its use in cognition of objects, still be said to belong to the realm of the sensible, that is, to the objects of the senses.[10]

Ontology (as a part of metaphysics) is the science that comprises a system of all concepts and principles of understanding, but only insofar as these extend to objects given by the senses and can, therefore, be justified by experience.[11] It does not deal with the supersensible, the ultimate end of metaphysics, and thus belongs to the latter only as a propadeutic. Ontology is the porch or entry way of metaphysics proper and will be called transcendental philosophy because it contains the conditions and elements of our a priori knowledge.

Ontology has made little progress since Aristotle's time. For just as a grammar is the analysis of a form of speech into its elementary rules and logic is the analysis of the form of thought, ontology is the analysis of experience into concepts that lie a priori in the understanding and that are used in experience. It is a system from whose tedious cultivation one can certainly exempt oneself if one only intends to determine the rules for the correct use of these concepts and principles in experiential knowledge; for experience always corroborates or corrects them; but this cannot happen if one proposes to progress from the sensible to the supersensible. If one has the latter intention, one must certainly make a complete and accurate inventory of understanding's powers and principles in order to know from what point and with what aid and support reason can risk attempting the transition from objects that are experienced to those that are not.[12]

Für die Ontologie hat nun der berühmte Wolf durch die Klarheit und Bestimmtheit in Zergliederung jenes Vermögens, aber nicht zur Erweiterung der Erkenntniß in derselben, weil der Stoff erschöpft war, unstreitige Verdienste.

5 Die obige Definition aber, welche nur anzeigt, was man mit der Metaphysik will, nicht aber, was in ihr zu thun sey, würde sie nur als eine zur Philosophie in der eigenthümlichen Bedeutung des Wortes, d. i. zur Weisheitslehre gehörige Unterweisung, von anderen Lehren auszeichnen und dem schlechterdings nothwendigen practischen Gebrauch 10 der Vernunft seine Prinzipien vorschreiben, welches nur eine indirecte Beziehung der Metaphysik ist, unter der man eine scholastische Wissenschaft und System von gewissen theoretischen Erkenntnissen a priori versteht, welche man sich unmittelbar zum Geschäfte macht. Daher wird die Erklärung der Metaphysik nach dem Begriff der Schule sein: — sie 15 ist das System aller Prinzipien der reinen theoretischen Vernunfterkenntniß durch Begriffe; oder kurz gesagt: sie ist das System der reinen theoretischen Philosophie.

Sie enthält also keine praktischen Lehren der reinen Vernunft, aber doch die theoretischen, die dieser ihrer Möglichkeit zum Grunde liegen. 20 Sie enthält nicht mathematische Sätze, d. i. solche, welche durch die Construktion der Begriffe Vernunfterkenntniß hervorbringen, aber die Prinzipien der Möglichkeit einer Mathematik überhaupt. Unter Vernunft aber wird in dieser Definition nur das Vermögen der Erkenntniß a priori, d. i. die nicht empirisch ist, verstanden.

25 Um nun einen Maasstab zu dem zu haben, was neuerdings in der Metaphysik geschehen ist, muß man dasjenige, was in ihr von jeher gethan worden, beydes aber mit dem vergleichen, was darin hätte gethan werden sollen. — Wir werden aber den überlegten vorsätzlichen Rückgang nach Maximen der Denkungsart, mit zum Fortschreiten, d. i. als einen 30 negativen Fortgang in Anschlag bringen können, weil dadurch, wenn es auch nur die Aufhebung eines eingewurzelten, sich in seinen Folgen weit verbreitenden Irrtums wäre, doch etwas zum Besten der Metaphysik bewirkt werden kann, so wie von dem, der vom rechten Wege abgekommen ist, und zu der Stelle, von der er ausging, zurückkehrt, um seinen Compaß 35 zur Hand zu nehmen, zum wenigstens gerühmt wird, daß er nicht auf dem unrechten Wege zu wandern fortgefahren, noch auch still gestanden, sondern sich wieder an den Punkt seines Ausganges gestellt hat, um sich zu orientiren.

Die ersten und ältesten Schritte in der Metaphysik wurden nicht etwa

Because of his clarity and precision in analyzing that faculty [understanding], the esteemed Wolff did ontology an uncontested service; but [he did not attempt an] extension of its knowledge, since its subject matter had been exhausted.

The foregoing definition — which only indicates what one *intends* with respect to metaphysics, not what is to be done *in it* — would only distinguish metaphysics from other teachings that belong to philosophy in the proper sense of the word, i.e., as a doctrine of wisdom, [distinguishing it from] the prescription of principles for the absolutely necessary practical use of reason.[13] This latter is only indirectly related to metaphysics understood as a scholastic science and system of a priori certain theoretical knowledge, which one makes one's immediate concern. Accordingly, the scholastic conception of metaphysics will be defined as follows: Metaphysics is the system of all of the principles of pure theoretical rational knowledge derivable from concepts [alone]; in short, it is the system of all pure rational philosophy.[14]

Metaphysics does not contain a practical doctrine of pure reason, but rather a theoretical one that underlies the possibility of the practical one. It does not contain mathematical propositions, i.e., those that the concepts of rational cognition produce by construction; instead, [it contains] only the principles of the possibility of mathematics in general. In this defintion one should understand "reason" to mean only the capacity for a priori knowledge, i.e., knowledge that is not empirical.[15]

In order to have a criterion to assess what has *recently* occurred in metaphysics, one must be aware of what *previously* happened. And both of these must be compared with what should have happened. However, in accordance with [received] maxims of method,[16] we shall go back through and reconsider the progress that has been made in metaphysics, that is, intentionally regard it as negative progress. Even if the errors are deeply rooted and their results widely circulated, something to the good of metaphysics can be achieved, just as he who has lost his way and returns to the point from which he set out and takes compass in hand is at least praised for not continuing to wander on along the wrong path; nor has he stood still, but has rather gone back to his point of departure in order to orient himself.

The first and oldest steps taken in metaphysics were not merely

als bedenkliche Versuche blos gewagt, sondern geschahen mit völliger Zu-
versicht, ohne vorher über die Möglichkeit der Erkenntnisse a priori sorg-
same Untersuchungen anzustellen. Was war die Ursache von diesem Vertrauen der Vernunft zu sich selbst? Das vermeynte Gelingen. Denn in
der Mathematik gelang es der Vernunft, die Beschaffenheit der Dinge
a priori zu erkennen, über alle Erwartung der Philosophen vortrefflich;
warum sollte es nicht eben so gut in der Philosophie gelingen? Daß die
Mathematik auf dem Boden des Sinnlichen wandelt, da die Vernunft
selbst ihm Begriffe construiren, d. i. a priori in der Anschauung darstellen und so die Gegenstände a priori erkennen kann, die Philosophie
hingegen eine Erweiterung der Erkenntniß der Vernunft durch bloße
Begriffe, wo man seinen Gegenstand nicht, so wie dort, vor sich hinstellen
kann, sondern die uns gleichsam in der Luft vorschweben, unternimmt,
fiel den Metaphysikern nicht ein, als einen himmelweiten Unterschied, in
Ansehung der Möglichkeit der Erkenntniß a priori, zur wichtigen Aufgabe
zu machen. Genug, Erweiterung der Erkenntniß a priori, auch außer der
Mathematik, durch bloße Begriffe, und daß sie Wahrheit enthalte, beweiset sich durch die Übereinstimmung solcher Urtheile und Grundsätze
mit der Erfahrung.

Ob nun zwar das Übersinnliche, worauf doch der Endzweck der Vernunft in der Metaphysik gerichtet ist, für die theoretische Erkenntniß
eigentlich gar keinen Boden hat: so wanderten die Metaphysiker doch an
dem Leitfaden ihrer ontologischen Prinzipien, die freylich wohl eines
Ursprunges a priori sind, aber nur für Gegenstände der Erfahrung gelten,
doch getrost fort, und obzwar die vermeynte Erwerbung überschwenglicher Einsichten auf diesem Wege durch keine Erfahrung bestätigt werden
konnte, so konnte sie doch eben darum, weil sie das Übersinnliche betrifft,
auch durch keine Erfahrung widerlegt werden: nur mußte man sich wohl
in Acht nehmen, in seine Urtheile keinen Widerspruch mit sich selbst ein-
laufen zu lassen, welches sich auch gar wohl thun läßt, obgleich diese
Urtheile, und die ihnen unterliegenden Begriffe, übrigens ganz leer
seyn mögen.

Dieser Gang der Dogmatiker von noch älterer Zeit, als der des Plato
und Aristoteles, selbst die eines Leibnitz und Wolf mit eingeschlossen, ist,
wenn gleich nicht der rechte, doch der natürlichste nach dem Zweck der
Vernunft und der scheinbaren Überredung, daß Alles, was die Vernunft
nach der Analogie ihres Verfahrens, womit es ihr gelang, vornimmt, ihr
eben so wohl gelingen müsse.

Der zweyte, beynahe ebenso alte, Schritt der Metaphysik war

dubious attempts, but were actually made in complete confidence, without having previously investigated carefully the possibility of a priori knowledge. What was the source of reason's self-confidence? Its imagined *success*. Because in mathematics reason succeeded in knowing a priori the nature of things, exceeding philosophers' highest expectations, why should it not succeed equally well in philosophy? That mathematics travels on the ground of the sensible — where reason itself constructs its concepts, i.e., displays them a priori in intuition and consequently can know its objects a priori — and that, by contrast, philosophy attempts to extend knowledge by means of mere concepts — where its object cannot be placed before one, as it can be in mathematics, but hovers before one, as if in thin air — did not strike metaphysicians as a vast difference in respect to the possibility of a priori cognition, one that had to be made an important issue. It was enough that the truth of the extension of a priori cognition — even outside of mathematics — was [thought to be] sufficiently demonstrated by the conformity *with experience* of such judgments and principles.[17]

However, the supersensible, which is reason's ultimate end in metaphysics, provides no proper ground for theoretical knowledge. So, guided by the lead strings of their ontological principles — whose origin is certainly a priori, even though they are valid only for objects of experience — metaphysicians wandered confidently on. And although the putative acquisition of transcendent insights that they gain in this way cannot be confirmed by any experience, neither, since they concern the supersensible, can they be disproved by it. The metaphysician has only to be careful not to allow his judgments to contradict one another — something it is perfectly possible to succeed at — even though these judgments and the concepts they are based on may be utterly empty.

This path of the dogmatic philosophers — including those from times even more ancient than Plato's and Aristotle's through Leibniz's and Wolff's period — is, if not the correct one, the one that most naturally agrees with reason's end and its apparent conviction that everything it undertakes on an analogy with its successful procedure [in mathematics] must itself be equally successful.[18]

By contrast, the second step in metaphysics — a step almost as old

dagegen ein Rückgang, welcher weise und der Metaphysik vortheilhaft
gewesen seyn würde, wenn er nur bis zum Anfangspunkte des Ausganges gereicht wäre, aber nicht um dabey stehen zu bleiben mit der Entschließung, keinen Fortgang ferner zu versuchen, sondern ihn vielmehr
5 in einer neuen Richtung vorzunehmen.

Dieser, alle ferneren Anschläge vernichtende, Rückgang, gründete sich
auf das gänzliche Mißlingen aller Versuche in der Metaphysik. Woran
aber konnte man dieses Mißlingen und die Verunglückung ihrer großen
Anschläge erkennen? Ist es etwa die Erfahrung, welche sie widerlegte?
10 Keineswegs! Denn was die Vernunft als Erweiterung a priori von ihrer
Erkenntniß der Gegenstände möglicher Erfahrung, in der Mathematik
sowohl, als in der Ontologie sagt, das sind wirkliche Schritte, die vor-
wärts gehen, und wodurch sie Feld zu gewinnen sicher ist. Nein, es sind
beabsichtigte und vermeynte Eroberungen im Felde des Übersinnlichen,
15 wo vom absoluten Naturganzen, was kein Sinn fasset, imgleichen von
Gott, Freyheit und Unsterblichkeit die Frage ist, die hauptsächlich die
letztern drey Gegenstände betrifft, daran die Vernunft ein praktisches
Interesse nimmt, in Ansehung deren nun alle Versuche der Erweiterung
scheitern, welches man aber nicht etwa daran sieht, daß uns eine tiefere
20 Erkenntniß des Übersinnlichen, als höhere Metaphysik, etwa das Gegentheil
jener Meynungen lehre, denn mit dem können wir diese nicht vergleichen,
weil wir sie als überschwenglich nicht kennen, sondern weil in unserer
Vernunft Prinzipien liegen, welche jedem erweiternden Satz über diese
Gegenstände einen, dem Ansehen nach, ebenso gründlichen Gegensatz
25 entgegen stellen, und die Vernunft ihre Versuche selbst zernichtet.

Dieser Gang der Sceptiker ist natürlicher Weise etwas spätern
Ursprungs, aber doch alt genug, zugleich aber dauert er noch immer
in sehr guten Köpfen allenthalben fort, obwohl ein anderes Interesse, als
das der reinen Vernunft, Viele nöthiget, das Unvermögen der Vernunft
30 hierin zu verhehlen. Die Ausdehnung der Zweifellehre, sogar auf die
Prinzipien der Erkenntniß des Sinnlichen, und auf die Erfahrung selbst,
kann man nicht füglich für eine ernstliche Meynung halten, die in irgend
einem Zeitalter der Philosophie statt gefunden habe, sondern ist vielleicht
eine Aufforderung an die Dogmatiker gewesen, diejenigen Prinzipien
35 a priori, auf welchen selbst die Möglichkeit der Erfahrung beruht, zu beweisen, und da sie dieses nicht vermochten, die letztere ihnen auch als
zweifelhaft vorzustellen.

Der dritte und neueste Schritt, den die Metaphysik gethan hat, und
der über ihr Schicksal entscheiden muß, ist die Kritik der reinen Vernunft

as the first one — was a retreat that might have been prudent and profitable for metaphysics had it only returned metaphysics to its original point of departure — not for the purpose of merely remaining in place, resolving to pursue no further advance, but instead determined to seek advancement in some new direction.[19]

This retreat, one that denied all further efforts, was based on the complete *failure* of all attempts in metaphysics. How can one recognize the failures and misfortunes of these great projects? Is it perhaps experience that refutes it? Certainly not! For what reason regards as extensions of its a priori cognition of the objects of possible experience in mathematics as well as in ontology are actual steps forward, and the area it wins is secure. On the other hand, there are intended and imagined conquests in the realm of the supersensible, where nature in its absolute entirety, which no sense grasps, as well as God, freedom and immortality, are in question, and reason takes a particular practical interest in the latter three, but in regard to which all attempts at an 'extension [of reason's knowledge] fail. This is perhaps something that one cannot see — [namely,] that a deeper knowledge of the supersensible, as a higher metaphysics, is perhaps the contrary of the doctrine [it is] intended [to be like] — for we cannot compare this [metaphysics] with that [mathematics and ontology], since as transcendent, we cannot know the supersensible. On the contrary, because reason can meet every ampliative proposition concerning these objects with a contrary proposition that seems equally well supported, reason itself denies its own attempts.

Naturally, while ancient enough, this procedure of the skeptics is somewhat later in origin, and it always endures in good minds everywhere, although some interest other than that of pure reason compels many to seek in [skepticism] a refuge from reason's inability [to know the supersensible]. The extension of doubt even to the principles of sensible cognition and to experience itself cannot properly be regarded as an attitude that was earnestly held during any epoch of philosophy. Perhaps it was instead a demand placed on dogmatic philosophers to justify even the a priori principles underlying the possiblity of experience. Since they were unable to do this, skeptics contended that those principles were dubious.[20]

The third and most recent step in metaphysics, whose fate must now be decided, is the critique of pure reason's general ability to extend a priori human knowledge, be it in relation to the sensible or the

59

selbst, in Ansehung ihres Vermögens, das menschliche Erkenntniß überhaupt, es sey in Ansehung des Sinnlichen oder Übersinnlichen, a priori
zu erweitern. Wenn diese, was sie verheißt, geleistet hat, nämlich den
Umfang, den Inhalt und die Grenzen desselben zu bestimmen, — wenn
sie dieses in Deutschland und zwar seit Leibnitzens und Wolfs Zeit ge- 5
leistet hat, so würde die Aufgabe der Königlichen Akademie der Wissenschaften aufgelöset seyn.

Es sind also drey Stadien, welche die Philosophie zum Behuf der
Metaphysik durchzugehen hatte. Das erste war das Stadium des Dogmatism; das zweyte das des Sceptizism; das dritte das des Kriticism der 10
reinen Vernunft.

Diese Zeitordnung ist in der Natur des menschlichen Erkenntnißvermögens gegründet. Wenn die zwey erstern zurückgelegt sind, so kann
der Zustand der Metaphysik viele Zeitalter hindurch schwankend seyn,
vom unbegrenzten Vertrauen der Vernunft auf sich selbst, zum grenzen- 15
losen Mißtrauen, und wiederum von diesem zu jenem abspringen. Durch
eine Kritik ihres Vermögens selbst aber würde sie in einen beharrlichen
Zustand, nicht allein des Äußern, sondern auch des Innern, fernerhin
weder einer Vermehrung noch Verminderung bedürftig, oder auch nur
fähig zu seyn, versetzt werden. 20

---

supersensible. When a determination of the scope, content, and limits of human knowledge has been completed — when this has been done with reference to Germany, particularly since the time of Liebniz and Wolff — then the Royal Academy of Science's task will have been completed.

Thus, philosophy has gone through three stages in regard to metaphysics. The first was the stage of dogmatism, the second skepticism, and the third the criticism of pure reason.

This temporal order is based on the nature of the human capacity for knowledge. When the first two had been gone through, metaphysics was in such a state that for many generations it swung from unbounded trust in reason in itself to boundless mistrust and then back again. Through a critique of its capacities it itself would have been able to establish reason's permanent status in regard not only to external but also to internal [matters], neither requiring nor permitting either extension or restriction.

Abhandlung.

Man kann die Lösung der vorliegenden Aufgabe unter zwey Ab-
theilungen bringen, davon die eine das Formale des Verfahrens der
Vernunft, sie als theoretische Wissenschaft zustande zu bringen, die
5 andere das Materiale — den Endzweck, den die Vernunft mit der
Metaphysik beabsichtiget, wiefern er erreicht, oder nicht erreicht ist, von
jenem Verfahren ableitet.

Der erste Theil wird also nur die neuerdings geschehenen Schritte
zur Metaphysik, der zweyte die Fortschritte der Metaphysik selber im
10 Felde der reinen Vernunft vorstellig machen. Der erste enthält den
neuern Zustand der Transscendentalphilosophie, der zweyte den der
eigentlichen Metaphysik.

Die erste Abtheilung.

Geschichte der Transscendentalphilosophie
15 ### unter uns in neuerer Zeit.

Der erste Schritt, der in dieser Vernunftforschung geschehen ist,
ist die Unterscheidung der analytischen von den synthetischen Urtheilen
überhaupt. — Wäre diese zu Leibnitzens oder Wolfs Zeiten deutlich erkannt worden, wir würden diesen Unterschied irgend in einer seitdem
20 erschienenen Logik oder Metaphysik, nicht allein berührt, sondern auch
als wichtig eingeschärft finden. Denn die erste Art Urtheile ist jederzeit
Urtheil a priori und mit dem Bewußtseyn seiner Nothwendigkeit verbunden. Das zweyte kann empirisch seyn, und die Logik vermag nicht
die Bedingung anzuführen, unter der ein synthetisches Urtheil a priori
25 statt finden würde.

Treatise

One can separate the solution to the foregoing problem into two parts. The first deals with reason's *formal* procedure in making metaphysics a theoretical science. The other deals with *content* — the ultimate end that reason intends to attain in metaphysics — and its success or failure in attaining it, which depends on that procedure.

The *first part* will thus present only the recent steps in metaphysics, the *second*, metaphysics' progress in the realm of pure reason. The first contains transcendental philosophy's new position, the second metaphysics proper.

———

FIRST SECTION

The History of Transcendental Philosophy in Modern Times

The *first step* to be taken in this rational investigation is to make the general distinction between analytic and synthetic judgments.[21] Had this distinction been clearly understood during Leibniz's or Wolff's time, we would have found every logic or metaphysics that has since appeared not only to have depended on it but also to have stressed its importance. For the first form of judgment is always a priori and accompanied by the consciousness of its necessity. The second can be empirical, and logic cannot permit specification of the conditions under which a synthetic judgment a priori will occur.

Der zwehte Schritt ist, die Frage auch nur aufgeworfen zu haben: Wie sind synthetische Urtheile a priori möglich? Denn daß es deren gebe, beweisen zahlreiche Behspiele der allgemeinen Naturlehre, vornehmlich aber der reinen Mathematik. Hume hat schon ein Verdienst, einen Fall anzuführen, nämlich den vom Gesetze der Kausalität, wodurch er alle 5 Metaphysiker in Verlegenheit setzte. Was wäre geschehen, wenn er oder irgend ein Anderer, sie im Allgemeinen vorgestellt hätte! Die ganze Metaphysik hätte so lange müssen zur Seite gelegt bleiben, bis sie wäre aufgelöst worden.

Der dritte Schritt ist die Aufgabe: „Wie ist.aus synthetischen 10 Urtheilen ein Erkenntniß a priori möglich?" Erkenntniß ist ein Urtheil, aus welchem ein Begriff hervorgeht, der objective Realität hat, d. i. dem ein correspondirender Gegenstand in der Erfahrung gegeben werden kann. Alle Erfahrung aber besteht aus Anschauung eines Gegenstandes, d. i. einer unmittelbaren und einzelnen Vorstellung, durch die der Gegenstand, 15 als zum Erkenntniß gegeben, und aus einem Begriff, d. i. einer mittelbaren Vorstellung durch ein Merkmal, was mehreren Gegenständen gemein ist, dadurch er also gedacht wird. — Eine von behden Arten der Vorstellungen für sich allein macht kein Erkenntniß aus, und soll es synthetische Erkenntnisse a priori geben: so muß es auch Anschauungen sowohl 20 als Begriffe a priori geben, deren Möglichkeit also zuerst erörtert, und dann die objective Realität derselben durch den nothwendigen Gebrauch derselben, zum Behuf der Möglichkeit der Erfahrung bewiesen werden muß.

Eine Anschauung, die a priori möglich sehn soll, kann nur die Form betreffen, unter welcher der Gegenstand angeschauet wird, denn das 25 heißt, etwas sich a priori vorstellen, sich vor der Wahrnehmung, d. i. dem empirischen Bewußtsehn, und unabhängig von demselben, eine Vorstellung davon machen. Das Empirische aber in der Wahrnehmung, die Empfindung oder der Eindruck (impressio), ist die Materie der Anschauung, beh welcher also die Anschauung nicht eine Vorstellung a priori sehn würde. 30 Eine solche nun, die blos die Form betrifft, heißt reine Anschauung, die, wenn sie möglich sehn soll, von der Erfahrung unabhängig sehn muß.

Es ist aber nicht die Form des Objectes, wie es an sich beschaffen ist, sondern die des Subjectes, nämlich des Sinnes, welcher Art Vorstellung er fähig ist, welche die Anschauung a priori möglich macht. Denn sollte 35 diese Form von den Objecten selbst hergenommen werden, so müßten wir dieses vorher wahrnehmen, und könnten uns nur in dieser Wahrnehmung der Beschaffenheit desselben bewußt werden. Das wäre aber alsdenn eine empirische Anschauung a priori. Ob sie aber das letztere seh

The *second step* consists solely in raising the question: How are synthetic judgments a priori possible? For that there are such is proven by numerous examples drawn from the general science of nature, but principally, from pure mathematics. *Hume* had already performed a service by bringing forth a case — the one concerning the law of causality — that constituted an embarrassment for all metaphysicians. What would have happened if he or any one else had stated the problem in universal form! All metaphysics would have had to have been set to one side until it was solved.[22]

The *third step* is the problem: How is it possible to gain a priori cognition from synthetic judgments? Cognition is a judgment from which arises a concept possessing objective reality, that is, one for which a corresponding object can be given in experience.[23] However, all experience is constituted from [1] an intuition of an object, i.e., an immediate, singular presentation through which an object is given for knowledge, and [2] a concept, i.e., a mediate representation through a characteristic common to several objects, by means of which, therefore, the object is thought. By themselves neither of the kinds of representation constitutes cognition. For there to be a priori synthetic cognition, then, there must be a priori intuitions and a priori concepts, whose possibility must be discussed; after that, their objective reality must be demonstrated by showing that their use is necessary for the possibility of experience.

An intuition that is to be possible a priori can concern only the form under which an object is intuited. For to intuit something a priori means to represent it a priori, before perception — i.e., empirical consciousness — and to make a representation of this object independently of perception. The empirical element of perception — sensation or the impression (*impressio*) — is the matter of intuition, with respect to which intuition would not thus be an a priori representation. An intuition concerned only with form is called pure intuition. And if such be possible, it must be independent of experience.[24]

However, it is not the form of the object as it is constituted in itself, but rather that of the subject — specifically, the kind of representations its senses are capable [of having] — that makes intuition a priori possible. For if this form were taken from objects themselves, we would have had previously to perceive those objects, and we could be conscious of their constitution only in this perception. But that would then be an empirical intuition a priori. We can

ober nicht, davon können wir uns alsbald überzeugen, wenn wir darauf
Acht haben, ob das Urtheil, welches dem Object diese Form beylegt, Nothwendigkeit bey sich führe, ober nicht, denn im letztern Falle ist es blos
empirisch.

5 Die Form des Objectes, wie es allein in einer Anschauung a priori
vorgestellt werden kann, gründet sich also nicht auf die Beschaffenheit dieses
Objectes an sich, sondern auf die Naturbeschaffenheit des Subjects,
welches einer anschaulichen Vorstellung des Gegenstandes fähig ist, und
dieses Subjective in der formalen Beschaffenheit des Sinnes, als der
10 Empfänglichkeit für die Anschauung eines Gegenstandes, ist allein dasjenige, was a priori, b. i. vor aller Wahrnehmung vorhergehend, Anschauung a priori möglich macht, und nun läßt sich diese und die Möglichkeit synthetischer Urtheile a priori von Seiten der Anschauung gar wohl
begreifen.

15 Denn man kann a priori wissen, wie und unter welcher Form die
Gegenstände der Sinne werden angeschaut werden, nämlich so, wie
es die subjective Form der Sinnlichkeit, b. i. der Empfänglichkeit des
Subjectes für die Anschauung jener Objecte, mit sich bringt, und man
müßte, um genau zu sprechen, eigentlich nicht sagen, daß von uns die
20 Form des Objectes in der reinen Anschauung vorgestellt werde, sondern
daß es blos formale und subjective Bedingung der Sinnlichkeit sey,
unter welcher wir gegebene Gegenstände a priori anschauen.

Das ist also die eigenthümliche Beschaffenheit unsrer (menschlichen)
Anschauung, sofern die Vorstellung der Gegenstände uns nur als sinnlichen
25 Wesen möglich ist. Wir könnten uns wohl eine unmittelbare (directe)
Vorstellungsart eines Gegenstandes denken, die nicht nach Sinnlichkeits-
bedingungen, also durch den Verstand, die Objecte anschaut. Aber von
einer solchen haben wir keinen haltbaren Begriff; doch ist es nöthig, sich
einen solchen zu denken, um unsrer Anschauungsform nicht alle Wesen,
30 die Erkenntnißvermögen haben, zu unterwerfen. Denn es mag seyn,
daß einige Weltwesen unter andrer Form dieselben Gegenstände anschauen dürften; es kann auch seyn, daß diese Form in allen Weltwesen
und zwar nothwendig, eben dieselbe sey, so sehen wir diese Nothwendigkeit doch nicht ein, so wenig, als die Möglichkeit eines höchsten Verstandes,
35 der in seiner Erkenntniß von aller Sinnlichkeit und zugleich vom Bedürfniß, durch Begriffe zu erkennen, frey, die Gegenstände in der bloßen
(intellectuellen) Anschauung vollkommen erkennt.

Nun beweiset die Kritik der reinen Vernunft an den Vorstellungen
von Raum und Zeit, daß sie solche reine Anschauungen sind, als wir eben

be satisfied as to whether or not the latter can exist as soon as we take note of whether or not the judgment that attributes this form to objects is necessary; for if not, the judgment is merely empirical.[25]

The form of objects, which is all that can be presented in an intuition a priori, is not based on the constitution of this object in itself but on the natural constitution of a subject capable of representing objects in intuition.[26] And it is only this subjective [element] in the formal constitution of the senses — as the receptivity to sensation in intuiting objects — which a priori makes possible a priori intuition, i.e., intuition preceding all perception. This, and the possibility of a priori synthetic judgments, is easily conceived from the point of view of intuition.

One can know a priori, then, how and under what form the objects of the senses will be intuited, namely, in accordance with the subjective form of sensibility — that is, in accordance with the inherent capacity for receiving sensations that the subject brings with it — and in order to speak precisely, one must not, as a matter of fact, say that the form of objects is represented by us in pure intuition, but that what is represented is merely the formal and subjective condition of sensibility under which we a priori intuit given objects.[27]

That is the special constitution of our (human) intuition insofar as the representation of objects is possible for us simply as sensuous beings. We can, to be sure, think of an immediate (*direkte*) manner of representing an object, one that does not depend on conditions of sensibility and, consequently, that intuits objects through the understanding. However, we do not have a defensible concept of such [a mode of intuiting], even though it is necessary to think of such an understanding in order not to attribute our form of intuition to all beings possessing capacities for knowledge. For it may be that some beings in this world are able to intuit the same objects under another form; it may also be that this form is the same in all beings in this world, and, indeed, necessarily so. But we have just as little insight into this necessity as into the possibility of a supreme understanding, which, free from all reliance on sensibility and the need to use concepts in knowing, knows objects perfectly by means of mere (intellectual) intuition.[28]

Now the *Critique of Pure Reason* proves that the presentations of space and time are precisely such pure intuitions as we require — that

gefordert haben, daß sie seyn müssen, um a priori allem unserm Erkenntniß der Dinge zum Grunde zu liegen, und ich kann mich mit Zutrauen darauf berufen, ohne wegen Einwürfe besorgt zu seyn. —

Nur will ich noch anmerken, daß in Ansehung des innern Sinnes
das doppelte Ich im Bewußtseyn meiner selbst, nämlich das der innern
sinnlichen Anschauung und das des denkenden Subjects, Vielen scheint
zwey Subjecte in einer Person vorauszusetzen.

Dieses ist nun die Theorie, daß Raum und Zeit nichts als subjective
Formen unsrer sinnlichen Anschauung sind, und gar nicht den Objecten
an sich zuständige Bestimmungen, daß aber gerade nur darum wir
a priori diese unsre Anschauungen bestimmen können mit dem Bewußtseyn der Nothwendigkeit der Urtheile in Bestimmung derselben, wie z. B.
in der Geometrie. Bestimmen aber heißt synthetisch urtheilen.

Diese Theorie kann die Lehre der Idealität des Raumes und der
Zeit heißen, weil diese als etwas, was gar nicht den Sachen an sich selbst
anhängt, vorgestellt werden; eine Lehre, die nicht etwa blos Hypothese,
um die Möglichkeit der synthetischen Erkenntniß a priori erklären zu
können, sondern demonstrirte Wahrheit ist, weil es schlechterdings unmöglich ist, sein Erkenntniß über den gegebenen Begriff zu erweitern,
ohne irgend eine Anschauung, und wenn diese Erweiterung a priori
geschehen soll, ohne eine Anschauung a priori unterzulegen, und eine
Anschauung a priori gleichfalls unmöglich ist, ohne sie in der formalen
Beschaffenheit des Subjects, nicht in der des Objects, zu suchen, weil
unter Voraussetzung der erstern alle Gegenstände der Sinne jener gemäß
in der Anschauung vorgestellt werden, also sie a priori, und dieser Beschaffenheit nach als nothwendig erkannt werden müssen, anstatt daß,
wenn das letztere angenommen wurde, die synthetischen Urtheile a priori
empirisch und zufällig seyn würden, welches sich widerspricht.

Diese Idealität des Raumes und der Zeit ist gleichwohl zugleich
eine Lehre der vollkommenen Realität derselben in Ansehung der Gegenstände der Sinne (der äußern und des innern) als Erscheinungen,
d. i. als Anschauungen, so fern ihre Form von der subjectiven Beschaffenheit der Sinne abhängt, deren Erkenntniß, da sie auf Prinzipien a priori
der reinen Anschauung gegründet ist, eine sichere und demonstrable
Wissenschaft zuläßt, daher dasjenige Subjective, was die Beschaffenheit
der Sinnenanschauung, in Ansehung ihres Materialen, nämlich der
Empfindung betrifft, z. B. Körper im Licht als Farbe, im Schalle als

they must be in order to provide an a priori basis for all our knowledge of things — and I can confidently refer to it, without being concerned about objections.

Regarding inner sense, I will now remark only that to many the double I in the consciousness of myself — namely, the I of inner sensuous intuition and the I of the thinking subject — seems to presuppose two subjects in a single person.[29]

———————

Now this is the theory: space and time are nothing but subjective forms of our sensible intuition and in no way proper determinations of objects themselves; but for precisely this reason, we can determine our intuitions a priori with a consciousness of the necessity of the judgments that determine them, as, e.g., in geometry. To determine means, however, to judge synthetically.

This theory can be called the doctrine of the ideality of space and time, since it presents them as being absolutely independent of things in themselves, a doctrine that is not merely an hypothesis to clarify the possibility of synthetic knowledge a priori, but one that is rather a demonstrated truth; for without intuition it is absolutely impossible to extend knowledge beyond [the content of] a given concept. And if this extension is to occur a priori, it must be based on a priori intuition, because unless one seeks such an a priori intuition in the formal constitution of the subject, rather than in that of the object, it is impossible. For on the former assumption, all objects of the senses will be represented as in conformity with intuition, and it must thus be possible to know them a priori and as necessarily conforming with the constitution of the subject, while on the latter assumption, a priori synthetic judgments would have to be empirical and contingent, which is self-contradictory.

This [doctrine of the] ideality of space and time is nonetheless at the same time a doctrine of their complete reality in respect to the objects of the senses (both outer and inner) as *appearances*, that is, as intuitions. This is true insofar as the form of appearances depends on the subjective constitution of the senses, whose knowledge, since it is based on a priori principles of pure intuition, provides for a secure and demonstrable science. Therefore, what is subjective, what concerns the properties of sensuous intuition in regard to its material content, namely sensation — for example, bodies in light as colors, in vibration as sounds, in salts as acids, and so on — remains merely

Töne, oder im Salze als Säuern usw., blos subjectiv bleiben, und kein Erkenntniß des Objects, mithin keine für jedermann gültige Vorstellung in der empirischen Anschauung darlegen, kein Beyspiel von jenen abgeben können, indem sie nicht, so wie Raum und Zeit, Data zu Er-
5 kenntnissen a priori enthalten, und überhaupt nicht einmal zur Erkenntniß der Objecte gezählt werden können.

Ferner ist noch anzumerken, daß Erscheinung, im transscendentalen Sinn genommen, da man von Dingen sagt, sie sind Erscheinungen (Phaenomena), ein Begriff von ganz anderer Bedeutung ist, als wenn
10 ich sage, dieses Ding erscheint mir so oder so, welches die physische Erscheinung anzeigen soll, und Apparenz, oder Schein, genannt werden kann. Denn in der Sprache der Erfahrung sind diese Gegenstände der Sinne, weil ich sie nur mit andern Gegenständen der Sinne vergleichen kann, z. B. der Himmel mit allen seinen Sternen, ob er zwar blos Er-
15 scheinung ist, wie Dinge an sich selbst gedacht, und wenn von diesem gesagt wird, er hat den Anschein von einem Gewölbe, so bedeutet hier der Schein das Subjective in der Vorstellung eines Dinges, was eine Ursache seyn kann, es in einem Urtheil fälschlich für objectiv zu halten.

Und so ist der Satz, daß alle Vorstellungen der Sinne uns nur die
20 Gegenstände als Erscheinungen zu erkennen geben, ganz und gar nicht mit dem Urtheile einerley, sie. enthielten nur den Schein von Gegenständen, wie es der Idealist behaupten würde.

In der Theorie aber aller Gegenstände der Sinne, als bloßer Erscheinungen, ist nichts, was befremdlich//auffallender ist, als daß ich,
25 als der Gegenstand des innern Sinnes, d. i. als Seele betrachtet, mir selbst blos als Erscheinung bekannt werden könne, nicht nach demjenigen, was ich als Ding an sich selbst bin, und doch verstattet die Vorstellung der Zeit, als blos formale innere Anschauung a priori, welche allem Erkenntniß meiner selbst zum Grunde liegt, keine andre Erklärungsart
30 der Möglichkeit, jene Form als Bedingung des Selbstbewußtseyns anzuerkennen.

Das Subjective in der Form der Sinnlichkeit, welches a priori aller Anschauung der Objecte zum Grunde liegt, machte es uns möglich, a priori von Objecten ein Erkenntniß zu haben, wie sie uns erscheinen.
35 Jetzt wollen wir diesen Ausdruck noch näher bestimmen, indem wir dieses Subjective als die Vorstellungsart erklären, wie unser Sinn von Gegenständen, den äußern oder dem innern (d. i. von uns selbst), afficirt wird, um sagen zu können, daß wir diese nur als Erscheinungen erkennen.

subjective and yields no knowledge of objects, and, consequently, what is subjective cannot provide examples of representations in empirical intuition that are valid for everyone, for it contains no data for a priori cognition, as do space and time. In general, then, the subjective element [of sensible intuition] cannot be counted as knowledge of objects.[30]

It has further to be noted that appearance, taken in the transcendental sense, where one says of things that they are appearances (*Phaenomena*), is a concept that means something entirely different from when I say, this thing appears to me in this or that way. Saying the latter merely indicates physical appearance, which can be regarded as [its] appearance (*Apparenz*) or semblance. In the language of experience, the objects of the senses are regarded as things in themselves, for I can only compare them with other objects of the senses thought of as things in themselves — e.g., heaven with all its stars, even though it is merely appearance; and if one says of the starry heaven that it gives the illusion of a vault, the term semblance [denotes] the subjective [element] in the representation of a thing, which can be a reason for falsely judging that it [the thing] is objective.[31]

And so the proposition that all sensuous representations provide knowledge of objects only as appearances is altogether different from the proposition that such representations comprise only the semblance of objects, which the idealist would maintain.

But nothing is as strange or more astounding in the theory that all objects of the senses are mere appearances, than that I, as the object of inner sense, that is, considered as soul, am acquainted with myself only as appearance, not as that which I am as a thing in itself. Yet the representation of time, as mere a priori form of inner intuition underlying all knowledge of myself, permits of no other explanation of the possibility of recognizing that form to be the condition of self-consciousness.

The *subjective* [element] that constitutes the form of sensibility, which a priori underlies all intuition of objects, makes it possible for us to have a priori knowledge of objects as they *appear* to us. We want now to define this expression still more explicitly, since we explain this subjective (element of representation) as the manner of representing how those objects — outer or inner (i.e., ourselves) — affect our senses, and thus we can say that we know these objects only as appearances.

71

Ich bin mir meiner selbst bewußt, ist ein Gedanke, der schon ein zweifaches Ich enthält, das Ich als Subject, und das Ich als Object. Wie es möglich sey, daß ich, der ich denke, mir selber ein Gegenstand (der Anschauung) seyn, und so mich von mir selbst unterscheiden könne, ist schlechterdings unmöglich zu erklären, obwohl es ein unbezweifeltes Factum ist; es zeigt aber ein über alle Sinnenanschauung so weit erhabenes Vermögen an, daß es, als der Grund der Möglichkeit eines Verstandes, die gänzliche Absonderung von allem Vieh, dem wir das Vermögen, zu sich selbst Ich zu sagen, nicht Ursache haben beyzulegen, zur Folge hat, und in eine Unendlichkeit von selbstgemachten Vorstellungen 10 und Begriffen hinaussieht. Es wird dadurch aber nicht eine doppelte Persönlichkeit gemeynt, sondern nur Ich, der ich denke und anschaue, ist die Person, das Ich aber des Objectes, was von mir angeschauet wird, ist gleich andern Gegenständen außer mir, die Sache.

Von dem Ich in der erstern Bedeutung (dem Subject der Apper- 15 ception), dem logischen Ich, als Vorstellung a .priori, ist schlechterdings nichts weiter zu erkennen möglich, was es für ein Wesen, und von welcher Naturbeschaffenheit es sey; es ist gleichsam, wie das Substanziale, was übrig bleibt, wenn ich alle Accidenzen, die ihm inhäriren, weggelassen habe, das aber schlechterdings gar nicht weiter erkannt werden kann, 20 weil die Accidenzen gerade das waren, woran ich seine Natur erkennen konnte.

Das Ich aber in der zweyten Bedeutung (als Subject der Perception), das psychologische Ich, als empirisches Bewußtseyn, ist mannigfacher Erkenntniß fähig, worunter die Form der inneren Anschauung, 25 die Zeit, diejenige ist, welche a priori allen Wahrnehmungen und deren Verbindung zum Grunde liegt, deren Auffassung (apprehensio) der Art, wie das Subject dadurch afficirt wird, d. i. der Zeitbedingung gemäß ist, indem das sinnliche Ich vom intellectuellen, zur Aufnahme derselben ins Bewußtseyn, bestimmt wird. 30

Daß dieses so sey, davon kann uns jede innere, von uns angestellte psychologische Beobachtung zum Beleg und Beyspiel dienen; denn es wird dazu erfordert, daß wir den innern Sinn, zum Theil auch wohl bis zum Grade der Beschwerlichkeit, vermittelst der Aufmerksamkeit afficiren (denn Gedanken, als factische Bestimmungen des Vorstellungs- 35 vermögens, gehören auch mit zur empirischen Vorstellung unsers Zustandes), um ein Erkenntniß von dem, was uns der innere Sinn darlegt, zuvörderst in der Anschauung unsrer selbst zu haben, welche uns dann uns selbst nur vorstellig macht, wie wir uns erscheinen, indessen daß das

That I am conscious of myself is a thought that already contains a twofold self, the I as subject and the I as object. How it might be possible for the I that I think to be an object (of intuition) for me, one that enables me to distinguish me from myself, is absolutely impossible to explain, even though it is an indubitable fact; it indicates, however, a capacity so highly elevated above sensuous intuition that, as the basis for the possibility of understanding, it has the effect of separating us from all animals, to which we have no reason for ascribing the ability to say I to themselves, and results in an infinity of self-constituted representations and concepts. But a double personality is not meant by this double I. Only the I that I think and intuit is a person; the I that belongs to the object that is intuited by me is, similarly to other objects outside me, a thing.

Absolutely no further knowledge regarding the I in the first sense (the subject of apperception) — the logical I, considered as an a priori representation — is possible, neither with respect to what sort of being it is nor [with regard to] its natural constitution. It is as if the substance were what remains when all of its inhering accidents have been stripped away, but cannot in any way be further known [when stripped of its accidents], because its accidents are precisely that by means of which I can know its nature.[32]

But the I in the second sense (as subject of perception), the psychological I, as empirical consciousness, is capable of [providing] all sorts of cognition, and in regard to it the form of inner sense, time, is the a priori ground underlying all perceptions and their connection, whose apprehension (*apprehensio*) is the way the subject is thereby affected, i.e., in conformity with the condition of time, whereas the sensible I is determined by the intellectual I in the former's reception of the latter into consciousness.

Every inner psychological observation we make serves as a proof and example that this is so; for such observation requires that one can affect inner sense by means of attention — even if doing so involves a certain degree of difficulty (for thoughts, as factual determinations of the capacity for representing, belong to the empirical represenation of our state) — so as to gain knowledge of what in the first place inner sense discloses in the intuition of our own selves. This, of course, presents us to ourselves only in the way in which we appear, whereas the logical I, which is indeed the subject as it is in

logische Ich das Subject zwar, wie es an sich ist, im reinen Bewußtseyn, nicht als Receptivität, sondern reine Spontaneität anzeigt, weiter aber auch keiner Erkenntniß seiner Natur fähig ist.

Von Begriffen a priori.

5 Die subjective Form der Sinnlichkeit, wenn sie, wie es nach der Theorie der Gegenstände derselben als Erscheinungen geschehen muß, auf Objecte, als Formen derselben, angewandt wird, führt in ihrer Bestimmung eine Vorstellung herbey, die von dieser unzertrennlich ist, nämlich die des Zusammengesetzten. Denn einen bestimmten Raum 10 können wir uns nicht anders vorstellen, als, indem wir ihn ziehen, d. i. einen Raum zu dem andern hinzuthun, und ebenso ist es mit der Zeit bewandt.

Nun ist die Vorstellung eines Zusammengesetzten, als eines solchen, nicht bloße Anschauung, sondern erfordert den Begriff einer Zusammen-
15 setzung, sofern er auf die Anschauung in Raum und Zeit angewandt wird. Dieser Begriff also (sammt dem seines Gegentheiles, des Ein-fachen) ist ein Begriff, der nicht von Anschauungen, als eine in diesen enthaltene Theilvorstellung abgezogen, sondern ein Grundbegriff ist, und zwar a priori, endlich der einzige Grundbegriff a priori, der allen Be-
20 griffen von Gegenständen der Sinne ursprünglich im Verstande zum Grunde liegt.

Es werden also so viel Begriffe a priori im Verstande liegen, wo-runter die Gegenstände, die den Sinnen gegeben werden, stehen müssen, als es Arten der Zusammensetzung (Synthesis) mit Bewußtseyn, d. i.
25 als es Arten der synthetischen Einheit der Apperception des in der An-schauung gegebenen Mannigfaltigen giebt.

Diese Begriffe nun sind die reinen Verstandesbegriffe von allen Gegenständen, die unsern Sinnen vorkommen mögen, und die unter dem Namen der Kategorien vom Aristoteles, obzwar mit frembartigen
30 Begriffen untermengt, und von den Scholastikern unter dem der Prä-dicamente mit eben denselben Fehlern vorgestellt, wohl hätten in eine systematisch geordnete Tafel gebracht werden können, wenn das, was die Logik von dem Mannigfaltigen in der Form der Urtheile lehrt, vorher in dem Zusammenhange eines Systems wäre aufgeführt worden.

35 Der Verstand zeigt sein Vermögen lediglich in Urtheilen, welche nichts anders sind, als die Einheit des Bewußtseyns im Verhältniß der Begriffe überhaupt, unbestimmt, ob jene Einheit analytisch oder synthe-

74

itself in pure consciousness, signifies pure spontaneity, not receptivity. Beyond this no knowledge of the nature of the logical I is possible.

Of A Priori Concepts

When the subjective form of sensibility is applied to objects as their form — and this must occur, given the theory that sensuous objects are appearances — its determination of objects entails a representation that is inseparable from those objects, namely, that of composedness. For we cannot represent a determinate space to ourselves except by drawing it, i.e., by joining one [portion of] space to another, and it is exactly the same for time.[33]

Now the representation of a composedness as such is not a mere intuition, but instead requires the concept of a composition, insofar as it is applied to intuition in space and time. Thus, this concept (together with that of its contrary, simplicity) is not abstracted from intuitions, as one of the partial representations they contain. Rather, it is a fundamental concept, indeed an a priori one. Finally, it is the sole a priori fundamental concept originally in the understanding that is the basis for all concepts of the objects of the senses.[34]

Thus, in understanding there will be as many a priori concepts, under which the objects given by the senses must be subsumed, as there are modes of conscious composition (*Synthesis*), that is, as there are modes of synthetic unity of apperception of the manifold given in intuition.

These concepts are the pure concepts of the understanding that pertain to all objects that may be met with by our senses. They were presented by Aristotle under the name of categories, although mixed with heterogeneous concepts, and by the Scholastics under the name of *predicaments*, with the very same errors. They probably could have been presented in a systematically ordered table if what logic teaches concerning the manifold in the form of judgments had previously been presented with the coherence of a system.

Understanding manifests its power solely in judgments, which are nothing but the unity of consciousness in the relation of concepts in general, regardless of whether this unity is analytic or synthetic. Now

tisch ist. — Nun sind die reinen Verstandesbegriffe von in der Anschauung gegebenen Gegenständen überhaupt eben dieselbe logische Functionen, aber nur so fern sie die synthetische Einheit der Apperception des in einer Anschauung überhaupt gegebenen Mannigfaltigen a priori vorstellen; also konnte die Tafel der Kategorien, jener logischen parallel, vollständig 5 entworfen werden, welches aber vor Erscheinung der Kritik der reinen Vernunft nicht geschehen war.

Es ist aber wohl zu merken, daß diese Kategorien, oder, wie sie sonst heißen, Prädicamente, keine bestimmte Art der Anschauung (wie etwa die uns Menschen allein mögliche), wie Raum und Zeit, welche sinnlich 10 ist, voraussetzen, sondern nur Denkformen sind für den Begriff von einem Gegenstande der Anschauung überhaupt, welcher Art diese auch sey, wenn es auch eine übersinnliche Anschauung wäre, von der wir uns specifisch keinen Begriff machen können. Denn wir müssen uns immer einen Begriff von einem Gegenstande durch den reinen Verstand machen, 15 von dem wir etwas a priori urtheilen wollen, wenn wir auch nachher finden, daß er überschwenglich sey und ihm keine objective Realität verschafft werden könne, sodaß die Kategorie für sich von den Formen der Sinnlichkeit, Raum und Zeit, nicht abhängig ist, sondern auch andre für uns gar nicht denkbare Formen zur Unterlage haben mag, wenn 20 diese nur das Subjective betreffen, was a priori vor aller Erkenntniß vorhergeht, und synthetische Urtheile a priori möglich macht.

Noch gehören zu den Kategorien, als ursprünglichen Verstandesbegriffen, auch die Prädicabilien, als aus jener ihrer Zusammensetzung entspringende, und also abgeleitete, entweder reine Verstandes-, oder 25 sinnlich bedingte Begriffe a priori, von deren ersteren das Dasehn als Größe vorgestellt, d. i. die Dauer, oder die Veränderung, als Dasehn mit entgegengesetzten Bestimmungen, von den andern der Begriff der Bewegung, als Veränderung des Ortes im Raume, Beyspiele abgeben, die gleichfalls vollständig aufgezählt, und in einer Tafel syste- 30 matisch vorgestellt werden könnten.

Die Transscendentalphilosophie, d. i. die Lehre von der Möglichkeit aller Erkenntniß a priori überhaupt, welche die Kritik der reinen Vernunft ist, von der itzt die Elemente vollständig dargelegt worden, hat zu ihrem Zweck die Gründung einer Metaphysik, deren Zweck wiederum als 35 Endzweck der reinen Vernunft, dieser ihre Erweiterung von der Grenze des Sinnlichen zum Felde des Übersinnlichen beabsichtiget, welches ein

understanding's pure concepts of the objects given in intuition are the same logical functions, but only insofar as they represent the synthetic unity of apperception a priori with what is given in a manifold in an intuition in general. Thus, the table of categories could have been completely sketched out parallel to the [table of] logical [judgments]. But this did not happen until the appearance of the *Critique of Pure Reason.*[35]

But it is well to note that these categories, or, as they are otherwise known, *predicaments*, do not presuppose any determinate mode of intuition (as, for instance, the sole one possible for us humans), like space and time, that is sensible. They are forms of thought for the concept of an object of intuition in general, no matter what kind it may be, even if it is non-sensible, of which we can specifically form no concept. For by means of pure understanding we must always constitute a concept of an object about which we want to judge something a priori, even if we later find that it is transcendent and that no objective reality can be provided it. In itself, the category does not depend on the forms of sensibility, space and time, but may have other forms of which we simply cannot think as its foundation, if these [forms] pertain only to what is subjective that a priori precedes all cognition and makes synthetic a priori judgments possible.

Additionally, the predicaments belong among the categories as original concepts of the understanding; thus, they are derivative and are either pure concepts of the understanding or sensibly conditioned a priori concepts. The former are represented by existence as quantity, that is, duration, or as alteration, that is, as existence with opposing determinations; the latter sort are exemplified by the concept of motion as change of location in space, which likewise can be completely ennumerated and systematically presented in a table.[36]

Transcendental philosophy—that is, the doctrine of all a priori knowledge in general, which the *Critique of Pure Reason* is, and whose elements have now been completely laid out—has as its purpose the foundation of a metaphysics, which, as the ultimate end of pure reason, in turn has as its objective the extension of reason beyond the boundaries of the sensible to the field of the supersensible. This is a

Überschritt ist, der, damit er nicht ein gefährlicher Sprung sey, indessen daß er doch auch nicht ein continuirlicher Fortgang in derselben Ordnung der Prinzipien ist, eine den Fortschritt hemmende Bedenklichkeit an der Grenze beyder Gebiete nothwendig macht.

5 Hieraus folgt die Eintheilung der Stadien der reinen Vernunft, in die Wissenschaftslehre, als einen sichern Fortschritt, — die Zweifellehre, als einen Stillestand, — und die Weisheitslehre, als einen Überschritt zum Endzweck der Metaphysik: so daß die erste eine theoretisch-dogmatische Doctrin, die zweyte eine sceptische Disciplin, die dritte eine 10 practisch-dogmatische enthalten wird.

Erste Abtheilung.

Von dem Umfange des theoretisch-dogmatischen Gebrauches der reinen Vernunft.

Der Inhalt dieses Abschnittes ist der Satz: der Umfang der theo-
15 retischen Erkenntniß der reinen Vernunft erstreckt sich nicht weiter, als auf Gegenstände der Sinne.

In diesem Satze, als einem exponibeln Urtheile, sind zwey Sätze enthalten:

1) daß die Vernunft, als Vermögen der Erkenntniß der Dinge
20 a priori, sich auf Gegenstände der Sinne erstrecke,

2) daß sie in ihrem theoretischen Gebrauch zwar wohl der Begriffe, aber nie einer theoretischen Erkenntniß desjenigen fähig, was kein Gegenstand der Sinne seyn kann.

Zum Beweise des erstern Satzes gehört auch die Erörterung, wie
25 von Gegenständen der Sinne ein Erkenntniß a priori möglich sey, weil wir ohne das nicht recht sicher seyn würden, ob die Urtheile über jene Gegenstände auch in der That Erkenntnisse seyen; was aber die Beschaffenheit derselben, Urtheile a priori zu seyn, betrifft, so kündiget sie die von selbst durch das Bewußtseyn ihrer Nothwendigkeit an.

30 Damit eine Vorstellung Erkenntniß sey (ich verstehe aber hier immer ein theoretisches), dazu gehört Begriff und Anschauung von einem Gegenstande in derselben Vorstellung verbunden, so daß der erstere, so wie er die letztere unter sich enthält, vorgestellt wird. Wenn nun ein Begriff ein von der Sinnenvorstellung genommener, d. i. empirischer

transition that — if it is not to be a dangerous leap, inasmuch as it does not involve a continuous development is the same order of principles — requires careful consideration that checks progress at the boundaries of both realms.

From this there follows the division of the stages of pure reason into the doctrine of scientific knowledge, progress — the doctrine of doubt, as stagnation — and the doctrine of wisdom, as a transition to the ultimate end of metaphysics. The first contains a theoretical-dogmatic doctrine, the second a skeptical discipline, and the third a practical-dogmatic doctrine.*

FIRST SECTION [sic]

The Extent of Pure Reason's
Theoretical-Dogmatic Use

The content of this section is the proposition that the extent of pure reason's theoretical knowledge reaches only to objects of the senses.

This proposition, insofar as it is an exponible judgment, contains two propositions:

(1) As a capacity for a priori cognition of things, reason extends to objects of the senses.

(2) In its theoretical use, reason is certainly capable of concepts, but not of having theoretical cognition of what cannot be an object of the senses.

An explanation of how a priori cognition of the objects of the senses is possible belongs to the proof of the first proposition, for without an explanation we would not be genuinely certain whether the judgments concerning those objects would in fact be cognition; however, as regards the property [by virtue of which] they are a priori judgments, it announces itself through consciousness of their necessity.

For a representation to be cognition (here I always mean theoretical cognition), a concept must be combined in the same representation with an intuition of an object so that the former is represented as containing the latter. Now if a concept is taken as a sensible representation, that is, as empirical, it contains as a

*[This paragraph seems out of place; it fits better with the material on page 281. Trans.]

79

Begriff ist, so enthält er als Merkmal, d. i. als Theilvorstellung, etwas, was in der Sinnenanschauung schon begriffen war, und nur der logischen Form, nämlich der Gemeingültigkeit nach, sich von der Anschauung der Sinne unterscheidet, z. B. der Begriff eines vierfüßigen Thieres in der Vorstellung eines Pferdes. 5

Ist aber der Begriff eine Kategorie, ein reiner Verstandesbegriff, so liegt er ganz außerhalb aller Anschauung, und doch muß ihm eine solche untergelegt werden, wenn er zum Erkenntniß gebraucht werden soll, und wenn dies Erkenntniß ein Erkenntniß a priori seyn soll, so muß ihm reine Anschauung untergelegt werden, und zwar der synthetischen 10 Einheit der Apperception des Mannigfaltigen der Anschauung, welche durch die Kategorie gedacht wird, gemäß, d. i. die Vorstellungskraft muß dem reinen Verstandesbegriff ein Schema a priori unterlegen, ohne das er gar keinen Gegenstand haben, mithin zu keinem Erkenntniß dienen könnte.

Da nun alle Erkenntniß, deren der Mensch fähig, sinnlich, und 15 Anschauung a priori desselben Raum oder Zeit ist, beyde aber die Gegenstände nur als Gegenstände der Sinne, nicht aber als Dinge überhaupt vorstellen: so ist unser theoretisches Erkenntniß überhaupt, ob es gleich Erkenntniß a priori seyn mag, doch auf Gegenstände der Sinne eingeschränkt, und kann innerhalb diesem Umfange allerdings 20 dogmatisch verfahren, durch Gesetze, die sie der Natur, als Inbegriff der Gegenstände der Sinne, a priori vorschreibt, über diesen Kreis aber nie hinaus kommen, um sich auch theoretisch mit ihren Begriffen zu erweitern.

Das Erkenntniß der Gegenstände der Sinne, als solcher, d. i. durch 25 empirische Vorstellungen, deren man sich bewußt ist (durch verbundene Wahrnehmungen), ist Erfahrung. Demnach übersteigt unser theoretisches Erkenntniß niemals das Feld der Erfahrung. Weil nun alles theoretische Erkenntniß mit der Erfahrung zusammen stimmen muß: so wird dieses nur auf eine oder die andere Art möglich, nämlich daß entweder die 30 Erfahrung der Grund unserer Erkenntniß, oder das Erkenntniß der Grund der Erfahrung ist. Giebt es also ein synthetisches Erkenntniß a priori, so ist kein andrer Ausweg, als es muß Bedingungen a priori der Möglichkeit der Erfahrung überhaupt enthalten. Alsdann aber enthält sie auch die Bedingungen der Möglichkeit der Gegenstände der Er- 35 fahrung überhaupt, denn nur durch Erfahrung können sie für uns erkennbare Gegenstände seyn. Die Prinzipien a priori aber, nach denen allein Erfahrung möglich ist, sind die Formen der Gegenstände, Raum und Zeit, und die Kategorien, welche die synthetische Einheit des Be-

characteristic, i.e., as a partial representation, something already conceived in sensible intuition, and is distinguished from the intuition of the senses only by its logical form, namely, its general validity, e.g., the concept of a four footed animal in the representation of a horse.

However, if the concept is a category, a pure concept of the understanding, it is independent of all intuition; yet a concept must be given an intuition if it is to be employed in cognition. And if this cognition is to be a priori, it must be given a pure intuition, and, of course, this must conform to the synthetic unity of apperception of the manifold of intuition that is thought through the categories; that is, the power of representation must give an a priori schema to the pure concept of the understanding, without which it can have no object and cannot serve as cognition.[37]

Now because all the cognition of which man is capable is sensible, and because the a priori intuition of either space or time—both of which represent objects only as objects of sense, not as things in general—our theoretical cognition in general is limited to objects of the senses, even though it may be cognition a priori. To be sure, cognition can proceed dogmatically within these boundaries by using laws, as the essence of objects of sense, that it prescribes for nature a priori. However, it can never extend itself theoretically beyond this boundary.

Cognition of the objects of the senses as such, that is, through those empirical representations which one is conscious of (through connected perceptions), is experience. Accordingly, our theoretical cognition never transcends the field of experience.[38] Now since all theoretical cognition must agree with experience, and since this agreement is possible only in one or another way, that is, either experience is the foundation of our cognition, or cognition is the foundation of experience, then, if there is synthetic cognition a priori, there is no alternative but that it must contain the a priori conditions of the possibility of experience in general. But then it also contains the conditions of the possibility of objects of experience in general, for only through experience can objects of experience be cognizable objects for us. The a priori principles in accordance with which any experience is possible are the forms of objects—space, time, and the

wußtseyns a priori enthalten, so ferne unter sie empirische Vorstellungen subsumirt werden können.

Die höchste Aufgabe der Transscendentalphilosophie ist also: Wie ist Erfahrung möglich?

5 Der Grundsatz, daß alles Erkenntniß allein von der Erfahrung anhebe, welcher eine quaestio facti betrifft, gehört also nicht hieher, und die Thatsache wird ohne Bedenken zugestanden. Ob sie aber auch allein von der Erfahrung, als dem obersten Erkenntnißgrunde, abzuleiten sey, dies ist eine quaestio iuris, deren bejahende Beantwortung den 10 Empirism der Transscendentalphilosophie, die Verneinung den Rationalism derselben einführen würde.

Der erstere ist ein Widerspruch mit sich selbst; denn wenn alles Erkenntniß empirischen Ursprungs ist, so ist der Reflexion und deren ihrem logischen Prinzip, nach dem Satz des Widerspruchs, unbeschadet, welche 15 a priori im Verstande gegründet seyn mag, und die man immer einräumen kann, doch das Synthetische der Erkenntniß, welches das Wesentliche der Erfahrung ausmacht, bloß empirisch, und nur als Erkenntniß a posteriori möglich, und die Transscendentalphilosophie ist selbst ein Unding.

Da aber gleichwohl solchen Sätzen, welche der möglichen Erfahrung 20 a priori die Regel vorschreiben, als z. B. Alle Veränderung hat ihre Ursache, ihre strenge Allgemeinheit und Nothwendigkeit, und daß sie bey allem dem doch synthetisch sind, nicht bestritten werden kann: so ist der Empirism, welcher alle diese synthetische Einheit unsrer Vorstellungen im Erkenntnisse für bloße Gewohnheitssache ausgiebt, gänzlich 25 unhaltbar, und es ist eine Transscendentalphilosophie in unsrer Vernunft fest gegründet, wie denn auch, wenn man sie als sich selbst vernichtend vorstellig machen wollte, eine andre und schlechterdings unauflösliche Aufgabe eintreten würde. Woher kommt den Gegenständen der Sinne der Zusammenhang und die Regelmäßigkeit ihres Beyeinanderseyns, 30 daß es dem Verstande möglich ist, sie unter allgemeine Gesetze zu fassen, und die Einheit derselben nach Prinzipien aufzufinden, welcher der Satz des Widerspruchs allein nicht Genüge thut, da dann der Rationalism unvermeidlich herbeygerufen werden muß.

Finden wir uns also nothgedrungen, ein Prinzip a priori der Mög- 35 lichkeit der Erfahrung selbst aufzusuchen: so ist die Frage, was ist das für eines? Alle Vorstellungen, die eine Erfahrung ausmachen, können zur Sinnlichkeit gezählt werden, eine einzige ausgenommen, d. i. die des Zusammengesetzten, als eines solchen.

Da die Zusammensetzung nicht in die Sinne fallen kann, sondern

categories, which contain a priori the synthetic unity of consciousness, insofar as empirical representations can be subsumed under it.

The highest task of transcendental philosophy is thus [to determine]: how is experience possible?[39]

The principle that all cognition begins only with experience concerns a *quaestio facti* that does not properly belong here, and the fact will be conceded without scruple.[40] But whether it is to be derived from experience alone as its ultimate foundation is a *quaestio iuris*,[41] an affirmative answer to which would introduce an empiricism of transcendental philosophy and a denial of its rationalism.

The first view is self-contradictory. For if all cognition is of empirical origin, then, without prejudice to reflection and its logical principle in conformity to the law of contradiction, which may be grounded a priori in the understanding and whose existence one can always concede, synthetic cognition, which comprises the essence of experience, is merely empirical and is possible only as cognition a posteriori. Transcendental philosophy itself is then a non-entity.

But nevertheless — since propositions that prescribe a priori rules for possible experience, as for example, *All change has a cause*, are strictly universal and necessary, yet for all that it cannot be disputed that they are synthetic — empiricism, which construes all the synthetic unity of our representations in knowledge as mere matters of custom, is totally indefensible.[42] Transcendental philosophy is so firmly rooted in our reason that if one were to represent it as self-negating, another absolutely insoluble problem would arise. [That problem is] from whence comes the coherence and the regularity of sensible objects' existence together, [a coherence and regularity] that makes it possible for understanding to apprend them under universal law and to discover their unity in accordance with principles for which the principle of contradiction alone is not sufficient, since [if it were] rationalism would have inevitably to be invoked?

We find ourselves therefore compelled to seek an a priori principle of experience itself: So the question is, what can serve as one? All representations that constitute an experience can be ascribed to sensibility, excepting only one, namely, composedness as such.

Since composition cannot occur in the senses, but rather we must

wir sie selbst machen müssen: so gehört sie nicht zur Receptivität der Sinnlichkeit, sondern zur Spontaneität des Verstandes, als Begriff a priori.

Raum und Zeit sind, subjectiv betrachtet, Formen der Sinnlichkeit, aber um von ihnen, als Objecten der reinen Anschauung, sich einen Begriff zu machen, (ohne welchen wir gar nichts von ihnen sagen könnten) dazu 5 wird a priori der Begriff eines Zusammengesetzten, mithin der Zusammensetzung (Synthesis) des Mannigfaltigen erfordert, mithin synthetische Einheit der Apperception in Verbindung dieses Mannigfaltigen, welche Einheit des Bewußtseyns, nach Verschiedenheit der anschaulichen Vorstellungen der Gegenstände in Raum und Zeit, verschiedene Functionen 10 sie zu verbinden erfordert, welche Kategorien heißen, und Verstandesbegriffe a priori sind, die zwar für sich allein noch kein Erkenntniß von einem Gegenstande überhaupt, aber doch von dem, der in der empirischen Anschauung gegeben ist, begründen, welches alsdann Erfahrung seyn würde. Das Empirische aber, d. i. dasjenige, wodurch ein Gegen 15 stand seinem Daseyn nach als gegeben vorgestellt wird, heißt Empfindung (sensatio, impressio), welche die Materie der Erfahrung ausmacht, und, mit Bewußtsein verbunden, Wahrnehmung heißt, zu der noch die Form, d. i. die synthetische Einheit der Apperception derselben im Verstande, mithin die a priori gedacht wird, hinzukommen muß, um Er 20 fahrung als empirisches Erkenntniß hervorzubringen, wozu, weil wir Raum und Zeit selbst, als in denen wir jedem Object der Wahrnehmung seine Stelle durch Begriffe anweisen müssen, nicht unmittelbar wahrnehmen, Grundsätze a priori nach bloßen Verstandesbegriffen nothwendig sind, welche ihre Realität durch die sinnliche Anschauung beweisen, 25 und in Verbindung mit dieser, nach der a priori gegebenen Form derselben, Erfahrung möglich machen, welche ein ganz gewisses Erkenntniß a posteriori ist.

*   *

Wider diese Gewißheit aber regt sich, was die äußere Erfahrung 30 betrifft, ein wichtiger Zweifel, nicht zwar darin, daß das Erkenntniß der Objecte durch dieselbe etwa ungewiß sey, sondern ob das Object, welches wir außer uns setzen, nicht vielleicht immer in uns seyn könne, und es wohl gar unmöglich sey, etwas außer uns, als ein solches, mit Gewißheit anzuerkennen. Die Metaphysik würde dadurch, daß man 35 diese Frage ganz unentschieden ließe, an ihren Fortschritten nichts verlieren, weil, da die Wahrnehmungen, aus denen, und der Form der Anschauung in ihnen, wir nach Grundsätzen durch die Kategorien Erfahrung machen, doch immer in uns seyn mögen, und ob ihnen auch

do it ourselves, it does not belong to sensibility's receptivity, but to understanding's spontaneity, as an a priori concept.

Subjectively considered, space and time are forms of intuition; but in order to make concepts of them as objects of pure intuition (without doing which we could not say anything about them) an a priori concept of composedness, consequently, of a composition (*Synthesis*) of the manifold is required. [Consequently, there must be] synthetic unity of apperception in the connection of this manifold; this unity of consciousness requires different functions to connect elements in the manifold in accordance with the differences in the intuitive representations of the objects in space and time. These are called categories and are a priori concepts of the understanding. To be sure, by themselves, they are not sufficient for *cognition* of an object in general. But still, they are the basis of the cognition of an object given in empirical intuition, which would then be experience. But the empirical element, i.e., that by means of which the existence of an object is represented as given, is called sensation (*sensatio, impressio*), which constitutes the matter of experience and, when connected with consciousness, is called perception.[43] To produce experience as empirical cognition, the form of it — that is, the synthetic unity of apperception of it in the understanding, which is thus thought a priori — must still be added. For this, principles a priori in accord with mere concepts of the understanding are necessary, since we do not perceive space and time themselves directly and yet we must indicate the place of every object of perception in them through concepts. These concepts demonstrate their reality in sensible intuition, and in conjunction with intuition they make *experience* possible according to its form, which is given a priori.[44] This experience is completely certain cognition a posteriori.

*   *

But an important doubt arises so far as the certainty of outer experience is concerned, not, to be sure, regarding whether our cognition of objects by means of such experience might perhaps be uncertain; rather, [the doubt is] whether the object that we posit as outside ourselves could not perhaps always be in us and that it would be quite impossible to recognize something as external with certainty. In leaving this question wholly undecided metaphysics would lose nothing of its progress, for, since the perceptions out of which, and the form of intuition in which, we constitute experience acccording to principles by means of categories may always be in us, whether or not

etwas außer uns entspreche, oder nicht, in der Erweiterung der Erkenntniß keine Änderung macht, indem wir ohnedem uns deshalb nicht an den Objecten, sondern nur an unsrer Wahrnehmung, die jederzeit in uns ist, halten können.

5   *   *   *

Hieraus folgt das Prinzip der Eintheilung der ganzen Metaphysik: Vom Übersinnlichen ist, was das speculative Vermögen der Vernunft betrifft, kein Erkenntniß möglich (Noumenorum non datur scientia).

*   *

10 So viel ist in neuerer Zeit in der Transscendentalphilosophie ge= schehen, und hat geschehen müssen, ehe die Vernunft einen Schritt in der eigentlichen Metaphysik, ja, auch nur einen zu derselben hat thun können, indessen daß die Leibniß=Wolfische Philosophie immer in Deutschland bey einem andern Theile ihren Weg getrost fortwanderte, in der Meynung,
15 über den alten Aristotelischen Satz des Widerspruchs noch einen neuen Kompaß zur Leitung den Philosophen in die Hand gegeben zu haben, nämlich den Satz des zureichenden Grundes für die Existenz der Dinge, zum Unterschiede von ihrer bloßen Möglichkeit nach Begriffen, und den des Unterschiedes der dunkeln, klaren, aber noch verworrenen, und der
20 deutlichen Vorstellungen, für den Unterschied der Anschauung von der Erkenntniß nach Begriffen, indessen daß sie mit aller dieser ihrer Bear= beitung unwissentlich immer nur im Felde der Logik blieb, und zur Meta= physik keinen Schritt, noch weniger aber in ihr gewonnen hatte, und dadurch bewies, daß sie vom Unterschiede der synthetischen von den
25 analytischen Urtheilen gar keine deutliche Kenntniß hatte.

Der Satz: „Alles hat seinen Grund“, welcher mit dem: „Alles ist eine Folge“, zusammenhängt, kann nur so fern zur Logik gehören, und der Unterschied statthaben zwischen den Urtheilen, welche proble= matisch gedacht werden, von denen, die assertorisch gelten sollen, und ist
30 bloß analytisch, da, wenn er von Dingen gelten sollte, daß nämlich alle Dinge nur als Folge aus der Existenz eines andern müßten angesehen werden, der zureichende Grund, auf den es doch angesehen war, gar nirgend anzutreffen seyn würde, wider welche Ungereimtheit dann die Zuflucht in dem Satz gesucht würde, daß ein Ding (ens a se), zwar
35 auch noch immer einen Grund seines Daseyns, aber in sich selbst habe, d. i. als eine Folge von sich selbst existire, wo, wenn die Ungereimtheit nicht offenbar seyn soll, der Satz gar nicht von Dingen, sondern nur von

they correspond to something outside us effects no change in the extension of cognition. For we can never have any commerce with objects, but must always stop with our perception, which is always in us.[45]

*   *   *

From this follows the principle of the division of all metaphysics: knowledge of the supersensible, which is the concern of reason's speculative capacity, is not possible (*Noumenorum non datur scientia*).

*   *

This much has happened in recent times in transcendental philosophy and must have happened before reason could have taken one step in metaphysics proper, or even one step towards metaphysics. Indeed, it is the only thing that could have happened so long as for its part the Leibnizian-Wolffian philosophy still confidently proceeded on its way in Germany, believing that in addition to the old Aristotelian law of contradiction, it had given philosophy a new compass to guide it, namely, the principle of sufficient reason for the existence of things, as distinguished from their mere possibility according to concepts.[46] The new guide also used the principle of the distinction between obscure, and clear but still confused representations and distinct ones for the distinction between intuition and conceptual knowledge.[47] But with all of this, it [the Leibnizio-Wolffian Philosophy] unknowingly remained only in the field of logic — taking no steps into that of metaphysics, much less conquering any of it — proving that it had no clear knowledge of the distinction between synthetic and analytic judgments.

Now the proposition "Everything has its cause," which goes hand-in-hand with "Everything is an effect," can only belong to logic and permit the difference between judgments that are thought problematically and those supposed to have assertoric validity. It is merely analytic, because if it were to be valid for things, to wit, that all things must be regarded only as the effect of the existence of another, the sufficient reason that was so esteemed could be found nowhere. Refuge from this absurdity is then sought in the proposition that a thing (*ens a se*) does indeed always have a reason for its existence, but [that the] reason [may] be in itself, i.e., that the thing exists as an effect of itself. Here, assuming the absurdity is not apparent, the principle has nothing to do with things, but only judgments, and is

87

Urtheilen, und zwar blos von analytischen, gelten könnte. Z. B. der Satz: „Ein jeder Körper ist theilbar" hat allerdings einen Grund, und zwar in sich selbst, d. i. er kann als Folgerung des Prädicates aus dem Begriffe des Subjectes nach dem Satze des Widerspruches, mithin nach dem Prinzip analytischer Urtheile, eingesehen werden, mithin ist er blos auf 5 einem Prinzip a priori der Logik gegründet, und thut gar keinen Schritt im Felde der Metaphysik, wo es auf Erweiterung der Erkenntniß a priori ankommt, wozu analytische Urteile nichts beytragen. Wollte aber der vermeynte Metaphysiker über den Satz des Widerspruches noch den gleichfalls logischen Satz des Grundes einführen: so hätte der die Moda- 10 lität der Urtheile noch nicht vollständig aufgezählt; denn er müßte noch den Satz der Ausschließung eines Mittlern zwischen zwey contradictorisch einander entgegengesetzten Urtheilen hinzuthun, da er dann die logischen Prinzipien der Möglichkeit, der Wahrheit, oder logischen Wirklichkeit, und der Nothwendigkeit der Urtheile in den problematischen, assertorischen 15 und apodiktischen Urtheilen würde aufgestellt haben, so fern sie alle unter einem Prinzip, nämlich dem der analytischen Urtheile, stehen. Diese Un- terlassung beweiset, daß der Metaphysiker selbst nicht einmal mit der Logik, was die Vollständigkeit der Eintheilung betrifft, im Reinen war.

Was aber das Leibnitzische Prinzip von dem logischen Unterschiede 20 der Undeutlichkeit und Deutlichkeit der Vorstellungen betrifft, wenn er behauptet, daß die erstere diejenige Vorstellungsart, die wir bloße An- schauung nannten, eigentlich nur der verworrene Begriff von ihrem Gegenstande, mithin Anschauung von Begriffen der Dinge, nur dem Grade des Bewußtseyns nach, nicht specifisch, unterschieden sey, so daß 25 z. B. die Anschauung eines Körpers im durchgängigen Bewußtseyn aller darin enthaltenen Vorstellungen den Begriff von demselben, als einem Aggregat von Monaden abgeben würde: so wird der kritische Philosoph hingegen bemerken, daß auf die Art der Satz: „Die Körper bestehen aus Monaden" aus der Erfahrung, blos durch die Zergliederung der 30 Wahrnehmung, entspringen könne, wenn wir nur scharf genug (mit ge- hörigem Bewußtseyn der Theilvorstellungen) sehen könnten. Weil aber das Beysammensein dieser Monaden als nur im Raume möglich vorge- stellt wird, so muß dieser Metaphysiker von altem Schrot und Korn uns den Raum als blos empirische und verworrene Vorstellung des Neben- 35 einanderseyns des Mannigfaltigen außerhalb einander gelten lassen.

Wie ist er aber alsdann im Stande, den Satz, daß der Raum drey Abmessungen habe, als apodictischen Satz a priori zu behaupten, denn das hätte er auch durch das klarste Bewußtseyn aller Theilvorstellungen

only valid for those that are analytic. For example, the proposition, "Every body is divisible" surely has a reason and, indeed, in itself. That is, it can be regarded as a deduction of the predicate from the concept of the subject concept acccording to the law contradiction, thus according to the principle of analytic judgments. Thus it is based only on an a priori principle of logic and does not take one step into the field of metaphysics, where the concern at hand is to extend a priori knowledge, [an enterprise] to which analytic judgments contribute nothing. Should the putative metaphysician introduce in addition the equally logical law of [sufficient] reason to the law of contradiction, he would still not have completely enumerated the modality of judgments, because he would still have to add the law of excluded middle between two contradictory judgments. Then he would have established the logical principles of the possibility, truth or logical actuality, and the necessity of judgments as problematic, assertoric and apodictic judgments, so far as all of these stand under a single principle, that is, the principle of analytic judgments. The neglect of this proves that the metaphysician never got clear about logic, which concerns the completeness of the division.

But so far as the Leibnizian principle of the logical difference between indistinct and distinct representations is concerned, if it maintains that the former kind of representation that we called mere intuition is properly only the confused concept of its object and, consequently, intuition is distinguished from concepts of things only in virtue of the degree of consciousness, not specifically,[48] so that, for example, if one were completely conscious of all the representations contained in the intuition of a body, that would [Leibnizians contend] provide a concept of it as an aggregate of monads. In opposition, the critical philosopher will maintain that a proposition such as "Bodies are constituted of monads" can derive — if we could only see sufficiently acutely (i.e., with complete consciousness of all partial representations) — only from experience and solely by means of an analysis of perception. However, since the existence of these monads together can be represented only in space, the metaphysician of the good old kind can grant the validity of space only as a merely empirical and confused representation of the juxtaposition of the [elements of the] manifold outside one another.[49]

How, then, is he going to be in a position to maintain the proposition that space has three dimensions as an apodictic a priori proposition? He has not been able to show that this must be so from even the

eines Körpers nicht herausbringen können, daß es so seyn müsse, sondern
höchstens nur, daß es, wie ihm die Wahrnehmung lehrt, so sey. Nimmt
er aber den Raum mit seiner Eigenschaft der drey Abmessungen als nothwendig, und a priori aller Körpervorstellung zum Grunde liegend an,
5 wie will er sich diese Nothwendigkeit, die er doch nicht wegvernünfteln
kann, erklären, da diese Vorstellungsart, seiner eignen Behauptung nach,
doch blos empirischen Ursprungs ist, welcher keine Nothwendigkeit her-
giebt? Will er sich aber auch über diese Anforderung wegsetzen, und den
Raum mit dieser seiner Eigenschaft annehmen, wie es auch immer mit
10 jener vorgeblich verworrenen Vorstellung beschaffen seyn mag, so demon-
strirt ihm die Geometrie, mithin die Vernunft, nicht durch Begriffe,
die in der Luft schweben, sondern durch die Konstruktion der Begriffe,
daß der Raum, und daher auch das, was ihn erfüllet, der Körper, schlechterdings nicht aus einfachen Theilen bestehe, ob zwar, wenn wir die Mög-
15 lichkeit des letztern uns nach bloßen Begriffen begreiflich machen wollten,
wir freilich von den Theilen anhebend, und so zum Zusammengesetzten
aus denselben fortgehend, das Einfache zum Grunde legen müßten, wodurch
sie denn endlich zum Geständniß genöthigt wird, daß Anschauung (dergleichen die Vorstellung des Raumes ist) und Begriff der Species nach ganz
20 verschiedene Vorstellungsarten sind, und die erstere nicht durch bloße
Auflösung der Verworrenheit der Vorstellung in den letzteren verwandelt
werden könne. — Eben dasselbe gilt auch von der Zeitvorstellung!

Von der Art, den reinen Verstandes- und Vernunft-
begriffen objective Realität zu verschaffen.

25 Einen reinen Begriff des Verstandes, als an einem Gegenstande
möglicher Erfahrung denkbar vorstellen, heißt, ihm objective Realität
verschaffen, und überhaupt, ihn darstellen. Wo man dieses nicht zu
leisten vermag, ist der Begriff leer, d. i. er reicht zu keinem Erkenntniß
zu. Diese Handlung, wenn die objective Realität dem Begriff geradezu
30 (directe) durch die demselben correspondirende Anschauung zugetheilt,
d. i. dieser unmittelbar dargestellt wird, heißt der Schematism; kann er
aber nicht unmittelbar, sondern nur in seinen Folgen (indirecte) dargestellt werden, so kann sie die Symbolisirung des Begriffs genannt
werden. Das erste findet bey Begriffen des Sinnlichen statt, das zweyte
35 ist eine Nothülfe für Begriffe des Übersinnlichen, die also eigentlich
nicht dargestellt, und in keiner möglichen Erfahrung gegeben werden

clearest consciousness of all partial representations of a body. Rather, at best perception teaches him that it is so. But if he assumes that the existence of three dimensional space is necessary and that it a priori underlies all representations of bodies, how will he explain this necessity, which he cannot reason away? For this form of representation, according to his own contention, is of mere empirical origin, which provides no necessity. If he desires to set aside this demand and assume [the existence of] space with those of its properties as may be constituted by that allegedly confused presentation — then geometry demonstrates to him, and consequently to reason, not by means of concepts, which float in the mind, but by means of the construction of concepts, that space and therefore that which fills it, bodies, can in no way be constituted of simple parts. Although, of course, if we want to make the possibility of the latter comprehensible to ourselves through mere concepts, we begin with particles and procede from them to the composite, and the simples must then be the basis of this. In this way, we will be forced to confess that intuition (which is the type of representation that space is) and concept are wholly different species of presentation and that the former cannot be changed into the latter merely by analyzing the confusion in its presentation. Precisely the same holds for the representation of time!

How to Provide Objective Reality for Pure Concepts of Understanding and Reason

To represent a pure concept of the understanding as thinkable in an object of possible experience is to provide objective reality for it and to represent it in general. When this cannot be accomplished the concept is *empty*, that is, insufficient for cognition.[50] When objective reality is directly attributed (*directe*) to a concept by an intuition corresponding to it, that is, when the concept is immediately represented, this action is schematism; however, if the concept cannot be represented immediately, but rather only through its consequences (*indirecte*), it can be called the symbolization of the concept. The former occurs with concepts of the sensible; the latter is an aid for concepts of the supersensible, which are thus not represented and

können, aber doch nothwendig zu einem Erkenntnisse gehören, wenn es auch blos als ein practisches möglich wäre.

Das Symbol einer Idee (oder eines Vernunftbegriffes) ist eine Vorstellung des Gegenstandes nach der Analogie, d. i. dem gleichen Verhältnisse zu gewissen Folgen, als dasjenige ist, welches dem Gegenstande an 5 sich selbst, zu seinen Folgen beygelegt wird, obgleich die Gegenstände selbst von ganz verschiedener Art sind, z. B. wenn ich gewisse Producte der Natur, wie etwa die organisirten Dinge, Thiere oder Pflanzen, in Verhältniß auf ihre Ursache, mir wie eine Uhr, im Verhältniß auf den Menschen, als Urheber, vorstellig mache, nämlich das Verhältniß der 10 Kausalität überhaupt, als Kategorie, in beyden eben dasselbe, aber das Subject dieses Verhältnisses, nach seiner innern Beschaffenheit mir unbekannt bleibt, jenes also allein, diese aber gar nicht dargestellt werden kann.

Auf diese Art kann ich vom Übersinnlichen, z. B. von Gott, zwar eigentlich kein theoretisches Erkenntniß, aber doch ein Erkenntniß nach der 15 Analogie, und zwar die der Vernunft zu denken nothwendig ist, haben; wobey die Kategorien zum Grunde liegen, weil sie zur Form des Denkens nothwendig gehören, dieses mag auf das Sinnliche oder Übersinnliche gerichtet seyn, ob sie gleich, und gerade eben darum, weil sie für sich noch keinen Gegenstand bestimmen, kein Erkenntniß ausmachen. 20

Von der Trüglichkeit der Versuche, den Verstandesbegriffen, auch ohne Sinnlichkeit, objective Realität zuzugestehen.

Nach bloßen Verstandesbegriffen ist, zwey Dinge außer einander zu denken, die doch in Ansehung aller innern Bestimmungen (der Quantität und Qualität) ganz einerley wären, ein Widerspruch; es ist immer 25 nur ein und dasselbe Ding zweymal gedacht (numerisch Eines).

Dies ist Leibnizens Satz des Nichtzuunterscheidenden, dem er keine geringe Wichtigkeit beylegt, der aber doch stark wider die Vernunft verstößt, weil nicht zu begreifen ist, warum ein Tropfen Wasser an einem Orte hindern sollte, daß nicht an einem andern ein ebendergleichen 30 Tropfen angetroffen würde. Aber dieser Anstoß beweiset sofort, daß Dinge im Raum nicht blos durch Verstandesbegriffe als Dinge an sich, sondern auch ihrer sinnlichen Anschauung nach als Erscheinungen vorgestellt werden müssen, um erkannt zu werden, und daß der Raum nicht eine Beschaffenheit oder Verhältniß der Dinge an sich selbst sey, wie Leib= 35 niz annahm, und daß reine Verstandesbegriffe für sich allein kein Erkenntniß abgeben.

* * *

92

cannot be given in any possible experience; and yet they necessarily belong to knowledge, even if it is possible only as practical knowledge.[51]

The symbol of an idea (or a concept of reason) is an analogical representation of an object. That is, its relation to certain consequences is the same as the one that is attributed to the object in itself and its consequences, even though the objects themselves are of wholly different orders, as for example, when I represent to myself certain products of nature, perhaps the organized things, animals and plants, in relation to their cause, and a clock in relation to a man as its maker, because the relation of causality in general as a category is the same in the two cases. But the inner constitution of the subject of this relation remains unknown to me, and thus only the former can be represented, never the latter.[52]

In this way, although I can have no properly theoretical cognition of the nonsensible, e.g., God, I can have knowledge by analogy and, to be sure, knowledge that it is necessary for reason to think. The categories are the basis of this knowledge, since they necessarily belong to the form of thought, whether it be directed toward the sensible or the supersensible, even though and just because by themselves they determine no object and do not constitute cognition.

The Illusion in Attempting to Provide Objective Reality for the Concepts of Understanding Independently of Sensibility

According to mere concepts of understanding, it is contradictory to think of two things external to one another that are completely identical with respect to all inner determinations (of quantity and quality). It is always just one and the same (numerically identical) thing thought twice.

This is Leibniz's principle of the identity of indiscernibles, to which he ascribed no small importance, but which, nonetheless, grossly offends reason. For one cannot conceive why a drop of water in one place should prevent an exactly identical drop of water from being in another. However, this attack immediately proves [1] that things in space cannot be represented by rational concepts as things in themselves — rather, in order to be known, they must be represented in sensible intuition as appearances — [2] that space is not a property or relation of things-in-themselves, as Leibniz assumes, and [3] that by themselves pure rational concepts do not yield cognition.

*   *   *

SECTION
II

Zweyte Abtheilung.

Von dem, was seit der Leibnitz-Wolfischen Epoche, in Ansehung des Objectes der Metaphysik, d. i. ihres Endzweckes, ausgerichtet worden.

Man kann die Fortschritte der Metaphysik in diesem Zeitlaufe in
5 drey Stadien eintheilen: erstlich in das des theoretisch-dogmatischen Fortganges, zweytens in das des sceptischen Stillstandes, drittens in das der praktisch-dogmatischen Vollendung ihres Weges, und der Gelangung der Metaphysik zu ihrem Endzwecke*). Das erste läuft lediglich innerhalb der Grenzen der Ontologie, das zweyte in
10 denen der transscendentalen oder reinen Kosmologie, welche auch als Naturlehre, d. i. angewandte Kosmologie, die Metaphysik der körperlichen und die der denkenden Natur, jener als Gegenstandes der äußern Sinne, dieser als Gegenstandes des innern Sinnes (physica et psychologia rationalis), nach dem, was an ihnen a priori erkennbar ist, betrachtet.
15 Das dritte Stadium ist das der Theologie, mit allen den Erkenntnissen a priori, die darauf führen, und sie nothwendig machen. Eine empirische Psychologie, welche dem Universitätsgebrauche gemäß, episodisch in die Metaphysik eingeschoben worden, wird hier mit Recht übergangen.

Der Metaphysik
20 ### Erstes Stadium
in dem
genannten Zeit- und Länderraume.

Was die Zergliederung der reinen Verstandesbegriffe, und zu der Erfahrungserkenntniß gebrauchter Grundsätze a priori betrifft, als worin
25 die Ontologie besteht: so kann man beyden genannten Philosophen, vornehmlich dem berühmten Wolf, sein großes Verdienst nicht absprechen, mehr Deutlichkeit, Bestimmtheit und Bestreben nach demonstrativer Gründlichkeit, wie irgend vorher, oder außerhalb Deutschlands im Fache der Metaphysik geschehen, ausgeübt zu haben. Allein ohne den Mangel
30 an Vollständigkeit, da noch keine Kritik eine Tafel der Kategorien nach einem festen Prinzip aufgestellt hatte, zu rügen, so war die Ermangelung

*) S. oben.

96

SECOND SECTION

What has been Accomplished in Regard to the Object of
Metaphysics, i.e., its Ultimate End, Since Leibniz's and
Wolff's Time

The progress of metaphysics during this period can be divided into
three stages: *first*, the [stage of] its theoretical-dogmatic *departure*;
second, the [stage of] its skeptical *deadlock*; *third*, the [stage of] the
practically dogmatic *completion* of its pursuit and the arrival of
metaphysics at its ultimate end.* The first proceeds entirely within
the bounds of ontology. The second proceeds within those of
transcendental or pure cosmology, which as physics, that is, applied
cosmology, also studies the metaphysics of bodily and of thinking
nature in terms of what is cognizable a priori in them — the former
[bodily nature] as an object of outer sense, the latter [thinking
nature] as an object of inner sense (*physica et psychologia rationalis*).
The third stage is theology, including all a priori knowledge that leads
to it and that it makes necessary.[53] Empirical psychology, which, in
accordance with university practice, was inserted for a while into
metaphysics, is justly disregarded here.

Metaphysics
First Stage in the Period and Country Named

So far as the analysis of the pure concepts of understanding and
the a priori principles used in experiential cognition as that which
constitutes ontology is concerned, one cannot deny the contention
that the two previously mentioned philosophers — especially the
esteemed Wolff, whose great contribution is undeniable — have exer-
cised more clarity and precision and have striven for greater
demonstrative thoroughness in the area of metaphysics than has
obtained at any time, or [anywhere] outside of Germany. However,
without censuring the incompleteness [of their work] — since no critique had established a table of categories set out according to a solid

*See above [p. 273].

97

aller Anschauung a priori, welche man als Prinzip gar nicht kannte, die
vielmehr Leibnitz intellektuirte, d. i. in lauter verworrene Begriffe ver=
wandelte, doch die Ursache, das, was er nicht durch bloße Verstandes=
begriffe vorstellig machen konnte, für unmöglich zu halten, und so Grund=
sätze, die selbst dem gesunden Verstande Gewalt anthun, und die keine ⁵
Haltbarkeit haben, aufzustellen. Folgendes enthält die Beyspiele von dem
Irrgange mit solchen Prinzipien.

1) Der Grundsatz der Identität des Nichtzuunterscheidenden (principium identitatis indiscernibilium), daß, wenn wir uns von A
   und B, die in Ansehung aller ihrer innern Bestimmungen (der Quali= ¹⁰
   tät und Quantität) völlig einerley sind, einen Begriff als von zwey
   Dingen machen, wir irren und sie für ein und dasselbe Ding (numero
   eadem) anzunehmen haben. Daß wir sie doch durch die Örter im
   Raume unterscheiden kön̅en, weil ganz ähnliche und gleiche Räume
   außer einander vorgestellt werden können, ohne daß man darum ¹⁵
   sagen dürfe, es sey ein und derselbe Raum, weil wir auf die Art den
   ganzen unendlichen Raum in einen Kubikzoll und noch weniger
   bringen könnten, konnte er nicht zugeben, denn er ließ nur eine
   Unterscheidung durch Begriffe zu, und wollte keine von diesen speci=
   fisch unterschiedene Vorstellungsart, nämlich Anschauung, und zwar ²⁰
   a priori, anerkennen, die er vielmehr in lauter Begriffe der Koexistenz
   oder Succession auflösen zu müssen glaubte, und so verstieß er wider
   den gesunden Verstand, der sich nie wird überreden lassen, daß, wenn
   ein Tropfen Wasser an einem Orte ist, dieser einen ganz ähnlichen
   und gleichen Tropfen an einem anderen Orte zu seyn hindere. ²⁵

2) Sein Satz des zureichenden Grundes, da er dem letztern keine An=
   schauung a priori unterlegen zu dürfen glaubte, sondern die Vor=
   stellung desselben auf bloße Begriffe a priori zurückführte, brachte
   die Folgerung hervor, daß alle Dinge, metaphysisch betrachtet, aus
   Realität und Negation, aus dem Seyn und dem Nichtseyn, wie bey ³⁰
   dem Demokrit alle Dinge im Weltraume aus den Atomen und dem
   Leeren, zusammengesetzt wären, und der Grund einer Negation
   kein anderer seyn könne, als daß kein Grund, wodurch etwas gesetzt
   wird, nämlich keine Realität da ist, und so brachte er aus allem
   sogenannten metaphysischen Bösen, in Vereinigung mit dem Guten ³⁵
   dieser Art, eine Welt aus lauter Licht und Schatten hervor, ohne in
   Betrachtung zu ziehen, daß, um einen Raum in Schatten zu stellen,
   ein Körper da seyn müsse, also etwas Reales, was dem Licht wider=
   steht, in den Raum einzudringen. Nach ihm würde der Schmerz

principle—still the lack of any a priori intuition, which was not recognized as a principle, and which Leibniz instead intellectualized, i.e., transformed into nothing more than confused concepts, was the reason that he regarded what he could not represent by means of mere rational concepts as impossible, and set up fundamental principles that cannot stand scrutiny and that do violence to common sense. The following contain examples of futile effort with such principles:[54]

1) The principle of the identity of indiscernibles (*principium identitatis indiscernibilium*), that if we form a concept of A and B—which are completely identitical in regard to all their inner determinations (of quality and quantity)—as two things, we err and have instead to assume them to be the same thing (*numero eadem*). He could not admit that we can distinguish them by means of their locations in space, since quite similar and equivalent spaces can be represented outside one another without being able to say of them that they are one and the same space. For in this way, [were it the same space] we would be able to compress all infinite space into a cubic inch or even less. He admitted only distinctions by means of concepts and would not admit a specifically distinguishing mode of representation for these things, that is, intuition, nor of course a priori intuition, believing that it [space] must be analyzed into nothing but concepts of coexistence or succession.[55] Thus, he offended common sense, which never allows itself to be convinced that when there is a drop of water in one place this prevents an altogether identical and equal drop from being somewhere else.

2) His principle of sufficient reason—which he believed did not need to be supported by an a priori intuition, but rather is reduced in his representation of it to mere a priori concepts— produces the following [result]: Metaphysically considered, all things would be composed of reality and negation, of being and non-being, as, according to Democritus, all things in the universe are composed of atoms and the void. The only reason for a negation is that there is no ground for something to be postulated, that is, no reality exists. And so he produced a world of nothing but light and shadows from all the so-called metaphysical evil in combination with good of this sort, without taking into consideration that in order to place a space in shadow, a body, thus something real, must exist to stand in the way of the light penetrating the space. According to him, the

nur den Mangel an Luft, das Laster nur den Mangel an Tugend-
antrieben, und die Ruhe eines bewegten Körpers nur den Mangel
an bewegender Kraft zum Grunde haben, weil nach bloßen Begriffen
Realität = a nicht der Realität = b, sondern nur dem Mangel = 0
entgegengesetzt seyn kann, ohne in Betrachtung zu ziehen, daß in der
Anschauung, z. B. der äußern, a priori, nämlich im Raume, eine
Entgegensetzung des Realen (der bewegenden Kraft), gegen ein andres
Reale, nämlich einer bewegenden Kraft in entgegengesetzter Richtung
und so auch, nach der Analogie in der innern Anschauung, einander
entgegengesetzte reale Triebfedern in einem Subject verbunden
werden können, und die a priori erkennbare Folge von diesem Kon-
flikt der Realitäten, Negation seyn könne; aber freylich hätte er zu
diesem Behuf einander entgegenstehende Richtungen, die sich nur in
der Anschauung, nicht in bloßen Begriffen vorstellen lassen, annehmen
müssen, und dann entsprang das wider den gesunden Verstand, selbst
sogar wider die Moral verstoßende Prinzip, daß alles Böse als
Grund = 0, d. i. bloße Einschränkung, oder, wie die Metaphysiker
sagen, das Formale der Dinge sey. So half ihm also sein Satz des
zureichenden Grundes, da er diesen in bloße Begriffe setzte, auch nicht
das Mindeste, um über den Grundsatz analytischer Urtheile, den Satz
des Widerspruchs, hinauszukommen, und sich durch die Vernunft
a priori synthetisch zu erweitern.

3) Sein System der vorherbestimmten Harmonie, ob es zwar damit
eigentlich auf die Erklärung der Gemeinschaft zwischen Seele und
Körper abgezielt war, mußte doch vorher im Allgemeinen auf die
Erklärung der Möglichkeit der Gemeinschaft verschiedener Substanzen, durch die sie ein Ganzes ausmachen, gerichtet werden, und
da war es freylich unvermeidlich, darin zu gerathen, weil Substanzen
schon durch den Begriff von ihnen, wenn sonst nichts Andres dazu
kommt, als vollkommen isolirt vorgestellt werden müssen; denn
da einer jeden, vermöge ihrer Subsistenz, kein Accidenz inhäriren darf,
das sich auf einer andern Substanz gründet, sondern, wenn gleich
noch andre existiren, jene doch von diesen in nichts abhängen darf,
selbst dann nicht, wenn sie gleich alle von einer dritten (dem Urwesen),
als Wirkungen von ihrer Ursache abhingen, so ist gar kein Grund da,
warum die Accidenzen der einen Substanz sich auf einer andern
gleichartigen äußeren in Ansehung dieses ihres Zustandes gründen
müssen. Wenn sie also gleichwohl als Weltsubstanzen in Gemeinschaft
stehen sollen, so muß diese nur ideal, und kann kein realer (physischer)

only basis of pain would be the lack of pleasure, of vice only the lack of motives toward virtue, and the motionlessness of a body that had been moved, only the body's lack of moving force; for from a purely conceptual point of view, a reality $= a$ can be opposed only to a lack $= 0$, not another reality $= b$. He did not consider that in intuition—e.g., outer a priori [intuition], that is, in space, the opposition of one reality (a moving force) to another, that is, a moving force in an opposed direction—thus also by analogy, real motives in a subject—can be united and that the result of this conflict of realities, which can be known a priori, can be a negation. But of course for this purpose he would have to assume tendencies that are opposed to one another, which can be represented only in intuition, not in mere concepts. From that arose the principle, offensive to common sense as well as to morals, that all evil as cause $= 0$, i.e., is a mere limitation or, as metaphysicians say, the formal [nature of] things. Consequently, his principles of sufficient reason, being formulated in mere concepts, did not help him in the least to proceed beyond the fundamental principle of analytic judgments, the principle of contradiction, and to extend a priori [knowledge] synthetically by means of reason.[56]

3) His system of the pre-established harmony,—though properly it was aimed at clarifying the interaction between mind and body, yet it must be antecedently directed in general toward an explanation of the possibility of interaction among different substances, by virtue of which [interaction] they constitute a whole— and the monadology inevitably fell into this. For if nothing else is added to the concept of substances, they must be represented as completely isolated; since by virtue of its subsistence, no accident based upon another [substance] can possibly inhere in substance. Even if others do exist, the former can in no way depend upon the latter even if they all depend, as effects on their cause, upon a third substance (the original being). Consequently, there is absolutely no reason why the condition of the accidents of the one substance must be grounded with respect to another external, yet similar, substance. Thus, if they are to be substances associated as a community in the world, this must be only as ideal, and can be no real (physical)

Einfluß seyn, weil dieser die Möglichkeit der Wechselwirkung, als ob
sie sich aus ihrem bloßen Daseyn verstände (welches doch nicht ist),
annimmt, d. i. man muß den Urheber des Daseyns als einen
Künstler annehmen, der diese an sich völlig isolirte Substanzen, entweder gelegentlich, oder schon im Weltanfange, so modificirt, oder schon 5
eingerichtet, daß sie untereinander, gleich der Verknüpfung von Wirkung und Ursache, so harmonirten, als ob sie in einander wirklich
einflössen. So mußte also, da das System der Gelegenheitsursachen
nicht so schicklich zur Erklärung aus einem einzigen Prinzip zu seyn
scheint, als das letztere, das systema harmoniae praestabilitae, das 10
wunderlichste Figment, was je die Philosophie ausgedacht hat, entspringen, blos weil alles aus Begriffen erklärt und begreiflich gemacht
werden sollte.

Nimmt man dagegen die reine Anschauung des Raumes, so wie
dieser a priori allen äußern Relationen zum Grunde liegt, und nur 15
ein Raum ist: so sind dadurch alle Substanzen in Verhältnissen, die den
physischen Einfluß möglich machen, verbunden, und machen ein
Ganzes aus, sodaß alle Wesen, als Dinge im Raume, zusammen
nur eine Welt ausmachen, und nicht mehrere Welten außer einander
seyn können, welcher Satz von der Welteinheit, wenn er durch lauter 20
Begriffe, ohne jene Anschauung zum Grunde zu legen, geführt
werden soll, schlechterdings nicht bewiesen werden kann.

4) Seine Monadologie. Nach bloßen Begriffen sind alle Substanzen der
Welt entweder einfach, oder aus Einfachem zusammengesetzt. Denn
die Zusammensetzung ist nur ein Verhältniß, ohne welches sie gleich- 25
wohl als Substanzen ihre Existenz behalten müßten; das aber, was
übrig bleibt, wenn ich alle Zusammensetzung aufhebe, ist das Einfache. Also bestehen alle Körper, wenn man sie blos durch den Verstand als Aggregate von Substanzen denkt, aus einfachen Substanzen.
Alle Substanzen aber müssen außer ihrem Verhältnisse gegen ein- 30
ander, und den Kräften, dadurch sie auf einander Einfluß haben mögen,
doch gewisse, innerlich ihnen inhärirende reale Bestimmungen haben,
d. i. es ist nicht genug, ihnen Accidenzen beyzulegen, die nur in
äußeren Verhältnissen bestehen, sondern man muß ihnen auch solche,
die sich bloß auf das Subject beziehen, d. i. innere, zugestehen. Wir 35
kennen aber keine innere reale Bestimmungen, die einem Einfachen
beygelegt werden könnten, als Vorstellungen, und was von diesen
abhängt; diese aber, da man sie nicht den Körpern beylegen kann,
aber doch den einfachen Theilen desselben beylegen muß, wenn man

influence since this [physical influence] assumes the possibility of community as though it were understood through the mere existence of substances (which it certainly is not). That is, one must assume that the creator of being is an artist who either occasionally, or at the origin of the world, so modifies or immediately arranges these wholly isolated substances that they harmonize with one another, even in the relation of cause and effect, as if they really influence one another. Thus, since the system of occasional causes does not appear so simply explicable on the basis of a single principle, as the latter, the *systema harmoniae praeestablitae*, the most whimsical figment philosophy has ever contrived, had to develop merely because everything was to be explained and made comprehensible through concepts.

If, by contrast, one assumes the pure intuition of space so that it underlies a priori all outer relations and is only a single space, in that way all substances are united in a relation that makes physical influence possible so that they constitute a whole. Thus, all beings, as things in space, together constitute only a single world and cannot be several worlds extrinsic to one another. This principle of the world's unity cannot be proved at all if it is to be achieved by means of nothing but concepts — i.e., without basing it upon that [pure] intuition.

4) His monadology. Given mere concepts, all substances in the world are either simple or constituted by simples. Composition is only a relation, without which they can still maintain their existence as substances; what remains when I take away all composition is the simple. Thus, all bodies, if one thinks of them solely through the understanding as aggregates of substance, consist of simple substances. But besides their relations to one another and the powers by means of which they may influence one another, all substances must have certain inner inherent real determinations; that is, it is not sufficient to attribute accidents consisting only of outer relations to them; instead, such determinations as pertain exclusively to the subject — i.e., are internally in it — must also be recognized. However, we know no internal real determinations that can be attributed to a simple thing except representations and what depends on these representations. But since these cannot be attributed to bodies, they must be attributed to the simple parts of bodies if it is not to be

diese, als Substanzen, innerlich nicht als ganz leer annehmen will.
Einfache Substanzen aber, die in sich das Vermögen der Vorstellungen haben, werden von Leibnitz Monaden genannt. Also bestehen
die Körper aus Monaden, als Spiegel des Universums nämlich,
5 d. i. mit Vorstellungskräften begabt, die sich von denen der denkenden Substanzen nur durch den Mangel des Bewußtseins unterscheiden und daher schlummernde Monaden genannt werden, von
denen wir nicht wissen, ob das Schicksal sie nicht bereinst aufwecken
dürfte, vielleicht gar schon unendlich viel nach und nach zum Erwachen
10 gebracht und wieder in den Schlummer habe zurückfallen lassen, um
dereinst aufs neue zu erwachen, und als Thier nach und nach
in Menschenseelen, und so weiter zu höhern Stufen hinauf-
zustreben; eine Art von bezauberter Welt, zu deren Annehmung
der berühmte Mann nur dadurch hat verleitet werden können, daß
15 er Sinnenvorstellungen als Erscheinungen, nicht, wie es seyn sollte,
für eine von allen Begriffen ganz unterschiedene Vorstellungsart,
nämlich Anschauung, sondern für ein, aber nur verworrenes,
Erkenntniß durch Begriffe annahm, die im Verstande, nicht in der
Sinnlichkeit ihren Sitz haben.

20 Der Satz der Identität des Nichtzuunterscheidenden,
der Satz des zureichenden Grundes, das System der vorherbestimmten Harmonie, endlich die Monadologie, machen zusammen das Neue aus, was Leibnitz und nach ihm Wolf, dessen meta-
physisches Verdienst in der praktischen Philosophie bey weitem größer
25 war, in die Metaphysik der theoretischen Philosophie zu bringen versucht haben. Ob diese Versuche Fortschritte derselben genannt zu werden
verdienen, wenn man gleich nicht in Abrede zieht, daß sie dazu wohl
vorbereitet haben mögen, mag am Ende dieses Stadiums dem Urtheile
derer anheim gestellt bleiben, die sich darin durch große Nahmen nicht
30 irre machen lassen.

———

Zu dem theoretisch-dogmatischen Theile der Metaphysik gehört auch
die allgemeine rationale Naturlehre, d. i. reine Philosophie über Gegenstände der Sinne, der der äußern, d. i. rationale Körperlehre, und des
innern, die rationale Seelenlehre, wodurch die Prinzipien der Möglich-
35 keit einer Erfahrung überhaupt auf eine zwiefache Art Wahrnehmungen
angewandt werden, ohne sonst etwas Empirisches zum Grunde zu legen,
als daß es zwey dergleichen Gegenstände gebe. — In beyden kann nur

assumed that as substances these parts are completely empty. And Leibniz calls simple substances, which have the capacity for representation, monads. Thus, bodies are constituted by monads conceived as mirrors of the universe — that is, as endowed with powers of representation — distinguishable from thinking substances only by a lack of consciousness. They are, therefore, called sleeping monads. We do not know whether fortune may not someday awaken these monads, or whether, perhaps, they have already endlessly, gradually been awakened and have fallen back to sleep again in order to be newly awakened someday, and like animals strive gradually toward human souls and toward even higher levels. [This is] a kind of enchanted world that the famous man could have been misled into accepting only by taking sensible representations as appearances, that is, intuitions, not as they are — as a mode of representation completely different from all concepts — but rather as cognition, albeit only confused cognition from, concepts that have their seat in the understanding instead of in sensibility.

Together, *the law of the identity of indiscernibles, the law of sufficient reason, the system of preestablished harmony* and, finally, the *monadolgy* constitute the new elements that Leibniz and following him Wolff — whose metaphysical contribution to practical philosophy was by far greater — attempted to bring to the metaphysics of theoretical philosophy. Whether these attempts deserve to be called progress in theoretical metaphysics, even if one does not disagree that they probably prepared the way for the progress at the end of this stage, devolves upon the judgment of those who do not allow themselves to be led astray by their great names.

————

The universal rational doctrine of nature, i.e., the pure philosophy of the objects of the senses — the pure philosophy of outer sense, that is, rational physics — also belongs to the theoretical dogmatic part of metaphysics; so does the pure philosophy of inner sense, that is, rational psychology, through which the principles of the possibility of experience in general are applied to a twofold manner of perception without anything else empirical lying at the doctrine's foundation, except the fact that there are two kinds of objects.[57] — In both there

Wissenschaft seyn, als darin Mathematik, d. i. Konstruktion der Begriffe, angewandt werden kann, daher das Räumliche der Gegenstände der Physik mehr a priori vermag, als die Zeitform, welche der Anschauung durch den inneren Sinn zum Grunde liegt, die nur eine Dimension hat.

Die Begriffe vom vollen und leeren Raum, von Bewegung und 5 bewegenden Kräften, können und müssen in der rationalen Physik auf ihre Prinzipien a priori gebracht werden, indessen daß in der rationalen Psychologie nichts weiter, als der Begriff der Immaterialität einer denkenden Substanz, der Begriff ihrer Veränderung und der Identität der Person, bey den Veränderungen allein, Prinzipien a priori vorstellen, 10 alles übrige aber empirische Psychologie, oder vielmehr nur Anthropologie ist, weil bewiesen werden kann, daß es uns unmöglich ist, zu wissen, ob und was das Lebensprinzip im Menschen (die Seele) ohne Körper im Denken vermöge, und Alles hier nur auf empirische Erkenntniß, d. i. eine solche, die wir im Leben, mithin in der Verbindung der Seele mit dem 15 Körper, erwerben können, hinausläuft, und also dem Endzweck der Metaphysik, vom Sinnlichen zum Übersinnlichen einen Überschritt zu versuchen, nicht angemessen ist. Dieser ist in der zweyten Epoche der reinen Vernunftversuche in der Philosophie anzutreffen, die wir itzt vorstellig machen. 20

Der Metaphysik

Zweytes Stadium.

Im ersten Stadium der Metaphysik, welches darum das der Ontologie genannt werden kann, weil es nicht etwa das Wesentliche unserer Begriffe von Dingen, durch Auflösung in ihre Merkmale zu erforschen 25 lehrt, welches das Geschäft der Logik ist, sondern wie, und welche wir uns a priori von Dingen machen, um das, was uns in der Anschauung überhaupt gegeben werden mag, unter sie zu subsumiren, welches wiederum nicht anders geschehen konnte, als so fern die Form der Anschauung a priori in Raum und Zeit, diese Objecte uns blos als Erscheinungen, 30 nicht als Dinge an sich, erkennbar macht — in jenem Stadium sieht sich die Vernunft in einer Reihe einander untergeordneter Bedingungen, die ohne Ende immer wiederum bedingt sind, zum unaufhörlichen Fortschreiten zum Unbedingten aufgefordert, weil jeder Raum und jede Zeit nie anders, als wie Theil eines noch größern gegebenen Raumes oder 35

can be only so much science as mathematics can apply to it, that is, as can be [applied to it] through construction of concepts. Therefore, the spatiality of the objects of physics allows more to be known a priori than the form of time, which underlies the intuition of inner sense and has only one dimension.

In rational physics the concepts of full and empty space and of motion and moving forces, can and must be traced back to their a priori principles, while in rational psychology, as the concept of the immateriality of a thinking substance, nothing but the concepts of the alteration and identity of the person in alteration can be represented a priori.[58] But everything else is empirical psychology, or, rather, only anthropology, since it can be shown that it is impossible for us to know whether and to what extent the principle of life in men (the soul) can think without a body. Here everything derives from empirical cognition, that is, such as we can acquire in life, and hence in the combination of the soul with the body; and it is thus not adapted to the attempt to transcend from the sensible to the supersensible, the ultimate end of metaphysics. This is to be found in the second epoch of pure rational investigation in philosophy, which we shall now present.

Metaphysics
The Second Stage

The first stage of metaphysics can be called that of ontology, for it teaches nothing about investigating the essential [aspects] of our concepts of things by analyzing them into their distinctive characteristics, which is the role of logic, but instead, teaches how and which [characteristics] of things we make a priori in order to subsume what may be given to us in intuition in general under them; in turn, this can only occur insofar as the a priori forms of intuition, space and time, make cognition of these objects possible just as appearances, not as things in themselves. In that stage, reason sees itself summoned to an unceasing progress towards the unconditioned through a series of subordinated conditions that always and without end are conditioned.

Zeit vorgestellt werden kann, in denen doch die Bedingungen zu dem, was uns in jeder Anschauung gegeben ist, gesucht werden müssen, um zum Unbedingten zu gelangen.

Der zweyte große Fortschritt, welcher nun der Metaphysik zuge-
5 muthet wird, ist der, vom Bedingten an Gegenständen möglicher Erfahrung zum Unbedingten zu gelangen, und ihre Erkenntniß bis zur Vollendung dieser Reihe durch die Vernunft (denn was bis dahin geschehen war, geschah durch Verstand und Urtheilskraft) zu erweitern, und das Stadium, welches sie itzt zurücklegen soll, wird daher das der transscenden-
10 talen Kosmologie heißen können, weil Raum und Zeit in ihrer ganzen Größe, als Inbegriff aller Bedingungen betrachtet und als die Behälter aller verknüpften wirklichen Dinge vorgestellt, und so das Ganze von diesen, sofern sie jene ausfüllen, unter dem Begriffe einer Welt vorstellig gemacht werden sollen.

15 Die synthetischen Bedingungen (principia) der Möglichkeit der Dinge, d. i. die Bestimmungsgründe derselben (principia essendi), werden hier, und zwar in der Totalität der aufsteigenden Reihe, in der sie einander untergeordnet sind, zu dem Bedingten (den principiatis) gesucht, um zu dem Unbedingten (principium, quod non est principiatum) zu gelangen.
20 Das fordert die Vernunft, um ihr selbst genug zu thun. Mit der absteigenden Reihe von der Bedingung zum Bedingten hat es keine Noth, denn da bedarf es für sie keiner absoluten Totalität, und diese mag als Folge immer unvollendet bleiben, weil die Folgen sich von selbst ergeben, wenn der oberste Grund, von dem sie abhangen, nur gegeben ist.

25 Nun findet sich, daß in Raum und Zeit alles bedingt, und das Unbedingte in der aufsteigenden Reihe der Bedingungen schlechterdings unerreichbar ist. Den Begriff eines absoluten Ganzen von lauter Bedingtem sich als unbedingt zu denken, enthält einen Widerspruch; das Unbedingte kann also nur als Glied der Reihe betrachtet werden, welches diese als
30 Grund begrenzt, der selbst keine Folge aus einem andern Grunde ist, und die Unergründlichkeit, welche durch alle Klassen der Kategorien geht, so fern sie auf das Verhältniß der Folgen zu ihren Gründen angewandt werden, ist das, was die Vernunft mit sich selbst in einen nie beyzulegenden Streit verwickelt, solange die Gegenstände in Raum und Zeit für Dinge
35 an sich selbst, und nicht für bloße Erscheinungen, genommen werden, welches vor der Epoche der reinen Vernunftkritik unvermeidlich war, so daß Satz und Gegensatz sich unaufhörlich einander wechselweise vernichteten, und die Vernunft in den hoffnungslosesten Scepticism stürzen mußten, der darum für die Metaphysik traurig ausfallen mußte, weil,

For each space and each time can be represented only as part of a still greater space or time, in which, in order to arrive at the unconditioned, the condition of what is given in each intuition must be sought.[59]

The second great step that is now demanded of metaphysics is to proceed from the conditioned objects of possible experience to the unconditioned and, through reason, to expand knowledge through completion of this series. (What was previously accomplished was done by understanding and judgment.) The stage through which it must now progress can be called transcendental cosmology.[60] For space and time in their entire magnitude are considered the totality of all conditions and are represented as the containers of all connected actual things, so that the entirety of these, so far as they fill space and time, ought to be represented by the concept of a world.

In order to arrive at the unconditioned (*principium, quod non est principiatum*), the synthetic conditions (*principia*) of the possibility of things — i.e., their determining grounds (*principia essendi*), here and in the totality of the ascending series, in which they are subordinated to one another — are to be sought in their conditions (the *principiatis*). This requires reason in order to be accomplished. There is no problem with the series descending from condition to conditioned, since for this series no absolute totality is required, and as a consequence it may always remain incomplete, for the consequences follow by themselves if only the ultimate ground that they depend on is already given.

Now it turns out that everything in space and time is conditioned and that the unconditioned in the ascending series of conditions is absolutely unreachable. To think the concept of an absolute totality of nothing but conditioned [entities] as itself unconditioned is contradictary. The unconditioned can thus only be regarded as a member of the series that limits the series as a ground that is itself not the result of another ground. The unfathomableness that attaches to all classes of categories when they are used in conjunction with the relation of results to their grounds is what entangles reason in an unresolvable conflict so long as objects in space and time are taken for things in themselves and not for mere appearances, something unavoidable prior to the epoch of the criticism of pure reason. Thus, thesis and antithesis reciprocally annihilate one another without end, and reason necessarily plunges into the most hopeless skepticism, which must turn out tragically for metaphysics, since if reason can

wenn sie nicht einmal an Gegenständen der Sinne, ihre Forderung des Unbedingten betreffend, befriedigen kann, an einen Überschritt zum Übersinnlichen, der doch ihren Endzweck ausmacht, gar nicht zu denken war*).

Wenn wir nun in der aufsteigenden Reihe, vom Bedingten zu den Bedingungen, in einem Weltganzen fortschreiten, um zum Unbedingten zu gelangen: so finden sich folgende wahre, oder bloß scheinbare Widersprüche der Vernunft mit ihr selbst im theoretisch-dogmatischen Erkenntniß eines gegebenen Weltganzen vor. Erstlich nach mathematischen Ideen der Zusammensetzung oder Theilung des Gleichartigen; zweytens nach den dynamischen der Gründung der Existenz des Bedingten auf die unbedingte Existenz.

[I. In Ansehung der extensiven Größe der Welt in Messung derselben, d. i. der Hinzuthuung der gleichartigen und gleichen Einheit, als des Maaßes, einen bestimmten Begriff von ihr zu bekommen, und zwar a) von ihrer Raumes= und b) von ihrer Zeitgröße, so fern beyde gegeben sind, die letzte also die verflossene Zeit ihrer Dauer messen soll, von welchen beyden die Vernunft mit gleichem Grunde, daß sie unendlich, und daß sie doch nicht unendlich, mithin endlich sey, behauptet. Der Beweis aber von beyden kann — welches merkwürdig ist! — nicht direct, sondern nur apagogisch d. i. durch Widerlegung des Gegentheils geführt werden. Also

a) der Satz: Die Welt ist der Größe nach im Raum unendlich, denn, wäre sie endlich, so würde sie durch den leeren Raum begrenzt sein, der selbst unendlich, aber an sich nichts Existirendes ist, der aber dennoch die Existenz von Etwas, als dem Gegenstande möglicher Wahrnehmung, voraussetzte, nämlich der eines Raumes, der nichts Reales enthält, und doch als die Grenze des Realen, d. i. als die bemerkliche letzte Bedingung des im Raum an einander Grenzenden enthielte, welches sich widerspricht; denn der leere Raum kann nicht wahrgenommen werden, noch ein (spürbares) Dasehn bei sich führen. — b) Der Gegensatz: Die Welt ist auch der verflossenen Zeit nach unendlich. Denn, hätte sie einen

*) Der Satz: Das Ganze aller Bedingung in Zeit und Raum ist unbedingt, ist falsch. Denn wenn alles in Raum und Zeit bedingt ist (innerhalb), so ist kein Ganzes derselben möglich. Die also, welche ein absolutes Ganze von lauter bedingten Bedingungen annehmen, widersprechen sich selbst, sie mögen es als begrenzt (endlich) oder unbegrenzt (unendlich) annehmen, und doch ist der Raum als ein solches Ganze anzusehen, imgleichen die verflossene Zeit.

never be satisfied concerning its demand for the unconditioned in objects of sense, a transition to the supersensible, which constitutes its ultimate goal, cannot be contemplated.*[60]

Now if, in order to arrive at the unconditioned, we proceed in the ascending series from conditioned entities to the conditions in a world whole, the following genuine or merely apparent contradiction of reason with itself is to be met with in its theoretically dogmatic knowledge of an actually given world whole, *first*, from the mathematical ideas of combining or dividing the homogeneous and, *second*, from the dynamic grounding of the existence of conditioned upon unconditioned existence.[62]

[I.[63] With regard to measuring the *extensive magnitude*[64] of the world — to get a determinate concept of the addition of homogeneous and equal unit[s], as of a mass, that is, of its a) spatial and b) temporal magnitude, so far as both are given (the latter is to measure the duration of elapsed time), reason can maintain with equal justification of both that they are infinite and yet not infinite, consequently finite. The proof of neither can never be achieved directly — a point worthy of note — but only apogogically, i.e., by refutation of the antithesis.[65] Thus,

a) *The Thesis* is: "The spatial extent of the world is infinite." For were it finite, it would be limited by empty space, which is itself infinite, but in itself nothing existent. But this [thesis] would nevertheless presuppose the existence of something as an object of possible perception, namely, that of a space that contains nothing real and yet, as the boundary of the real, that is, as the sensible final condition of what is in space, it would contain limiting conditions of another space. And this is self-contradictory, for empty space cannot be perceived, nor have a perceptible existence. b) *The Antithesis* is: "The world is also infinite in age." For, if it had a beginning, there would have had to have been an empty time before it; however, this makes the genesis of the world, consequently the nothingness that preceded it, into an object of possible experience, which is self-contradictory.

---

*The proposition "The Totality of all conditions in space and time is unconditioned" is false. For if everything within space and time is conditioned (internally), no totality of them is possible. Those who assume an absolute totality of nothing but conditioned conditions contradict themselves, whether they assume them to be bounded (finite) or unbounded (infinite). Yet, space, just as past time, is regarded as such a whole.

Zweiter Entwurf

Anfang, so wäre eine leere Zeit vor ihr vorhergegangen, welche gleichwohl das Entstehen der Welt, mithin des Nichts, was vorherging, zu
einem Gegenstande möglicher Erfahrung machte, welches sich widerspricht.
II. In Ansehung der intensiven Größe, d. i. des Grades, in welchem
5 diese den Raum oder die Zeit erfüllet, zeigt sich folgende Antinomie.
a) Satz: Die körperlichen Dinge im Raum bestehen aus einfachen Theilen;
denn, setzet das Gegentheil, so würden die Theile zwar Substanzen seyn,
wenn aber alle ihre Zusammensetzung als eine bloße Relation aufgehoben
würde: so würde nichts als der bloße Raum, als das bloße Subject aller
10 Relationen, übrig bleiben. Die Körper würden also nicht aus Substanzen
bestehen, welches der Voraussetzung widerspricht. — b) Gegensatz: Die
Körper bestehen nicht aus einfachen Theilen.]

Nach den ersteren findet sich eine Antinomie hervor, wir mögen nun
im Größenbegriff von den Dingen der Welt, im Raume sowohl als der
15 Zeit, von den durchgängig bedingt gegebenen Theilen zum unbedingten
Ganzen in der Zusammensetzung aufsteigen, oder von dem gegebenen
Ganzen zu den unbedingt gedachten Theilen durch Theilung hinabgehen.
— Man mag nämlich, was das erstere betrifft, annehmen, die Welt sey
dem Raume und der verflossenen Zeit nach unendlich, oder, sie sey endlich,
20 so verwickelt man sich unvermeidlich in Widersprüche mit sich selbst. Denn,
ist die Welt, so wie der Raum und die verflossene Zeit, die sie einnimmt,
als unendliche Größe gegeben, so ist sie eine gegebene Größe, die niemals
ganz gegeben werden kann, welches sich widerspricht. — Besteht jeder
Körper, oder jede Zeit, in der Veränderung des Zustandes der Dinge,
25 aus einfachen Theilen: so muß, weil Raum sowohl als Zeit ins Unendliche theilbar sind (welches die Mathematik beweiset), eine unendliche
Menge gegeben seyn, die doch ihrem Begriffe nach niemals ganz gegeben
seyn kann, welches sich gleichfalls widerspricht.

Mit der zweyten Klasse der Ideen, des dynamisch Unbedingten, ist es
30 eben so bestellt. Denn so heißt es einerseits: Es ist keine Freyheit, sondern
alles in der Welt geschieht nach Naturnothwendigkeit. Denn: in der Reihe
der Wirkungen, in Beziehung auf ihre Ursachen, herrscht durchaus Natur-
mechanism, nämlich daß jede Veränderung durch den vorhergehenden
Zustand prädeterminirt ist. Andrerseits steht dieser allgemeinen Be-
35 hauptung der Gegensatz entgegen: Einige Begebenheiten müssen als durch
Freyheit möglich gedacht werden, und sie können nicht alle unter dem
Gesetze der Naturnothwendigkeit stehen, weil sonst alles nur bedingt
geschehen, und also in der Reihe der Ursachen nichts Unbedingtes anzu-

II. The following antinomy arises with respect to *intensive magnitudes*,[66] i.e., the degrees to which space or time is filled: a) *Thesis*: "Simple parts constitute bodily things in space." For, if one assumed the contrary, the parts would certainly be substances, and if all their composition were negated as mere relation, nothing would remain as the subject of all relations except mere space. Bodies would then not consist of substances, which contradicts the original presupposition. b) *Antithesis*: "Bodies do not consist of simple parts."]

In the first instance, an antinomy is produced, either when we ascend in the quantitative concept of things in the world, in space as well as in time, from the thoroughly conditioned given particles to the unconditioned whole in composition, or when we descend by analysis from the given whole to the unconditioned imagined particles. So far as the first [antinomy] is concerned, whether it be assumed that the spatial extent of the world and its age are infinite or that they are finite, one is inevitably entangled in self-contradiction. For, if the world, and the space and past time that it occupies, is given as an infinite quantity, it is a given quantity that can never be completely given, which is self-contradictory. If every body, or every time in which the condition of things changed, consisted of simple parts, then, because space and time are infinitely divisible (which mathematics proves), an infinite number would be given, but yet conceptually this infinite quantity can never be given, which is likewise self-contradictory.

The second class of ideas, those of the dynamically unconditioned, are ordered in precisely the same way. On the one hand, it is claimed that there is no freedom and that everything in the world happens in accordance with natural necessity. For in the series of effects in relation to their causes, natural mechanism thoroughly dominates, that is, every change is predetermined by a preceding condition. Contrary to this stands the universal claim of the antithesis: Some occurrences must be thought as possible through freedom, and they cannot all stand under the law of natural necessity, since otherwise everything happens only conditionally, and thus nothing unconditioned could be found

treffen seyn würde, eine Totalität aber der Bedingungen, in einer Reihe
von lauter Bedingtem anzunehmen, ein Widerspruch ist.

Endlich leidet der zur dynamischen Klasse gehörende Satz, der sonst
klar genug ist, nämlich, daß in der Reihe der Ursachen nicht alles zufällig,
sondern doch irgend ein schlechterdings nothwendig existirendes Wesen 5
seyn möge, dennoch an dem Gegensatze, daß kein von uns immer denk-
bares Wesen als schlechthin nothwendige Ursache anderer Weltwesen
gedacht werden könne, einen gegründeten Widerspruch, weil es alsdann
als Glied in die aufsteigende Reihe der Wirkungen und Ursachen mit den
Dingen der Welt gehören würde, in der keine Kausalität unbedingt ist, 10
die aber hier doch als unbedingt müßte angenommen werden, welches
sich widerspricht.

Anmerkung. Wenn der Satz: Die Welt ist an sich unendlich, soviel
bedeuten soll, sie ist größer als alle Zahl (in Vergleichung mit
einem gegebenen Maß): so ist der Satz falsch, denn eine unend- 15
liche Zahl ist ein Widerspruch. — Heißt es, sie ist nicht unendlich,
so ist dieses wohl wahr, aber man weiß dann nicht, was sie denn
sey. Sage ich: sie ist endlich, so ist das auch falsch, denn ihre
Grenze ist kein Gegenstand möglicher Erfahrung. Ich sage also,
sowohl was gegebnen Raum, als auch verflossene Zeit betrifft, 20
wird nur als zur Opposition erfordert. Beydes ist dann falsch,
weil mögliche Erfahrung weder eine Grenze hat, noch unendlich
seyn kann, und die Welt als Erscheinung nur das Object möglicher Erfahrung ist.

*   *   *   25

Hiebey zeigen sich nun folgende Bemerkungen:

Erstlich der Satz, daß zu allem Bedingten ein schlechthin Unbedingtes
müsse gegeben seyn, gilt als Grundsatz von allen Dingen, so wie ihre Verbindung durch reine Vernunft, d. i. als die der Dinge an sich selbst, gedacht
wird. Findet sich nun in der Anwendung desselben, daß er nicht auf 30
Gegenstände in Raum und Zeit ohne Widerspruch angewandt werden
könne: so ist keine Ausflucht aus diesem Widerspruche möglich, als daß
man annimmt, die Gegenstände in Raum und Zeit, als Objecte möglicher
Erfahrung, sind nicht als Dinge an sich selbst, sondern als bloße Erscheinungen anzusehen, deren Form auf der subjectiven Beschaffenheit unsrer 35
Art sie anzuschauen beruhet.

Die Antinomie der reinen Vernunft führt also unvermeidlich auf jene

in the series of causes. However, it is contradictory to assume a totality of conditions in a series of nothing but conditioned events or beings.

Finally, the otherwise clear thesis that belongs to the dynamic class — that not everything in the series of causes is contingent, but rather that there may be an absolutely necessary existing being — is subject to a fundamental contradiction of the antithesis — that none of the beings of which we can ever think may be thought of as the absolutely necessary origin of another being in the world. For, then, as a member of the ascending series of causes and origins, [that absolutely necessary cause] would belong to the things of the world, in which no causality is unconditioned; yet here it must be taken as unconditioned, which is self-contradictory.

> *Remark*: If the thesis, "The world is in itself infinite," means that it is greater than all number (in comparison with a given quantity), it is false. For an infinite number is a contradiction. If it means that it is not infinite, this is certainly true; but one does not then know what the world may be. If I say, "It is finite," that also is false, because its boundary is no object of a possible experience. Thus, I say that what concerns a given space as well as time past is required only for contrast. Both are false because possible experience neither has a limit nor can it be infinite, and the world as appearance is only the object of possible experience.

*   *
*

This leads to the following remarks:

First, the proposition that "For all conditioned entities an absolutely unconditioned one must be given," is valid as a fundamental principle for all things so far as their connection is thought through pure reason, i.e., insofar as they are thought of as things in themselves. If, in applying this principle, one finds that it cannot be employed in relation to objects in space and time without contradiction, escape from this contradiction is possible only if it be assumed that objects in space and time, as objects of possible experience, cannot be regarded as things in themselves but as mere appearances, the form of which is based on the subjective constitution of our manner of intuiting them.

115

Beschränkung unsrer Erkenntniß zurück, und was in der Analytik vorher
a priori dogmatisch bewiesen worden war, wird hier in der Dialektik gleich=
sam durch ein Experiment der Vernunft, das sie an ihrem eignen Ver=
mögen anstellt, unwidersprechlich bestätigt. In Raum und Zeit ist das
5 Unbedingte nicht anzutreffen, was die Vernunft bedarf, und es bleibt
dieser nichts, als das immerwährende Fortschreiten zu Bedingungen
übrig, ohne Vollendung desselben zu hoffen.

Zweytens: Der Widerstreit dieser ihrer Sätze ist nicht bloß logisch,
der analytischen Entgegensetzung (contradictorie oppositorum), d. i.
10 ein bloßer Widerspruch, denn da würde, wenn einer derselben wahr ist,
der andre falsch sein müssen, und umgekehrt. Z. B. die Welt ist dem
Raume nach unendlich, verglichen mit dem Gegensatze, sie ist im
Raume nicht unendlich; sondern ein transscendentaler der synthethi=
schen Opposition (contrarie oppositorum), z. B. die Welt ist dem
15 Raume nach endlich, welcher Satz mehr sagt, als zur logischen Ent=
gegensetzung erfordert wird; denn er sagt nicht bloß, daß im Fortschreiten
zu den Bedingungen das Unbedingte nicht angetroffen werde, sondern
noch, daß diese Reihe der einander untergeordneten Bedingungen dennoch
ganz ein absolutes Ganze sey; welche zwey Sätze darum alle beyde falsch
20 seyn können — wie in der Logik zwey einander als Widerspiel entgegen=
gesetzte (contrarie opposita) Urtheile — und in der That sind sie es auch,
weil von Erscheinungen, als von Dingen an sich selbst, geredet wird.

Drittens können Satz und Gegensatz auch weniger enthalten, als
zur logischen Entgegensetzung erfordert wird, und so beyde wahr seyn, —
25 wie in der Logik zwey einander bloß durch Verschiedenheit der Subjecte
entgegengesetzte Urtheile (judicia subcontraria) — wie dieses mit der
Antinomie der dynamischen Grundsätze sich in der Tat so verhält, wenn
nämlich das Subject der entgegengesetzten Urtheile in beyden in ver=
schiedener Bedeutung genommen wird, z. B. der Begriff der Ursache, als
30 causa phaenomenon in dem Satz: Alle Kausalität der Phäno=
mene in der Sinnenwelt ist dem Mechanism der Natur
unterworfen, scheint mit dem Gegensatz: Einige Kausalität die=
ser Phänomene ist diesem Gesetz nicht unterworfen, im Wider=
spruch zu stehen, aber dieser ist darin doch nicht nothwendig anzutreffen,
35 denn in dem Gegensatze kann das Subject in einem andern Sinne ge=
nommen seyn, als es in dem Satze geschah, nämlich es kann dasselbe
Subject als causa noumenon gedacht werden, und da können beyde
Sätze wahr seyn, und daßelbe Subject kann als Ding an sich selbst frey
von der Bestimmung nach Naturnothwendigkeit seyn, was als Erschei=

The antinomy of pure reason unfailingly leads back to that restriction of our cognition. Here in the Dialectic what was proven dogmatically in the Analytic is likewise incontrovertibly confirmed by an experiment of reason that it employs upon its own capacities.[67] The unconditioned that reason requires cannot be found in space and time; it only remains for it to progress unceasingly through conditions, without hope of completing this progress.

Second, the conflict of these of its propositions is not merely logical[68] or analytical opposition (*contradictorie oppositorum*), i.e., a mere contradiction, since if it were, then, if one of these were true, the other would have necessarily to be false and vice versa, e.g., "*the world is spatially infinite*," compared with the contrary "*it is not spatially infinite*." Rather, the conflict is transcendental, a synthetic opposition (*contrarie oppositorum*), e.g., "*the world is spatially finite*." This proposition maintains more than is necessary for logical opposition because it asserts not just that the unconditioned will not be found in the progress to conditions, but rather also that the series of subordinated conditions comprises an absolute whole. Consequently, both propositions may be false — as two judgments as contraries can be set over against one another (*contrarie opposita*) in logic.[69] And in fact these are (both false) because appearances are spoken of as things in themselves.

Third, thesis and antithesis may also contain less than is required for a logical opposition and can thus both be true, as in logic when two judgments are opposed to one another by virtue of differences in their subjects (*judicia subcontraria*), as in fact happens with the antinomies of fundamental, dynamic principles, that is, when the same subject of opposed judgments is taken in different senses in both [the thesis and antithesis]. For example, the concept of cause, *causa phaenomenon* in the proposition, "*In the sensuous world all causality of phenomena is subject to the mechanism of nature*" appears to contradict the antithesis, "*some causality of these phenomena is not subject to this law.*" However, a contradiction is not necessarily to be found in this because in the antithesis the subject can be taken in a sense other than it is in the thesis, namely, the same subject can be thought as *causa noumenon*. Therefore, both propositions can be true, and the same subject can, as

117

nung, in Anſehung derſelben Handlung, doch nicht frey iſt. Und ſo auch
mit dem Begriffe eines nothwendigen Weſens.

Viertens: Dieſe Antinomie der reinen Vernunft, welche den
ſceptiſchen Stillſtand der reinen Vernunft nothwendig zu bewirken
ſcheint, führt am Ende, vermittelſt der Kritik, auf dogmatiſche Fortſchritte 5
derſelben, wenn es ſich nämlich hervor thut, daß ein ſolches Noumenon,
als Sache an ſich, wirklich und ſelbſt nach ſeinen Geſetzen, wenigſtens in
praktiſcher Abſicht, erkennbar iſt, ob es gleich überſinnlich iſt.

Freyheit der Willkür iſt dieſes Überſinnliche, welches durch moraliſche
Geſetze nicht allein als wirklich im Subject gegeben, ſondern auch in 10
praktiſcher Rückſicht, in Anſehung des Objectes, beſtimmend iſt, welches in
theoretiſcher gar nicht erkennbar ſeyn würde, welches dann der eigentliche Endzweck der Metaphyſik iſt.

Die Möglichkeit eines ſolchen Fortſchrittes der Vernunft mit dynamiſchen Ideen gründet ſich darauf, daß in ihnen die Zuſammenſetzung der 15
eigentlichen Verknüpfung der Wirkung mit ihrer Urſache, oder des Zufälligen mit dem Nothwendigen, nicht eine Verbindung des Gleichartigen ſeyn darf, wie in der mathematiſchen Syntheſis, ſondern Grund
und Folge, die Bedingung und das Bedingte, von verſchiedner Art ſeyn
können, und ſo in dem Fortſchritte vom Bedingten zur Bedingung, vom 20
Sinnlichen zum Überſinnlichen, als der oberſten Bedingung, ein Über-
ſchritt nach Grundſätzen geſchehen kann.

*   *   *

Die zwey dynamiſchen Antinomien ſagen weniger, als zur Oppo-
ſition erfordert wird, z. B. wie zwey particuläre Sätze. Daher beyde 25
wahr ſeyn können.

In den dynamiſchen Antinomien kann etwas Ungleichartiges zur
Bedingung angenommen werden. — Ingleichen hat man da Etwas,
wodurch das Überſinnliche (Gott, worauf der Zweck eigentlich geht)
erkannt werden kann, weil ein Geſetz der Freyheit als überſinnlich ge- 30
geben iſt.

Auf das Überſinnliche in der Welt (die geiſtige Natur der Seele)
und das außer der Welt (Gott), alſo Unſterblichkeit und Theologie,
iſt der Endzweck gerichtet.

thing in itself, be free from determination in accordance with natural necessity, and yet, as appearance, with respect to the same action, not be free. The same is true with the concept of a necessary being.

Fourth, this antinomy of pure reason, which appears necessarily to effect the sceptical stagnation of pure reason, leads in the end to its dogmatic advancement by means of critique, namely, when it emerges that such a *noumenon* as a thing in itself really is knowable, even from its own laws, at least for practical purpose[s], even though it is supersensible.

This supersensible is freedom of the will, which is not only actually given through moral laws in the subject, but also is practically determinative with respect to objects; yet theoretically it would not be knowable.[70] This then is metaphysics' proper ultimate end.

The possiblity of such progress of reason with dynamic ideas is based on the fact that with them the proper connection of an effect with its cause, or the accidental with the necessary cannot be a unification of homogeneous objects, as in mathematical synthesis, but of ground and consequence, the condition and the conditioned, which can be of different kinds. Thus, a transition based on principles can occur in the progression from the conditioned to the condition, from the sensible to the supersensible as the highest condition.

*   *   *

The two dynamic antinomies assert less than is required for an opposition, e.g., as in two existential propositions. Thus, both can be true.

In the dynamic antinomies something heterogeneous can be assumed as the condition. — In that way one has something whereby the supersensible (God, which is what the end really is) can be known, since a law of freedom as supersensible is given.

The supersensible in the world (the spiritual nature of the soul) and out of the world (God), hence immortality and theology, are the ultimate ends towards which metaphysics is directed.

Zweiter Entwurf

Der Metaphysik
drittes Stadium.

Praktisch=dogmatischer Überschritt zum Übersinnlichen.

Zuvörderst muß man wohl vor Augen haben, daß in dieser ganzen
5 Abhandlung der vorliegenden academischen Aufgabe gemäß, die Meta=
physik blos als theoretische Wissenschaft, oder, wie man sie sonst nennen
kann, als Metaphysik der Natur gemeynt sey, mithin der Überschritt
derselben zum Übersinnlichen nicht als ein Schreiten zu einer ganz andern,
nämlich moralisch=praktischen Vernunftwissenschaft, welche Meta=
10 physik der Sitten genannt werden kann, verstanden werden müsse,
indem dieses eine Verirrung in ein ganz andres Feld (μετάβασις εἰς ἄλλο
γένος) seyn würde, obgleich die letztere auch etwas Übersinnliches, näm=
lich die Freyheit, aber nicht nach dem, was es seiner Natur nach ist, son=
dern nach demjenigen, was es in Ansehung des Thuns und Lassens für
15 praktische Prinzipien begründet, zum Gegenstande hat.

Nun ist das Unbedingte nach allen im zweyten Stadium angestellten
Untersuchungen in der Natur, d. i. in der Sinnenwelt, schlechterdings nicht
anzutreffen, ob es gleich nothwendig angenommen werden muß. Von
dem Übersinnlichen aber gibt es kein theoretisch=dogmatisches Erkenntniß
20 (noumenorum non datur scientia). Also scheint ein praktisch=dogmatischer
Überschritt der Metaphysik der Natur sich selbst zu widersprechen, und
dieses dritte Stadium derselben unmöglich zu seyn.

· Allein wir finden unter den zur Erkenntniß der Natur, auf welche
Art es auch sey, gehörigen Begriffen, noch einen von der besondern
25 Beschaffenheit, daß wir dadurch nicht, was in dem Object ist, sondern
was wir, bloß dadurch, daß wir es in ihn legen, uns verständlich machen
können, der also eigentlich zwar kein Bestandtheil der Erkenntniß des
Gegenstandes, aber doch ein von der Vernunft gegebenes Mittel oder
Erkenntnißgrund ist, und zwar der theoretischen, aber in so fern doch nicht
30 dogmatischen Erkenntniß, und dies ist der Begriff von einer Zweck=
mäßigkeit der Natur, welche auch ein Gegenstand der Erfahrung seyn
kann, mithin ein immanenter, nicht transscendenter, Begriff ist, wie der
von der Struktur der Augen und Ohren, von der aber, was Erfahrung
betrifft, es kein weiteres Erkenntniß gibt, als was Epikur ihm zustand,
35 nämlich daß, nachdem die Natur Augen und Ohren gebildet hat, wir
sie zum Sehen und Hören brauchen, nicht aber beweiset, daß die sie
hervorbringende Ursache selbst die Absicht gehabt habe, diese Struktur
dem genannten ·Zwecke gemäß zu bilden, denn diesen kann man nicht

Metaphysics
The Third Stage

The Practical-Dogmatic Transition to the Supersensible

In the first place, one must not lose sight of [the fact] that through-out this entire treatise, in accord with the problem proposed by the Academy, by metaphysics is meant a merely theoretical science, or, as it might otherwise be called, the *metaphysics of nature*. Consequently, the transition of metaphysics to the supersensible must not be understood as a passage to a rational science of an entirely different kind, that is to a moral-practical science, which can be called the *metaphysics of morals*, for that would be a confusion in a completely different field (μετάβασις εἰς ἄλλο γένος), even though the latter also has something supersensible, that is freedom, as its object. Rather, it is an object with respect to what it establishes as practical principles for commission and omission.

Now according to all the investigations employed in the second stage, the unconditioned can nowhere be found in nature, that is, in the world of sense, even though it must be assumed. But there is no theoretical-dogmatic knowledge of the supersensible (*noumenorum non datur scientia*). And so a practical-dogmatic transition to a metaphysics of nature seems to be a contradiction and this third stage of metaphysics impossible.

However, among the concepts belonging to the cognition of nature — of whatever kind this knowledge may be — we find one with a special characteristic: that we can understand it not through something in the object itself, but rather merely because we place it in the object. Thus this is, to be sure, properly no component of cognition of the object but still is a means to or ground of knowledge — certainly theoretical but not for that reason dogmatic — given by reason. And this is the concept of nature's *purposiveness*, which also can be an object of experience; it is thus an immanent, not a transcendent concept. It is like the concept of the structure of the eyes and ears. But the concept gives no further knowledge of what concerns experience than what Epicurus conceded: That is, after nature had formed eyes and ears, we use them to see and to hear. This does not prove that the cause that produced them itself had the intention of forming these structures in accord with the aforementioned purpose; for these cannot be

wahrnehmen, sondern nur durch Vernünfteln hineintragen, um auch nur eine Zweckmäßigkeit an solchen Gegenständen zu erkennen.

Wir haben also einen Begriff von einer Teleologie der Natur, und zwar a priori, weil wir sonst ihn nicht in unsre Vorstellung der Objecte derselben hineinlegen, sondern nur aus dieser, als empirischer Anschauung, 5 herausnehmen dürften, und die Möglichkeit a priori einer solchen Vorstellungsart, welche doch noch kein Erkenntniß ist, gründet sich darauf, daß wir in uns selbst ein Vermögen der Verknüpfung nach Zwecken (nexus finalis) wahrnehmen.

Obzwar nun also die physisch-teleologischen Lehren (von Natur- 10 zwecken) niemals dogmatisch seyn, noch weniger den Begriff von einem Endzweck, d. i. dem Unbedingten in der Reihe der Zwecke, an die Hand geben können: so bleibt doch der Begriff der Freyheit, so wie er, als sinnlich-unbedingte Kausalität, selbst in der Kosmologie vorkommt, zwar sceptisch angefochten, aber doch unwiderlegt, und mit ihm auch 15 der Begriff von einem Endzweck; ja, dieser gilt in moralisch-praktischer Rücksicht als unumgänglich, ob ihm gleich seine objective Realität, wie überhaupt aller Zweckmäßigkeit gegebener oder gedachter Gegenstände, nicht theoretisch-dogmatisch gesichert werden kann.

Dieser Endzweck der reinen praktischen Vernunft ist das höchste 20 Gut, sofern es in der Welt möglich ist, welches aber nicht blos in dem, was Natur verschaffen kann, nämlich der Glückseligkeit (die größeste Summe der Lust), sondern was das höchste Erforderniß, nämlich die Bedingung ist, unter der allein die Vernunft sie den vernünftigen Weltwesen zuerkennen kann, nämlich zugleich im sittlich-gesetzmäßigsten 25 Verhalten derselben zu suchen ist.

Dieser Gegenstand der Vernunft ist übersinnlich; zu ihm als Endzweck fortzuschreiten, ist Pflicht; daß es also ein Stadium der Metaphysik für diesen Überschritt und das Fortschreiten in demselben geben müsse, ist unzweifelhaft. Ohne alle Theorie ist dies aber doch unmöglich, 30 denn der Endzweck ist nicht völlig in unsrer Gewalt, daher müssen wir uns einen theoretischen Begriff von der Quelle, woraus er entspringen kann, machen. Gleichwohl kann eine solche Theorie nicht nach demjenigen, was wir an den Objecten erkennen, sondern allenfalls nach dem, was wir hineinlegen, Statt finden, weil der Gegenstand übersinnlich ist. — 35 Also wird diese Theorie nur in praktisch-dogmatischer Rücksicht Statt finden, und der Idee des Endzweckes auch nur eine in dieser Rücksicht hinreichende objective Realität zusichern können.

Was den Begriff des Zweckes betrifft: so ist er jederzeit von uns

perceived, but can only be introduced by specious argument which also recognizes only one purpose in such objects.

Thus, we have a concept of a *teleology of nature*. Moreover, it is a priori; if it were not, we could not put it into our representation of objects of nature, but instead, as an empirical intuition, we would only be able to extract it from this representation. The a priori possibility of such a manner of representation, which is not cognition, is based on the fact that we perceive in ourselves a capacity to combine in accordance with ends (*nexus finalis*).

Thus, although physico-teleological doctrines (of the ends of nature) can never be dogmatic, and even less can they provide the concept of an ultimate end, i.e., of something unconditioned in the series of ends, yet the concept of freedom remains, appearing as sensibly unconditioned causality, even in cosmology; skeptically challenged but certainly unrefuted. And with the concept of freedom the concept of an ultimate end also remains. Indeed, this is indispensibly valid in moral-practical contexts, even though its objective reality cannot be theoretically guaranteed in a dogmatic fashion, as is in general the case for all purposive objects — either given or thought.

This ultimate end of pure practical reason is the highest good, so far as this is possible in the world, which [good], however, is not merely to be sought in what nature can provide, that is to say, in happiness (the greatest amount of pleasure). Instead, it is to be sought in the supreme requirement, that is, the only condition under which reason can award it to rational beings in the world, and, of course, at the same time in the ethical, law abiding conduct of rational beings.[71]

This object of reason is supersensible; to strive towards it as an ultimate end is duty. Thus, there must indubitably be a stage of metaphysics for this transition and for progress in it. This is impossible without a theory, however; for the ultimate end is not entirely within our power, and we must, therefore, construct for ourselves a theoretical concept of the source from which it can arise. Nevertheless, such a theory cannot arise in accordance with what we cognize in objects, but at most in accordance with what we put into them, for its object is supersensible. — Thus, this theory will arise only in a practical-dogmatic context, and only in this context can sufficient objective reality for the idea of an ultimate final end be guaranteed.

What pertains to the concepts of an end: it is always made by us, and

selbst gemacht, und der des Endzweckes muß a priori durch die Vernunft gemacht seyn.

Dieser gemachten Begriffe, oder vielmehr, in theoretischer Rücksicht, transscendenten Ideen sind, wenn man sie nach analytischer Methode
5 aufstellt, drey, das Übersinnliche nämlich, in uns, über uns, und nach uns:

1) Die Freyheit, von welcher der Anfang muß gemacht werden, weil wir von diesem Übersinnlichen der Weltwesen allein die Gesetze, unter dem Namen der moralischen, a priori, mithin dogmatisch, aber nur in praktischer Absicht, nach welcher der End-
10 zweck allein möglich ist, erkennen, nach denen also die Autonomie der reinen praktischen Vernunft zugleich als Autokratie, d. i. als Vermögen angenommen wird, diesen, was die formale Bedingung desselben, die Sittlichkeit, betrifft, unter allen Hindernissen, welche die Einflüsse der Natur auf uns, als Sinnenwesen,
15 verüben mögen, doch als zugleich intelligible Wesen, noch hier im Erdenleben zu erreichen, d. i. der Glaube an die Tugend, als das Prinzip in uns, zum höchsten Gut zu gelangen.

2) Gott, das allgnügsame Prinzip des höchsten Gutes über uns, was, als moralischer Welturheber, unser Unvermögen auch in
20 Ansehung der materialen Bedingung dieses Endzweckes einer der Sittlichkeit angemessenen Glückseligkeit in der Welt ergänzet.

3) Unsterblichkeit, d. i. die Fortdauer unsrer Existenz nach uns, als Erdensöhne, mit denen ins Unendliche fortgehenden moralischen und physischen Folgen, die dem moralischen Verhalten derselben
25 angemessen sind.

Eben diese Momente der praktisch-dogmatischen Erkenntniß des Übersinnlichen, nach synthetischer Methode aufgestellt, fangen von dem unbeschränkten Inhaber des höchsten ursprünglichen Gutes an, schreiten zu dem (durch Freyheit) Abgeleiteten in der Sinnenwelt fort, und endigen
30 mit den Folgen dieses objectiven Endzweckes der Menschen in einer künftigen intelligibeln, stehen also in der Ordnung: Gott, Freyheit und Unsterblichkeit systematisch verbunden da.

Was das Anliegen der menschlichen Vernunft in Bestimmung dieser Begriffe zu einem wirklichen Erkenntniß betrifft: so bedarf es
35 keines Beweises, und die Metaphysik, die gerade darum, nämlich nur um jenem zu gnügen, eine nothwendige Nachforschung geworden ist, bedarf wegen ihrer unablässigen Bearbeitung zu diesem Zwecke keiner Rechtfertigung. — Aber hat sie in Ansehung jenes Übersinnlichen, dessen

the concept of an ultimate end must be made a priori by reason.

These constructed concepts — or, rather, in theoretical perspective, transcendent ideas — are, if displayed according to the analytic method, three, namely, the supersensible *in us, over us*, and *after us*.[72]

1) *Freedom*: We must begin here, for only from this supersensible aspect of worldly beings do we know the laws — under the rubric of moral laws, which are a priori and consequently dogmatic, but only from a practical perspective — in accordance with which alone the ultimate end is possible, and in accord with which the *autonomy* of pure practical reason is thus simultaneously assumed as *autocracy*. That is, even here in earthly life, amidst all the hindrances that the influences of nature may place upon us as sensible creatures, still at the same time as intelligible beings this autocracy is assumed as the ability to achieve what pertains to the formal condition of freedom,[73] morality, that is the *faith in virtue* as the principle *in us* of achieving the supreme good.

2) *God*: the entirely sufficient principle of the highest good *over us* who, as moral creator of the world, supplements proportionate to our morality our incapacity, even with respect to the material condition of this ultimate goal of happiness in the world.

3) *Immortality*: that is, the continuation of our existence *after us*, as mortals with such moral and physical consequences, continued to infinity, as are appropriate to the moral behavior of such creatures.

Arranged in accord with synthetic method, these are the very moments of practical-dogmatic knowledge of the supersensible. They begin with the unlimited possessor of the highest original good, proceed (through freedom) to what derives from it in the world of sense, and conclude with the consequences of this objective goal of mankind in a future intelligible world. They stand, therefore, systematically connected in the order: God, freedom and immortality.

What concerns the interest of human reason in designating these concepts actual cognition requires no proof, and metaphysics, which has become a necessary inquiry just precisely in order to satisfy that interest, needs no justification for its unremitting cultivation of this

Erkenntniß ihr Endzweck ist, seit der Leibniz-Wolfischen Epoche irgend etwas, und wie viel ausgerichtet, und was kann sie überhaupt ausrichten? Das ist die Frage, welche beantwortet werden soll, wenn sie auf die Erfüllung des Endzweckes, wozu es überhaupt Metaphysik geben soll, gerichtet ist. 5

Auflösung
der academischen Aufgabe.

I.
Was für Fortschritte kann die Metaphysik in Ansehung des Übersinnlichen thun? 10

Durch die Kritik der reinen Vernunft ist hinreichend bewiesen, daß über die Gegenstände der Sinne hinaus es schlechterdings kein theoretisches Erkenntniß, und, weil in diesem Falle alles a priori durch Begriffe erkannt werden müßte, kein theoretisch-dogmatisches Erkenntniß geben könne, und zwar aus dem einfachen Grunde, weil allen Begriffen 15 irgend eine Anschauung, dadurch ihnen objective Realität verschafft wird, muß untergelegt werden können, alle unsre Anschauung aber sinnlich ist. Das heißt mit andern Worten, wir können von der Natur übersinnlicher Gegenstände, Gottes, unsers eigenen Freyheitsvermögens, und der unsrer Seele (abgesondert vom Körper) gar nichts erkennen, was dieses 20 innere Prinzip alles dessen, was zum Daseyn dieser Dinge gehört, die Folgen und Wirkungen desselben betrifft, durch welche die Erscheinungen derselben uns auch nur im mindesten Grade erklärlich, und ihr Prinzip, das Object selbst, für uns erkennbar sein könnte.

Nun kommt es also nur noch darauf an, ob es nicht demohngeachtet 25 von diesen übersinnlichen Gegenständen ein praktisch-dogmatisches Erkenntniß geben könne, welches dann das dritte, und den ganzen Zweck der Metaphysik erfüllende Stadium derselben seyn würde.

In diesem Falle würden wir das übersinnliche Ding nicht nach dem, was es an sich ist, sondern nur, wie wir es zu denken, und seine Be- 30 schaffenheit anzunehmen haben, um dem praktisch-dogmatischen Object des reinen sittlichen Prinzipes, nämlich dem Endzweck, welcher das höchste Gut ist, für uns selbst angemessen zu seyn, zu untersuchen haben. Wir würden da nicht Nachforschungen über die Natur der Dinge anstellen, die wir uns, und zwar blos zum nothwendigen praktischen Behuf, selbst 35

goal. — But has it accomplished anything in respect to the supersensible, cognition of which is its ultimate goal, since the Leibniz-Wolff epoch? And how much has it accomplished and what in general can it accomplish? That is the question that must be answered if it is directed towards the fulfillment of the ultimate goal for which in general there must be metaphysics.

Solution to the Academy's Problem

I.
What Progress Can Metaphysics Make in Regard to the Supersensible?

The *Critique of Pure Reason* adequately demonstrates that absolutely no theoretical knowledge of objects beyond the senses is possible, and since in this case everything must be known a priori through concepts there can be no theoretical-dogmatic cognition, for the simple reason, of course, that all concepts must be attached to some intuition, through which their objective reality is provided, and that all our intuition is sensible. That means, in other words, that we can cognize absolutely nothing of the nature of supersensible objects — of God, of our own capacity for freedom, and of the nature of our soul (separated from the body) — that could make even slightly cognizable to us what pertains to this internal principle of everything that belongs to the existence of these things, [as well as] their consequences and effects, by which their appearances, and their source, the object itself, are explicable.

But the question is whether, nonetheless, there could not be practical-dogmatic knowledge of these supersensible objects,[74] which then would be the third stage of metaphysics, and one that fulfills its entire end.

In this case, we would not have to investigate a supersensible thing in virtue of what it is in itself, but rather only in virtue of how we must think it and what we must assume about its nature in order that it may be appropriate for us as the practical-dogmatic object of the pure moral principle that is the ultimate end, which is the highest good. Here we would not engage in an investigation of the nature of things that we make for ourselves, solely for necessary practical purposes to

machen, und die vielleicht außer unsrer Idee gar nicht existiren, vielleicht
nicht seyn können (ob diese gleich sonst keinen Widerspruch enthält),
weil wir uns dabey nur ins Überschwängliche verlaufen dürften, sondern
nur wissen wollen, was jener Idee gemäß, die uns durch die Vernunft
unumgänglich nothwendig gemacht wird, für moralische Grundsätze
der Handlungen obliegen, und da würde ein praktisch-dogmatisches
Erkennen und Wissen der Beschaffenheit des Gegenstandes, bey völliger
Verzichtthuung auf ein theoretisches (suspensio judicii) eintreten, von
welchem ersteren es fast allein auf den Namen ankommt, mit dem
wir diese Modalität unseres Fürwahrhaltens belegen, damit er für eine
solche Absicht nicht zu wenig (wie bey dem bloßen Meynen), aber doch
auch nicht zu viel (wie bey dem Für-wahrscheinlich-annehmen) enthalte,
und so dem Sceptiker gewonnen Spiel gebe.

Überredung aber, welche ein Fürwahrhalten ist, von dem man
bey sich selbst nicht ausmachen kann, ob es auf blos subjectiven, oder
auf objectiven Gründen beruhe, im Gegensatz der blos gefühlten Überzeugung, bey welcher sich das Subject der letztern und ihrer Zulänglich-
keit bewußt zu seyn glaubt, ob es zwar dieselbe nicht nennen, mithin
nach ihrer Verknüpfung mit dem Object sich nicht deutlich machen kann,
können beyde nicht zu Modalitäten des Fürwahrhaltens im dogmatischen
Erkenntniß, es mag theoretisch oder praktisch seyn, gezählt werden, weil
diese ein Erkenntniß aus Prinzipien seyn soll, die also auch einer deutlichen, verständlichen und mittheilbaren Vorstellung fähig seyn muß.

Die Bedeutung dieses, vom Meynen und Wissen, als eines auf
Beurtheilung in theoretischer Absicht gegründeten, verschiedenen Fürwahrhaltens, kann nun in den Ausdruck Glauben gelegt werden, wo-
runter eine Annehmung, Voraussetzung (Hypothesis) verstanden wird, die
nur darum nothwendig ist, weil eine objective praktische Regel des Ver-
haltens als nothwendig zum Grunde liegt, bey der wir die Möglichkeit
der Ausführung und des daraus hervorgehenden Objectes an sich, zwar
nicht theoretisch einsehen, aber doch die einzige Art der Zusammenstimmung derselben zum Endzweck subjectiv erkennen.

Ein solcher Glaube ist das Fürwahrhalten eines theoretischen Satzes,
z. B. es ist ein Gott, durch praktische Vernunft, und in diesem Falle
als reine praktische Vernunft betrachtet, wo, indem der Endzweck die
Zusammenstimmung unsrer Bestrebung zum höchsten Gut, unter einer
schlechterdings nothwendigen praktischen, nämlich moralischen Regel
steht, deren Effekt wir uns aber nicht anders, als unter Voraussetzung
der Existenz eines ursprünglichen höchsten Gutes, als möglich denken

be sure — things that perhaps may not exist independently of our idea, perhaps cannot even be (although they otherwise contain no contradiction) — for in so doing we would only venture to lose our way in excess. Rather, we only want to know what kind of moral principles of action apply, consistent with that idea which is made unavoidably necessary for us by reason. And here enters a practical-dogmatic knowledge and science of the nature of the object, with a complete renunciation of theoretical cognition (*suspensio judicii*). About the only issue left is to determine what name to give the modality of our assent so that it does not contain too little for such a purpose (as with mere opinion) or yet too much (as with what is assumed to be probable), and so give up the game as lost to the skeptic.[75]

However, persuasion is assent and, in itself, it cannot be determined whether it rests on subjective or objective grounds in contrast to mere felt conviction, where the subject believes himself to be aware of objective reasons and their sufficiency, even though of course he cannot name them and thus make them clear according to their connection with the object. Neither of these can be counted among the modalities of assent in dogmatic knowledge, be it theoretical or practical, since this should be knowledge from principles and must thus be also capable of a clear, understandable and communicable representation.

The significance of this kind of assent, which differs from opinion and knowledge, inasmuch as it is based on judgment with a theoretical purpose, can be seen in the term *faith*. By this is understood an assumption or presupposition (hypothesis), which is necessary only because an objective practical rule of conduct that is necessary supports it. With the rule we subjectively know the possibility of its performance and [the possibility] of the object which proceeds from it in itself. Of course, this is not theoretical insight, but yet it is the only way subjectively to know the agreement of this possibility with the ultimate end.

Such faith is assent to a theoretical proposition, e.g., *there is a God*, through practical reason, considered in this case as pure practical reason, where — since the ultimate end or the agreement of our striving for the highest good stands under an absolutely necessary practical, that is, moral rule, whose effect we can think of as possible only under

können, wir dieses in praktischer Absicht anzunehmen, a priori genöthigt werden.

So ist für den Theil des Publikums, der nichts mit dem Getreide-handel zu thun hat, das Voraussehen einer schlechten Ernte ein bloßes Meynen, nachdem die Dürre den ganzen Frühling hindurch anhaltend 5 gewesen, nach derselben ein Wissen, für den Kaufmann aber, dessen Zweck und Angelegenheit es ist, durch diesen Handel zu gewinnen, ein Glauben, daß sie schlecht ausfallen werde, und er also seine Vorräthe sparen müsse, weil er etwas hiebey zu thun beschließen muß, indem es in seine Angelegenheit und Geschäfte einschlägt, nur daß die Noth- 10 wendigkeit dieser nach Regeln der Klugheit genommenen Entschließung nur bedingt ist, statt dessen eine solche, die eine sittliche Maxime voraus-setzt, auf einem Prinzip beruhet, das schlechterdings nothwendig ist.

Daher hat der Glaube in moralisch-praktischer Rücksicht auch an sich einen moralischen Werth, weil er ein freyes Annehmen enthält. Das 15 Credo in den drey Artikeln des Bekenntnisses der reinen praktischen Vernunft: Ich glaube an einen einigen Gott, als den Urquell alles Guten in der Welt, als seinen Endzweck; — ich glaube an die Möglichkeit, zu diesem Endzweck, dem höchsten Gut in der Welt, sofern es am Menschen liegt, zusammenzustimmen; — ich glaube an ein künftiges ewiges Leben, 20 als der Bedingung einer immerwährenden Annäherung der Welt zum höchsten in ihr möglichen Gut; — dieses Credo, sage ich, ist ein freyes Fürwahrhalten, ohne welches es auch keinen moralischen Wert haben würde. Es verstattet also keinen Imperativ (kein crede), und der Beweis-grund dieser seiner Richtigkeit ist kein Beweis von der Wahrheit dieser 25 Sätze, als theoretischer betrachtet, mithin keine objective Belehrung von der Wirklichkeit der Gegenstände derselben, denn die ist in Ansehung des Über-sinnlichen unmöglich, sondern nur eine subjectiv-, und zwar praktisch-gültige, und in dieser Absicht hinreichende Belehrung, so zu handeln, als ob wir wüßten, daß diese Gegenstände wirklich wären, welche Vorstellungsart hier 30 auch nicht in technisch-praktischer Absicht als Klugheitslehre (lieber zu viel, als zu wenig anzunehmen) für nothwendig angesehen werden muß, weil sonst der Glaube nicht aufrichtig seyn würde, sondern nur in mo-ralischer Absicht nothwendig ist, um dem, wozu wir so schon von selbst verbunden sind, nämlich der Beförderung des höchsten Gutes in der Welt 35 nachzustreben, noch ein Ergänzungsstück zur Theorie der Möglichkeit desselben, allenfalls durch bloße Vernunftideen hinzuzufügen, indem wir uns jene Objecte, Gott, Freyheit in praktischer Qualität, und Unsterb-

the assumption of an original supreme good — we are a priori constrained to assume this for a practical purpose.

Thus, for that part of the public having nothing to do with the grain trade, the forecast of a bad harvest is a mere *opinion*. After the drought has continued throughout the entire spring, it is *knowledge* for that same public. However, for the merchant, whose goal and business it is to profit from the trade, it is a *belief* that the harvest will be bad and that he must therefore conserve his supply; for in this he must decide what to do, since his interest and business involve only that the necessity of the decision taken be conditioned solely by the rules of prudence, instead of being one that presupposes an ethical maxim or rests upon a principle that is absolutely necessary.

Therefore, in its moral-practical aspect, belief has in itself a moral worth, for it includes a free commitment. The Credo in the three articles of confession of pure practical reason are: I believe in one God, original source of all good in the world, as its ultimate end; — I believe in the possibility of harmonizing this ultimate end with the highest good in the world, as far as it pertains to men; — I believe in a future eternal life as the condition of the perpetual approach of the world to the highest good possible in it. This Credo, I say, is a free assent, without which it would have no moral worth. Thus it authorizes no imperative (no *crede*), and the basis for the proof of its correctness is not a proof of the truth of these propositions considered theoretically. Consequently, it does not objectively teach the actuality of the objects of these propositions, for such is impossible with respect to the supersensible. It is rather only a subjectively and, of course, practically valid instruction — which is adequate for this purpose — to act as though we knew that these objects were actual. Neither may this mode of representation be considered as necessary from a technical-practical perspective, as a doctrine of prudence (better to assume too much than too little), for then faith would not be sincere. Rather this form of representation is necessary only for a moral purpose in order to append, by means of mere ideas of reason, if need be, a final touch to the theory of the possibility of that to which we already are committed, that is, to strive for promotion of the supreme good in the world. For

Zweiter Entwurf

lichkeit, nur der Forderung der moralischen Gesetze an uns zu Folge
selbst machen und ihnen objective Realität freywillig geben, da wir ver-
sichert sind, daß in diesen Ideen kein Widerspruch gefunden werden
könne, von der Annahme derselben die Zurückwirkung auf die subjectiven
5 Prinzipien der Moralität und deren Bestärkung, mithin auf das Thun
und Lassen selbst, wiederum in der Intention moralisch ist.

Aber sollte es nicht auch theoretische Beweise der Wahrheit jener
Glaubenslehren geben, von denen sich sagen ließe, daß ihnen zu Folge
es wahrscheinlich sey, daß ein Gott sey, daß ein sittliches, seinem Willen
10 gemäßes und der Idee des höchsten Gutes angemessenes Verhältniß
in der Welt angetroffen werde, und daß es ein künftiges Leben für jeden
Menschen gebe? — Die Antwort ist, der Ausdruck der Wahrscheinlichkeit
ist in dieser Anwendung völlig ungereimt. Denn wahrscheinlich (probabile)
ist das, was einen Grund des Fürwahrhaltens für sich hat, der größer
15 ist als die Hälfte des zureichenden Grundes, also eine mathematische
Bestimmung der Modalität des Fürwahrhaltens, wo Momente derselben
als gleichartig angenommen werden müssen, und so eine Annäherung
zur Gewißheit möglich ist, dagegen der Grund des mehr oder weniger
Scheinbaren (verosimile) auch aus ungleichartigen Gründen bestehen,
20 eben darum aber sein Verhältnis zum zureichenden Grunde gar nicht
erkannt werden kann.

Nun ist aber das Übersinnliche von dem sinnlich Erkennbaren,
selbst der Species nach (toto genere), unterschieden, weil es über alle uns
mögliche Erkenntniß hinaus liegt. Also giebt es gar keinen Weg, durch
25 eben dieselbe Fortschritte zu ihm zu gelangen, wodurch wir im Felde
des Sinnlichen zur Gewißheit zu kommen hoffen dürfen: also auch keine
Annäherung zu dieser, mithin kein Fürwahrhalten, dessen logischer Werth
Wahrscheinlichkeit könnte genannt werden.

In theoretischer Rücksicht kommen wir der Überzeugung vom
30 Daseyn Gottes, dem Daseyn des höchsten Gutes, und dem Bevorstehen
eines künftigen Lebens, durch die stärksten Anstrengungen der Vernunft
nicht im mindesten näher, denn in die Natur übersinnlicher Gegenstände
giebt es für uns gar keine Einsicht. In praktischer Rücksicht aber machen
wir uns diese Gegenstände selbst, so wie wir die Idee derselben dem
35 Endzwecke unsrer reinen Vernunft behülflich zu seyn urtheilen, welcher
Endzweck, weil er moralisch nothwendig ist, dann freylich wohl die
Täuschung bewirken kann, das, was in subjectiver Beziehung, nämlich
für den Gebrauch der Freyheit des Menschen, Realität hat, weil es in
Handlungen, die dieser ihrem Gesetze gemäß sind, der Erfahrung dargelegt

we ourselves make those objects, God, freedom in its practical quality, and immortality, only as a result of the demand of the moral laws on us, and we freely grant them objective reality, since we are assured that no contradiction can be found in these ideas. The effect upon subjective principles of morality and their confirmation, thus upon conduct itself, of the assumption of this is again moral in intention.

However, should there not also be theoretical proofs of the truth of those doctrines of belief so that it may be said that as a result of them it is *probable* that there is a God, that a moral relation conformable to his will and proportionate to the idea of a supreme good is to be encountered in the world, and that there is a future life for every man? — The answer is that the expression probability is wholly absurd in such an application. For probability (*probabile*) is what has a basis for assent that is greater than half the sufficient reason. It is thus a mathematical determination of the modality of assent, where moments of the latter must be taken as homogeneous and so an approximation to certainty is possible. By contrast, the basis of the more or less apparent (*verosimile*) consists of heterogeneous grounds, and for that reason its relation to sufficient reason cannot be known.

But now, the supersensible is different even in kind (*toto genere*) from what is sensibly known, since it transcends all cognition possible for us. Thus there is no way to achieve progress to the supersensible through the sensible, through which we can hope to come to certainty in the field of the supersensible,[77] and so there is no approach to certainty and thus no assent whose logical value can be termed probability.

From a theoretical point of view, reason's greatest efforts do not in the least come closer to conviction in the existence of God, the existence of a supreme good, and the prospect of a future life, because there is absolutely no insight into the nature of supersensible objects for us. From a practical perspective, however, we make these objects for ourselves as we judge the idea[s] of them to be helpful to the ultimate end of our pure reason. That ultimate end, because it is morally necessary, certainly can effect an illusion: that what has reality in a subjective relation, that is, for the use of human freedom, holds for knowledge of the existence of objects conformable to this form,

worden, für Erkenntniß der Existenz des dieser Form gemäßen Objectes zu halten.

Nunmehro läßt sich das dritte Stadium der Metaphysik in den Fortschritten der reinen Vernunft zu ihrem Endzweck verzeichnen. — Es macht einen Kreis aus, dessen Grenzlinie in sich selbst zurückkehrt, und so ein Ganzes von Erkenntniß des Übersinnlichen beschließt, außer dem nichts von dieser Art weiter ist, und der doch auch alles befasset, was dem Bedürfnisse dieser Vernunft gnügen kann. — Nachdem sie sich nämlich von allem Empirischen, womit sie in den zwey ersten Stadien noch immer verwickelt war, und von den Bedingungen der sinnlichen Anschauung, die ihr die Gegenstände nur in der Erscheinung vorstelleten, losgemacht, und sich in den Standpunkt der Ideen, woraus sie ihre Gegenstände nach dem, was sie an sich selbst sind, betrachtet, gestellt hat, beschreibt sie ihren Horizont, der von der Freyheit als übersinnlichem, aber durch den Kanon der Moral erkennbarem Vermögen theoretisch-dogmatisch anhebend, eben dahin auch in praktisch-dogmatischer, d. i. einer auf den Endzweck, das höchste in der Welt zu befördernde Gut, gerichteten Absicht zurückkehrt, dessen Möglichkeit durch die Ideen von Gott, Unsterblichkeit, und das von der Sittlichkeit selbst diktirte Vertrauen zum Gelingen dieser Absicht ergänzet, und so diesem Begriffe objective, aber praktische Realität verschafft wird.

Die Sätze: es ist ein Gott, es ist in der Natur der Welt eine ursprüngliche, obzwar unbegreifliche, Anlage zur Übereinstimmung mit der moralischen Zweckmäßigkeit, es ist endlich in der menschlichen Seele eine solche, welche sie eines nie aufhörenden Fortschreitens zu derselben fähig macht, — diese Sätze selber theoretisch-dogmatisch beweisen zu wollen, würde so viel seyn, als sich ins Überschwängliche zu werfen, ob es zwar, was den zweyten Satz betrifft, die Erläuterung desselben durch die physische, in der Welt anzutreffende Zweckmäßigkeit, die Annehmung jener moralischen sehr befördern kann. Eben dasselbe gilt von der Modalität des Fürwahrhaltens, dem vermeynten Erkennen und Wissen, wobey man vergißt, daß jene Ideen von uns selbst willkürlich gemacht, und nicht von den Objecten abgeleitet sind, mithin zu nichts mehrerm, als dem Annehmen in theoretischer, aber doch auch zur Behauptung der Vernunftmäßigkeit dieser Annahme in praktischer Absicht berechtigen.

Hieraus ergiebt sich nun auch die merkwürdige Folge, daß der

for it is displayed in acts of experience conforming to the laws of freedom.

The third stage of metaphysics in the progress of pure reason towards its ultimate end may now be sketched. — It constitutes a circle whose boundary turns back on itself and so includes a totality of knowledge of the supersensible; beyond this circle there is nothing further of this sort, and indeed it includes everything that can satisfy the need of such reason. — That is, after it has separated itself from everything empirical with which it was always entangled in the first two stages, and from the conditions of sensible intuition, which represents objects only as appearances, and puts itself into the standpoint of ideas,[78] which considers its objects as they are in themselves, *reason* describes its outlook,[79] beginning theoretically and dogmatically with freedom as supersensible but as a faculty known by the moral canon. But it also returns to the same place in its practical-dogmatic intent, that is, to an ultimate end directed towards the advancement of the supreme good in the world, the possibility of which is completed by the ideas of God, immortality, and the confidence in the success of this intention, which confidence is dictated by morality itself. Thus these ideas are provided objective but practical reality.

The propositions — "There is a God," "There is in the nature of the world an original but inconceivable disposition to conform with moral purposiveness" and, finally, "There is in the human soul a disposition that makes unceasing progress toward that conformity possible" — to attempt to prove just these propositions theoretically or dogmatically would involve us in the transcendent, although, of course, the elucidation of what concerns the second proposition by physical purposiveness encountered in the world can greatly advance acceptance of moral purposiveness. The very same is true for the modality of that assent, that putative perceiving and cognizing, by virtue of which it is forgotten that those ideas are arbitrarily made by ourselves and not derived from objects. Consequently, for a theoretical purpose, they are no more than *assumptions*; but they also justify the assertion of the reasonableness of these assumptions for practical purposes.

Now from this also derives the notable consequence that the progress of metaphysics in its third stage, in the realm of theology, is the

Zweiter Entwurf

Fortschritt der Metaphysik in ihrem dritten Stadium, im Felde der
Theologie, eben darum, weil er auf den Endzweck geht, der leichteste
unter allen ist, und, ob sie sich gleich hier mit dem Übersinnlichen beschäftigt, doch nicht überschwänglich, sondern der gemeinen Menschen-
5 vernunft eben so begreiflich wird, als den Philosophen, und dies so sehr,
daß die letztern durch die erstere sich zu orientiren genöthigt sind, damit
sie sich nicht ins Überschwängliche verlaufen. Diesen Vorzug hat die
Philosophie als Weisheitslehre vor ihr als speculativer Wissenschaft,
von nichts anderm, als dem reinen praktischen Vernunftvermögen,
10 d. i. der Moral, sofern sie aus dem Begriffe der Freyheit, als einem
zwar übersinnlichen, aber praktischen, a priori erkennbaren Prinzip
abgeleitet worden.

Die Fruchtlosigkeit aller Versuche der Metaphysik, sich in dem,
was ihren Endzweck, das Übersinnliche, betrifft, theoretisch-dogmatisch
15 zu erweitern: erstens in Ansehung der Erkenntniß der göttlichen Natur,
als dem höchsten ursprünglichen Gut; zweytens der Erkenntniß der
Natur einer Welt, in der, und durch die das höchste abgeleitete Gut
möglich seyn soll; drittens der Erkenntniß der menschlichen Natur,
sofern sie zu dem, diesem Endzwecke angemessenen Fortschreiten, mit der
20 erforderlichen Naturbeschaffenheit angethan ist; — die Fruchtlosigkeit,
sage ich, aller darin bis zum Schlusse der Leibniz-Wolfischen Epoche
gemachten und sogleich das nothwendige Mißlingen aller künftig noch
anzustellenden Versuche soll itzt beweisen, daß auf dem theoretisch-
dogmatischen Wege für die Metaphysik zu ihrem Endzweck zu gelangen,
25 kein Heil sey, und daß alle vermeynte Erkenntniß in diesem Felde
transscendent, mithin gänzlich leer sey.

Transscendente Theologie.

Die Vernunft will in der Metaphysik von dem Ursprunge aller
Dinge, dem Urwesen (ens originarium), und dessen innerer Beschaffen-
30 heit sich einen Begriff machen, und fängt subjectiv vom Urbegriffe
(conceptus originarius) der Dingheit überhaupt (realitas), d. i. von
demjenigen an, dessen Begriff an sich selbst ein Seyn, zum Unterschiede
von dem, dessen Begriff ein Nichtseyn vorstellt, nur daß sie, um sich
objectiv auch das Unbedingte an diesem Urwesen zu denken, dieses, als
35 das All (omnitudo) der Realität enthaltend (ens realissimum) vorstellt,
und so den Begriff desselben, als des höchsten Wesens, durchgängig

easiest of all, precisely because it is concerned with the ultimate end. And although theology deals with the supersensible it is not transcendent, but rather is just as comprehensible to common human reason as to philosophers, so certainly so that the latter are forced to orient themselves by the former in order not to lose themselves in the transcendent. Philosophy as a doctrine of wisdom has this advantage over philosphy as a speculative science: it is deduced only from the pure practical faculty of reason, that is, from morality so far, to be sure, as it is derived from the concept of freedom as a supersensible principle, but a practical one knowable a priori.

The fruitlessness of all attempts of metaphysics to extend itself theoretically and dogmatically in what concerns its ultimate end, the supersensible: *first*, in respect to knowledge of God's nature as the supreme original good; *second*, in respect to knowledge of the nature of a world in which and through which the highest possible derived good may be possible; and *third*, with respect to knowledge of human nature so far as it is endowed with the constitution necessary to make suitable progress to this final end; — I say the fruitlessness of all such attempts up until the end of the Leibnizian-Wolffian era and, at the same time, the necessary miscarriage of all attempts that might still be made in the future, should now prove that there is no salvation along the theoretical-dogmatic path to the ultimate end of metaphysics, and that all purported knowledge in this field is transcendent, therefore completely empty.

Transcendent Theology

In metaphysics, reason attempts to form a concept of the origin of all things, of the primordial being (*ens originarium*), and of its internal constitution.[80] Reason begins subjectively with the primal concept of thinghood in general (*realitas*), i.e, it starts with that the concept of which represents being, in contrast with that whose concept represents a non-being. Now in order to think this primordial being as quite unconditioned objectively, reason represents it as containing the totality (*omnitudo*) of reality (*ens realissimum*). Consequently, its concept, as the supreme being, is completely determined, something that can occur with no other concept. And there is no difficulty so far as proving

bestimmt, welches kein anderer Begriff vermag, und was die Möglichkeit eines solchen Wesens betrifft, wie Leibnitz hinzusetzt, keine Schwierigkeit mache sie zu beweisen, weil Realitäten als lauter Bejahungen einander nicht widersprechen können, und was denkbar ist, weil sein Begriff sich nicht selbst widerspricht, d. i. alles, wovon der Begriff möglich, auch ein 5 mögliches Ding sey, wobey doch die Vernunft, durch Kritik geleitet, wohl den Kopf schütteln dürfte.

Wohl indessen der Metaphysik, wenn sie hier nur nicht etwa Begriffe für Sache, und Sache, oder vielmehr den Namen von ihr, für Begriffe nimmt und sich so gänzlich ins Leere hinein vernünftelt! 10

Wahr ist es, daß, wenn wir uns a priori von einem Dinge überhaupt, also ontologisch, einen Begriff machen wollen, wir immer zum Urbegriff den Begriff von einem allerrealesten Wesen in Gedanken zum Grunde legen, denn eine Negation, als Bestimmung eines Dinges, ist immer nur abgeleitete Vorstellung, weil man sie als Aufhebung (remotio) 15 nicht denken kann, ohne vorher die ihr entgegengesetzte Realität, als etwas, das gesetzt wird (positio s. reale), gedacht zu haben, und so, wenn wir diese subjective Bedingung des Denkens zur objectiven der Möglich=keit der Sachen selbst machen, alle Negationen blos wie Schranken des Allinbegriffes der Realitäten, mithin alle Dinge, außer diesem einen 20 ihrer Möglichkeit, nur als von diesem abgeleitet müssen angesehen werden.

Dieses Eine, welches sich die Metaphysik nun, man wundert sich selbst, wie, hingezaubert hat, ist das höchste metaphysische Gut. Es ent=hält den Stoff zur Erzeugung aller andern möglichen Dinge, wie das Marmorlager zu Bildsäulen von unendlicher Mannigfaltigkeit, welche 25 insgesammt nur durch Einschränkung (Absonderung des Übrigen von einem gewissen Theil des Ganzen, also nur durch Negation) möglich, und so das Böse sich blos als das Formale der Dinge vom Guten in der Welt unterscheidet, wie die Schatten in dem den ganzen Weltraum durchströmenden Sonnenlicht, und die Weltwesen sind darum nur böse, 30 weil sie nur Theile, und nicht das Ganze ausmachen, sondern zum Theil real, zum Theil negativ sind, bey welcher Zimmerung einer Welt dieser metaphysische Gott (das realissimum) gleichwohl sehr in den Ver=dacht kommt, daß er mit der Welt, (unerachtet aller Protestationen wider den Spinozism) als einem All existirender Wesen, einerley sey. 35

Aber auch über alle diese Einwürfe weggesehen, lasset uns nun die vorgeblichen Beweise vom Dasehn eines solchen Wesens, die daher ontologische genannt werden können, der Prüfung unterwerfen.

Der Argumente sind hier nur zwey, und können auch nicht mehr

the possibility of such a being is concerned because, as Leibniz added, as pure affirmations realities cannot contradict one another: and what is conceivable, since its concept is not contradictory, is also possible, that is, anything whose concept is possible is also a possible thing. Reason, guided by criticism, might well shake its head at this.[81]

However, metaphysics would do better if only it would not take concepts for things and things, or rather their names, for concepts and so argue sophistically [and] totally in the dark.

It is true that when we want a priori to make the concept of a thing in general, thus ontologically, we always base it on the primal concept in thought, the concept of the most real being, for a negation as determination is always only a derivative representation, since a determination cannot be cancelled (*remotio*) without the reality opposed to it as something posited (*positio s. reale*) having been thought. And so if we make this subjective condition of thought into an objective principle of the possibility of things themselves, all negations must be regarded as limitations of the complete essence of realities, and thus all things, except the one that is their possibility, must be considered as deriving only from this complete essence.

This One, which metaphysics now improvises, though it may be wondered how, is the supreme metaphysical good. It contains the material for production of all other possible things, as the supply of marble does for an infinite multitude of statues, which are altogether possible only through limitation (separation of the remainder from a certain part of the whole, thus only through negation). Thus, evil, merely as a formal property of things, is distinguished from the good in the world, like shadows in the sunlight streaming through all the space of the universe, and created things are evil only because they constitute parts and not the whole, and thus are partially real and partially negative. In a world fashioned this way one comes strongly to suspect that this *metaphysical God* (the *realissimum*) is one with the world (despite all protestations against Spinozism),[82] as the totality of all existing beings.

But let us disregard all of these objections and put these would-be proofs for the existence of such a being, which may hence be called ontological, to the test.

There are only two of those arguments here and indeed there can be no more. — Either the existence of a most real being is deduced

Zweiter Entwurf

seyn. — Entweder man schließt aus dem Begriff des allerrealesten
Wesens auf das Daseyn desselben, oder aus dem nothwendigen Daseyn
irgend eines Dinges auf einen bestimmten Begriff, den wir uns von ihm
zu machen haben.

5   Das erste Argument schließt so: Ein metaphysisch allervollkom-
menstes Wesen muß nothwendig existiren, denn wenn es nicht existirte,
so würde ihm eine Vollkommenheit, nämlich die Existenz, fehlen.

    Das zweyte schließt umgekehrt: Ein Wesen, das als ein nothwendiges
existirt, muß alle Vollkommenheit haben, denn wenn es nicht alle Voll-
10 kommenheit (Realität) in sich hätte, so würde es durch seinen Begriff
nicht als a priori durchgängig bestimmt, mithin nicht als nothwendiges
Wesen gedacht werden können.

    Der Ungrund des erstern Beweises, in welchem das Daseyn als
eine besondre, über den Begriff eines Dinges zu diesem hinzugesetzte,
15 Bestimmung gedacht wird, da es doch bloß die Setzung des Dinges mit
allen seinen Bestimmungen ist, wodurch dieser Begriff also gar nicht
erweitert wird, — dieser Ungrund, sage ich, ist so einleuchtend, daß
man sich bei diesem Beweise, der überdem als unhaltbar von den Metaphysikern schon aufgegeben zu seyn scheint, nicht aufhalten darf.

20   Der Schluß des zweyten ist dadurch scheinbarer, daß er die Erweiterung der Erkenntniß nicht durch bloße Begriffe a priori versucht, sondern Erfahrung, obzwar nur die Erfahrung überhaupt: es existirt etwas,
zum Grunde legt, und nun von diesem schließt: weil alle Existenz entweder
nothwendig, oder zufällig seyn müsse, die letztere aber immer eine Ursache
25 voraussetzt, die nur in einem nicht zufälligen, mithin in einem nothwendigen Wesen ihren vollständigen Grund haben könne, so existire
irgend ein Wesen von der letzteren Naturbeschaffenheit.

    Da wir nun die Nothwendigkeit der Existenz eines Dinges, wie
überhaupt jede Nothwendigkeit, nur so fern erkennen können, als dadurch,
30 daß wir dessen Daseyn aus Begriffen a priori ableiten, der Begriff aber
von etwas Existirendem ein Begriff von einem durchgängig bestimmten
Dinge ist: so wird der Begriff von einem nothwendigen Wesen ein solcher
seyn, der zugleich die durchgängige Bestimmung dieses Dinges enthält.
Dergleichen aber haben wir nur einen einzigen, nämlich des allerrealesten
35 Wesens. Also ist das nothwendige Wesen ein Wesen, das alle Realität
enthält, es sey als Grund, oder als Inbegriff.

    Dies ist ein Fortschritt der Metaphysik durch die Hinterthüre. Sie
will a priori beweisen und legt doch ein empirisches Datum zum Grunde,
welches sie, wie Archimedes seinen festen Punkt außer der Erde (hier

from its concept, or the determinate concept that we must form of it is deduced from the necessary existence of some being.

The first argument proceeds as follows: A metaphysically most perfect being must necessarily exist, because if it did not, it would lack a perfection, namely, existence.

The second infers conversely: A being that exists necessarily must have all perfections, because if it did not have all perfections (reality) in itself, it would not be completely determined a priori through its concept and thus could not be thought of as a necessary being.

The inadequacy of the first proof—a proof in which existence is regarded as a special property that must be appended to the concept of a thing, since existence is merely the postulation of the thing with all its determinations, through which the concept of the thing is not at all enlarged—this inadequacy I say, is so evident that one need not be detained by this proof,[83] which, moreover, metaphysicians seem to have already given up as untenable.

The conclusion of the second is more plausible because it attempts extension of knowledge not through mere a priori concepts, but rather through experience, although only experience in general: something exists is its foundation. Now from this it concludes that since all existence must be either necessary or contingent, and since the latter always presupposes a cause that can have its complete foundation only in a non-contingent, thus in a necessary being, that thus there exists a being with the latter sort of nature.[84]

Since we can know the necessity of the existence of a thing—as [we can know] any necessity in general—only insofar as we deduce this existence from a priori concepts, and since the concept of something existent is the concept of an entirely determined thing, the concept of a necessary being will be such an [a priori] one as simultaneously contains the thorough determination of this thing. However, we have only one single concept like that, namely [the concept] of the most real being. Thus, the necessary being is one which contains all reality, be it as ground or as essence.

This is progress of metaphysics through the back doors. It wants to demonstrate a priori and yet uses an empirical datum as its basis, which it employs in order to apply a lever to raise knowledge to the

aber ist er auf derselben) braucht, um ihren Hebel anzusetzen und das Erkenntniß bis zum Übersinnlichen zu heben.

Wenn aber, den Satz eingeräumt, daß irgend etwas schlechterdings-nothwendig existire, gleichwohl eben so gewiß ist, daß wir uns schlechter-dings keinen Begriff von irgend einem Dinge, das so existire, machen 5 und also dieses, als ein solches, nach seiner Naturbeschaffenheit ganz und gar nicht bestimmen können (denn die analytischen Prädikate, d. i. die, welche mit dem Begriffe der Nothwendigkeit einerley sind, z. B. die Unveränderlichkeit, Ewigkeit, auch sogar die Einfachheit der Substanz, sind keine Bestimmungen, daher auch die Einheit eines solchen Wesens 10 gar nicht bewiesen werden kann) — wenn es, sage ich, mit dem Versuche, sich einen Begriff davon zu machen, so schlecht bestellt ist, so bleibt der Begriff von diesem metaphysischen Gott immer ein leerer Begriff.

Nun ist es schlechterdings unmöglich, einen Begriff von einem Wesen bestimmt anzugeben, welches von solcher Natur sey, daß ein 15 Widerspruch entspränge, wenn ich es in Gedanken aufhebe, gesetzt auch, ich nehme es als das All der Realität an. Denn ein Widerspruch findet in einem Urtheile nur alsdenn Statt, wenn ich ein Prädicat in einem Urtheile aufhebe, und doch eines im Begriffe des Subjectes übrig behalte, was mit diesem identisch ist, niemals aber, wenn ich das Ding sammt 20 allen seinen Prädicaten aufhebe, und z. B. sage: es ist kein allerrealestes Wesen.

Also können wir uns von einem absolut-nothwendigen Dinge, als einem solchen, schlechterdings keinen Begriff machen (wovon der Grund der ist, daß es ein bloßer Modalitätsbegriff ist, der nicht als 25 Dinges-Beschaffenheit, sondern nur durch Verknüpfung der Vorstellung von ihm mit dem Erkenntnißvermögen die Beziehung auf das Object enthält). Also können wir aus seiner vorausgesetzten Existenz nicht im mindesten auf Bestimmungen schließen, die unsre Erkenntniß desselben über die Vorstellung seiner nothwendigen Existenz erweitern, und also 30 eine Art von Theologie begründen könnten.

Also sinkt der von einigen sogenannte kosmologische, aber doch transcendentale Beweis, (weil er doch eine existirende Welt annimmt) der gleichwohl, weil aus der Beschaffenheit einer Welt nichts ge-schlossen werden will, sondern nur aus der Voraussetzung des Begriffes 35 von einem nothwendigen Wesen, also einem reinen Vernunftbegriffe a priori, zur Ontologie gezählt werden kann, so wie der vorige, in sein Nichts zurück.

---

supersensible, as Archimedes used his fixed point beyond the earth. (Here however the point is on the earth.)

But even if the proposition that something absolutely necessary exists be granted, nevertheless it is just as certain that we cannot form for ourselves the concept of a thing which exists in that way. Therefore, the intrinsic nature of such a thing cannot be determined at all. For the analytic predicates, i.e., those that are necessarily identical with the concept of necessity, e.g., immutability, immortality, and even the simplicity of substance, are not determinations, and, consequently, not even the unity of such a being can be proven. If, I say, the attempt to form a concept of that [necessary being] is so badly disposed, the concept of this metaphysical God always remains empty.

Now it is simply impossible to make a concept of a determinate being that is of such a nature that a contradiction would arise if I deny it in thought, even if I assume it to be the All of reality. For a contradiction occurs only when I deny a predicate in a judgment and yet retain one in the concept of the subject which is identical to this, but never when I deny a thing together with all its predicates, and, say, for example, that there is no most real being.

Thus, we simply cannot form a concept of an absolutely necessary thing as such. (The reason for this is that as a mere modal concept it contains nothing concerning the constitutive features of the thing, but rather it only contains a relation to the object through conjunction of its representation with the faculty of knowledge.)[85] Thus, from its presupposed existence we cannot conclude, beyond the assertion of its necessary existence, the slightest thing about such determinations that might extend our knowledge of it and that could thereby provide a basis for a species of theology.

Thus, the proof called cosmological by some (because it assumes an existing world), but which is still transcendental — and can be classed as ontology, because it seeks to deduce nothing from the constitution of a world, but rather only from the assumption of the concept of a necessary being, thus from a pure a priori concept of reason — sinks, as the previous [ontological] one, back into nothingness.

Zweiter Entwurf

Überschritt der Metaphysik zum Übersinnlichen,
nach der Leibniz-Wolfischen Epoche.

Die erste Stufe des Überschrittes der Metaphysik zum Übersinnlichen, das der Natur, als die oberste Bedingung zu allem Bedingten
5 derselben zum Grunde liegt, also in der Theorie zum Grunde gelegt
wird, ist die zur Theologie, d. i. zur Erkenntniß Gottes, obzwar nur nach
der Analogie des Begriffes von demselben, mit dem eines verständigen
Wesens, als eines von der Welt wesentlich unterschiedenen Urgrundes
aller Dinge, welche Theorie selber nicht in theoretisch- sondern blos
10 praktisch-dogmatischer, mithin subjectiv-moralischer Absicht aus der
Vernunft hervorgeht, d. i. nicht um die Sittlichkeit ihren Gesetzen, und
selbst ihrem Endzwecke nach zu begründen, denn diese wird hier vielmehr,
als für sich selbst bestehend, zum Grunde gelegt, sondern um dieser Idee
vom höchsten in einer Welt möglichen Gut, welches, objectiv und theo
15 retisch betrachtet, über unser Vermögen hinausliegt, in Beziehung auf
dasselbe, mithin in praktischer Absicht, Realität zu verschaffen, wozu
die bloße Möglichkeit, sich ein solches Wesen zu denken, hinreichend, und
zugleich ein Überschritt zu diesem Übersinnlichen, ein Erkenntniß desselben,
aber nur in praktisch-dogmatischer Rücksicht, möglich wird.

20 Dies ist nun ein Argument, das Dasehn Gottes, als eines moralischen Wesens, für die Vernunft des Menschen, sofern sie moralisch-
praktisch ist, d. i. zur Annehmung desselben, hinreichend zu beweisen,
und eine Theorie des Übersinnlichen, aber nur als praktisch-dogmatischen
Überschritt zu demselben, zu begründen, also eigentlich nicht ein Beweis
25 von seinem Dasehn schlechthin (simpliciter), sondern nur in gewisser
Rücksicht (secundum quid), nämlich auf den Endzweck, den der moralische
Mensch hat, und haben soll, bezogen, mithin blos der Vernunftmäßigkeit,
ein solches anzunehmen, wo dann der Mensch befugt ist, einer Idee,
die er, moralischen Prinzipien gemäß, sich selbst macht, gleich als ob er sie
30 von einem gegebenen Gegenstande hergenommen, auf seine Entschlie
ßungen Einfluß zu verstatten.

Freylich ist auf solche Art Theologie nicht Theosophie, d. i. Erkenntniß der göttlichen Natur, welche unerreichbar ist, aber doch des
unerforschlichen Bestimmungsgrundes unsers Willens, den wir in uns
35 allein zu seinen Endzwecken nicht zureichend finden, und ihn daher
in einem Anderen, dem höchsten Wesen über uns, annehmen, um dem
letztern zur Befolgung dessen, was die praktische Vernunft ihm vorschreibt, die der Theorie annoch mangelnde Ergänzung, durch die Idee
einer übersinnlichen Natur, zu verschaffen.

Transition of Metaphysics to the Supersensible
after the Epoch of Leibniz and Wolff

The first step in the transition of metaphysics to the supersensible—that of nature as the primary condition that is the ground of all contingent natural things, and that is thus the foundation of all theory—is the step to theology, that is, to knowledge of God, though only according to the analogy between the concept of Him and that of an intelligent being, as original cause of all things that is essentially distinguished from the world. This theory proceeds merely from the practical-dogmatic and thus from the subjective-moral purpose of reason, not from its theoretical-dogmatic purpose, that is, not in order to ground morality in accord with its laws or even its ultimate goal, for, as self-subsistent this [morality] is fundamental. Rather [the theory is assumed] in order to provide reality in respect to our faculty [of reason]—thus for practical purposes—for the idea of a supreme possible good in the world, which objectively and theoretically conceived lies beyond our capacity. For this, the mere possibility of thinking of such a being suffices, and a transition to knowledge of this supersensible being becomes at the same time possible, although only in a practical-dogmatic perspective.

Now this is an argument sufficient to prove the existence of God as a moral being for human reason so far as it is morally practical, that is, for the assumption of God as moral being.[86] And it grounds a theory of the supersensible, but only as a practical-dogmatic transition to it. Thus, properly it is not a proof of his existence absolutely (*simpliciter*), but is one only from a particular perspective (*secundum quid*); that is, [from the perspective of] the ultimate purpose that the moral man does and should have. Thus, it is related to the rationality of such an *assumption*. With this, man is authorized to grant influence over his decisions to an idea that he has himself constituted in accord with moral principles just as if it had come from given objects.

Of course, theology of this sort is not *theosophy*, i.e., knowledge of a divine nature that is inaccessible;[87] yet it is knowledge of the fathomless ground of the determination of our will that we cannot find in ourselves alone sufficient for its ultimate ends. And we thus assume it in another being, the supreme being over us, in order to provide for this will the observance of that which practical reason prescribes for it [and], by means of the idea, a supersensible nature, a completion the theory still lacks.[88]

Das moralische Argument würde also ein argumentum κατ' ἄνθρωπον heißen können, gültig für Menschen, als vernünftige Weltwesen überhaupt, und nicht blos für dieses oder jenes Menschen zufällig angenommene Denkungsart, und vom theoretisch-dogmatischen κατ' ἀλήθειαν, welches mehr für gewiß behauptet, als der Mensch wohl wissen kann, unterschieden werden müssen.

II.

Vermeynte theoretisch-dogmatische Fortschritte in der moralischen Theologie, während der Leibnitz-Wolfischen Epoche.

Es ist zwar für diese Stufe des Fortschrittes der Metaphysik von gedachter Philosophie keine besondre Abtheilung gemacht, sondern sie vielmehr der Theologie, im Kapitel vom Endzweck der Schöpfung, angehängt worden, aber sie ist doch in der darüber gegebenen Erklärung, daß dieser Endzweck die Ehre Gottes sey, enthalten, wodurch nichts andres verstanden werden kann, als daß in der wirklichen Welt eine solche Zweckverbindung sey, die, im Ganzen genommen, das höchste in einer Welt mögliche Gut, mithin die teleologische oberste Bedingung des Daseyns derselben enthalte, und einer Gottheit als moralischen Urhebers würdig sey.

Es ist aber, wenn gleich nicht die ganze, doch die oberste Bedingung der Weltvollkommenheit, die Moralität der vernünftigen Weltwesen, welche wiederum auf dem Begriffe der Freyheit beruht, deren, als unbedingter Selbstthätigkeit, diese sich wiederum selbst bewußt seyn müssen, um moralisch gut seyn zu können, unter deren Voraussetzung aber es schlechterdings unmöglich ist, sie als durch Schöpfung, also durch den Willen eines Andern entstandene Wesen, theoretisch nach dieser ihrer Zweckmäßigkeit zu erkennen, so wie man diese wohl an vernunftlosen Naturwesen einer von der Welt unterschiedenen Ursache zuschreiben, und diese sich also mit physisch-teleologischer Vollkommenheit unendlich mannigfaltig versehen vorstellen kann, dagegen die moralisch-teleologische, die auf den Menschen selbst ursprünglich gegründet seyn muß, nicht die Wirkung, also auch nicht der Zweck seyn kann, den ein Anderer zu bewirken sich anmaßen könne.

Obgleich nun der Mensch in theoretisch-dogmatischer Rücksicht die Möglichkeit des Endzweckes, darnach er streben soll, den er aber nicht

The moral argument can thus be called an argument $\kappa\alpha\tau'\,\H{\alpha}\nu\theta\rho\omega\pi o\nu$ valid for men as rational beings in general, and not just for an arbitrarily assumed form of thought valid of this or that man. It must be distinguished from the theoretical-dogmatic argument $\kappa\alpha\tau'\,\grave{\alpha}\lambda\eta\theta\epsilon\iota\alpha\nu$ which maintains more to be certain than man can know.[89]

II.

Purported Theoretical-Dogmatic Progress in Moral Theology during the Epoch of Leibniz and Wolff

To be sure, no special division was made in the aforementioned philosophy for this step in the progress of metaphysics; instead, it was appended to Theology, in the chapter on the ultimate end of creation, and yet the step is included in the explanation that that ultimate end is the *Glory of God*. By this can be understood nothing other than that in the actual world there is a connection of ends that, taken as a whole, contains the highest possible good in the world and, consequently, its *teleologically* supreme condition of existence, and this would be worthy of a Divinity as a moral creator.

But the supreme, if not complete, condition of the world's perfection is the morality of rational beings, which in turn rests on the concept of freedom. As unconditioned self-activity, freedom must be self-consciousness in order to be able to be morally good, under which assumption, however, it is absolutely impossible to recognize theoretically this autonomous activity either through the creation — thus through the will — of another created[90] being or through their purposiveness in accordance with this will, as, indeed, one might imagine irrational beings endowed with this purposiveness, deriving from a cause distinct from the world, a purposiveness that would be of infinitely manifold physico-teleological perfection. By contrast, moral-teleological purposiveness, which must originally be based upon men themselves, cannot be the effect nor even the purpose that another may claim to bring about.

Now although man is wholly incapable of making the possibility of the ultimate end towards which he should strive — but which he does not have entirely within his power — comprehensible to himself and will negate morality, which is still the principle thing in this final end, if he makes such a teleology the foundation for the advancement of this [ultimate end] in respect to the physical; and if he bases

147

ganz in seiner Gewalt hat, sich gar nicht begreiflich machen kann, indem,
wenn er dessen Beförderung in Ansehung des Physischen einer solchen
Teleologie zum Grunde legt, er die Moralität, welche doch das Vor-
nehmste in diesem Endzweck ist, aufhebt; gründet er aber alles, worin er
5 den Endzweck setzt, aufs Moralische, er bey der Verbindung mit dem
Physischen, was gleichwohl vom Begriffe des höchsten Gutes, als seinem
Endzweck, nicht getrennt werden kann, die Ergänzung seines Unver-
mögens zur Darstellung desselben vermißt: so bleibt ihm doch ein praktisch-
dogmatisches Prinzip des Überschrittes zu diesem Ideal der Weltvoll-
10 kommenheit übrig, nämlich unerachtet des Einwurfes, den der Lauf
der Welt als Erscheinung gegen jenen Fortschritt in den Weg legt, doch
in ihr, als Object an sich selbst, eine solche moralisch-teleologische Verknüpfung, die auf den Endzweck als das übersinnliche Ziel seiner praktischen
Vernunft, das höchste Gut, nach einer für ihn unbegreiflichen Ordnung
15 der Natur hinausgeht, anzunehmen.

Daß die Welt im Ganzen immer zum Bessern fortschreite, dies
anzunehmen berechtiget ihn keine Theorie, aber wohl die reine praktische
Vernunft, welche nach einer solchen Hypothese zu handeln dogmatisch
gebietet, und so nach diesem Prinzip sich eine Theorie macht, der er zwar
20 in dieser Absicht nichts weiter als die Denkbarkeit unterlegen kann,
welches in theoretischer Rücksicht, die objective Realität dieses Ideals
darzuthun, bey weitem nicht hinreichend ist, in moralisch-praktischer aber
der Vernunft völlig Gnüge thut.

Was also in theoretischer Rücksicht unmöglich ist, nämlich der Fort-
25 schritt der Vernunft zum Übersinnlichen der Welt, darin wir leben
(mundus noumenon), nämlich dem höchsten abgeleiteten Gut, das ist in
praktischer Rücksicht, um nämlich den Wandel des Menschen hier auf
Erden gleichsam als einen Wandel im Himmel darzustellen, wirklich, d. i.
man kann und soll die Welt nach der Analogie mit der physischen Teleo-
30 logie, welche letztere uns die Natur wahrnehmen läßt, (auch unabhängig
von dieser Wahrnehmung) a priori, als bestimmt, mit dem Gegenstande
der moralischen Teleologie, nämlich dem Endzweck aller Dinge nach
Gesetzen der Freyheit zusammen anzutreffen annehmen, um der Idee
des höchsten Gutes nachzustreben, welches, als ein moralisches Produkt,
35 den Menschen selbst als Urheber, (soweit es in seinem Vermögen ist) auf-
fordert, dessen Möglichkeit weder durch die Schöpfung, welche einen äußern
Urheber zum Grunde legt, noch durch Einsicht in das Vermögen der
menschlichen Natur, einem solchen Zwecke angemessen zu seyn, in theoretischer Rücksicht, nicht, wie es die Leibnitz-Wolfische Philosophie vermeynt,

everything in which he postulates the ultimate end upon morality in conjunction with the physical — which of course cannot be separated from the concept of the supreme good — he will fail in the fulfillment of his own incapacity for representing such a supreme good; there yet remains open to him a practical-dogmatic principle for the transition to this ideal of cosmic perfection. That is, despite the objection that the course of the world considered as a phenomenon raises against such progress, he may assume such a moral-teleological connection in the world, as an object in itself, which turns upon the ultimate end as the supersensible goal of his practical reason, the supreme good, in accord with an order of nature incomprehensible to him.

No theory allows him to assume that the world as a whole always progresses towards the better, but pure practical reason does. It dogmatically commands action in accordance with such an hypothesis and constructs a theory in accord with this principle, which, of course, can in this respect be supported by nothing more than its conceivability, which is grossly inadequate to demonstrate objective reality for theoretical purposes, but fully satisfies reason for moral-practical ones.

Thus, what is impossible from a theoretical perspective, namely, the progress of reason to the supersensible in the world that we live in (*mundus noumenon*), namely the highest derived good, is actual from a practical point of view, in order to portray, as it were, the behavior of men on earth as behavior in heaven. In order to strive towards the idea of the supreme good one may and should assume that the world is to harmonize with the object of moral teleology, that is, with the ultimate end of all things according to the law of freedom, on analogy with physical teleology, which allows us to perceive nature a priori as determined (even independently of this perception). As a moral product, this supreme good challenges man himself to be a creator (so far as it is within his power), the possibility of which is not only [not] — as the Leibnizian-Wolffian philosophy maintained — a tenable but also an extravagant concept for theoretical purposes, [one given] either by means of such productivity as is based upon an external creator, or by means of insight into

149

ein haltbarer, sondern überschwenglicher, in praktisch-dogmatischer Rücksicht aber ein reeller, und durch die praktische Vernunft für unsre Pflicht
sanctionirter Begriff ist.

III.

Vermeynter theoretisch-dogmatischer Fortschritt der Metaphysik 5
in der Psychologie, während der Leibnitz-Wolfischen Epoche.

Die Psychologie ist für menschliche Einsichten nichts mehr, und kann
auch nichts mehr werden, als Anthropologie, d. i. als Kenntniß des
Menschen, nur auf die Bedingung eingeschränkt, sofern er sich als Gegenstand des inneren Sinnes kennet. Er ist sich selbst aber auch als Gegen- 10
stand seiner äußern Sinne bewußt, d. h. er hat einen Körper, mit dem
der Gegenstand des inneren Sinnes verbunden, der die Seele des
Menschen heißt.

Daß er nicht ganz und gar blos Körper sey, läßt sich, wenn diese
Erscheinung als Sache an sich selbst betrachtet wird, strenge beweisen, 15
weil die Einheit des Bewußtseyns, die in jedem Erkenntniß (mithin auch
in dem seiner selbst) nothwendig angetroffen werden muß, es unmöglich
macht, daß Vorstellungen, unter viele Subjecte vertheilt, Einheit des
Gedankens ausmachen sollten; daher kann der Materialism nie zum
Erklärungsprinzip der Natur unsrer Seele gebraucht werden. 20

Betrachten wir aber Körper sowohl als Seele nur als Phänomene,
welches, da beyde Gegenstände der Sinne sind, nicht unmöglich ist, und
bedenken, daß das Noumenon, was jener Erscheinung zum Grunde liegt,
d. i. der äußere Gegenstand, als Ding an sich selbst, vielleicht ein einfaches
Wesen sein möge — —* 25

Über diese Schwierigkeit aber weggesehen, d. i. wenn auch Seele
und Körper als zwey specifisch-verschiedene Substanzen, deren Gemeinschaft den Menschen ausmacht, angenommen werden, bleibt es für alle
Philosophie, vornehmlich für die Metaphysik, unmöglich auszumachen,
was und wie viel die Seele, und was, oder wieviel der Körper selbst zu 30
den Vorstellungen des innern Sinnes beytrage, ja, ob nicht vielleicht,
wenn eine dieser Substanzen von der andern geschieden wäre, die Seele
schlechterdings alle Art Vorstellungen (Anschauen, Empfinden und Denken) einbüßen würde.

* Hier ist im Manuscript eine leere Stelle geblieben (Rink).

the capacity of human nature to be suitable for such a purpose. But it is a real concept from the practical-dogmatic perspective, and it is sanctioned by practical reason for our duty.

III.

Purported Theoretical-Dogmatic Progress of Metaphysics in Psychology during Leibniz's and Wolff's Time

For human insight, psychology is and can become nothing more than anthropology, that is, knowledge of man limited only by the condition that he knows himself as an object of inner sense. But he is also conscious of himself as an object of outer sense, i.e., he has a body that is linked with the object of inner sense, which is called the soul of man.

That man is not just merely body may be strictly proven if this appearance is regarded as a thing in itself. For the unity of consciousness that must necessarily be found in all knowledge (consequently also in that of one's self) makes it impossible that representations divided among several subjects should constitute unified thought. Therefore, materialism can never be used as a principle for explaining the nature of our souls.[91]

If we regard body and soul only as phenomena which, since both are objects of sense, is not impossible, and consider that the noumenon which underlies every appearance, i.e., the outer object as thing in itself, may perhaps be a simple being _____ *[92]

Overlooking this difficulty — i.e., even if soul and body are assumed to be two specifically different substances whose community constitutes men — it is impossible for all philosophy, especially metaphysics, to determine what and how much the soul and what or how much the body contribute to the representations of inner sense, or even, supposing one of these substances were to be separated from the other, whether the soul would absolutely forfeit all kinds of representations (intuition, sensation and thought).

*A lacuna remains in the manuscript here *(Rink)*.

Zweiter Entwurf

Also ist es schlechterbings unmöglich zu wissen, ob nach dem Tode des Menschen, wo seine Materie zerstreuet wird, die Seele, wenn gleich ihre Substanz übrig bleibt, zu leben, d. i. zu denken und zu wollen fortfahren könne, d. i. ob sie ein Geist sey (denn unter diesem Worte versteht man
5 ein Wesen, was auch ohne Körper sich seiner und seiner Vorstellungen bewußt seyn kann), oder nicht.

Die Leibniß-Wolfische Metaphysik hat uns zwar hierüber theoretisch-dogmatisch viel vorbemonstrirt, d. i. nicht allein das künftige Leben der Seele, sondern sogar die Unmöglichkeit, es durch den Tod des Menschen
10 zu verlieren, d. i. die Unsterblichkeit derselben zu beweisen vorgegeben, aber Niemand überzeugen können; vielmehr läßt sich a priori einsehen, daß ein solcher Beweis ganz unmöglich sey, weil innere Erfahrung allein es ist, wodurch wir uns selbst kennen, alle Erfahrung aber nur im Leben, d. i. wenn Seele und Körper noch verbunden sind, angestellt werden kann,
15 wir mithin, was wir nach dem Tode seyn und vermögen werden, schlech-terbings nicht wissen, der Seele abgesonderte Natur also gar nicht er-kennen können, man müßte denn etwa den Versuch zu machen sich ge-trauen, die Seele noch im Leben außer den Körper zu versetzen, welcher ohngefähr dem Versuche ähnlich seyn würde, den jemand mit geschlossenen
20 Augen vor dem Spiegel zu machen gedachte, und auf Befragen, was er hiemit wolle, antwortete: ich wollte nur wissen, wie ich aussehe, wenn ich schlafe.

In moralischer Rücksicht aber haben wir hinreichenden Grund, ein Leben des Menschen nach dem Tode (dem Ende seines Erdenlebens) selbst
25 für die Ewigkeit, folglich Unsterblichkeit der Seele anzunehmen, und diese Lehre ist ein praktisch-dogmatischer Überschritt zum Übersinnlichen, d. i. demjenigen, was bloße Idee ist, und kein Gegenstand der Erfahrung seyn kann, gleichwohl aber objective, aber nur in praktischer Rücksicht gültige, Realität hat. Die Fortstrebung zum höchsten Gut, als Endzweck, treibt
30 zur Annehmung einer Dauer an, die jener ihrer Unendlichkeit proportio-nirt ist, und ergänzet unvermerkt den Mangel der theoretischen Beweise, so daß der Metaphysiker die Unzulänglichkeit seiner Theorie nicht fühlt, weil ihm in Geheim die moralische Einwirkung den Mangel seiner, ver-meyntlich aus der Natur der Dinge gezogenen Erkenntniß, welche in
35 diesem Fall unmöglich ist, nicht wahrnehmen läßt.

Das sind nun die drey Stufen des Überschrittes der Metaphysik zum Übersinnlichen, das ihren eigentlichen Endzweck ausmacht. Es war ver-

Thus it is absolutely impossible to know whether, after the death of the man, when his matter is dispersed, the soul can continue to live, i.e., to think and will even if its substance remains, that is, whether or not the soul is a spirit (because by this word one understands a being that can be conscious of itself and its representations, even without a body).

To be sure, Leibniz's and Wolff's metaphysics have attempted to demonstrate a great deal for us about this theoretically and dogmatically, viz., not only the future life of the soul, but also the impossibility of losing it through the death of men, i.e., the pretended proof of the immortality of the soul—but they can convince no one. Rather, it can be seen a priori that such a proof is wholly impossible, since it is only through internal experience that we know ourselves, but all experience can be employed only in life, i.e., when soul and body are still united. Consequently, we absolutely cannot know what we are and can do after death; thus, we cannot know the soul at all in its separated nature. One would that way venture to make the attempt to remove the soul from the body while it is still alive. This would be similar to the experiment that someone attempted by standing before a mirror with closed eyes and, when asked what he was doing, replied: "I just want to know what I look like when I am asleep."

From a moral point of view, however, we have a sufficient reason to assume there to be life for men after death (the end of their earthly life), even for eternity, consequently immortality of soul.[93] This teaching is a practical-dogmatic transition to the supersensible, that is, to what is a mere idea and can be no object of experience, but nonetheless has objectively valid reality, though only from a practical perspective. The continued aspiration for the supreme good as the ultimate end leads to the assumption of a duration that is proportional to that end, and without being noticed it completes the deficiency of the theoretical proof so that the metaphysician does not feel the inadequacy of his theory, for the moral influence secretly prevents him from perceiving that his putative knowledge, derived from the nature of things—which knowledge is in this case impossible—is inadequate.

These are the three steps in metaphysics' transition to the supersensible, which constitutes its unique ultimate end. The effort devoted to

gebliche Mühe, die sie sich von jeher gegeben hat, diesen auf dem Wege
der Speculation und der theoretischen Erkenntniß zu erreichen, und so
wurde jene Wissenschaft das durchlöcherte Faß der Danaiden. Allererst
nachdem die moralischen Gesetze das Übersinnliche im Menschen, die
Freyheit, deren Möglichkeit keine Vernunft erklären, ihre Realität aber 5
in jenen praktisch-dogmatischen Lehren beweisen kann, entschleyert haben:
so hat die Vernunft gerechten Anspruch auf Erkenntniß des Übersinnlichen,
aber nur mit Einschränkung auf den Gebrauch in der letztern Rücksicht
gemacht, da sich dann eine gewisse Organisation der reinen praktischen
Vernunft zeigt, wo erstlich das Subject der allgemeinen Gesetzgebung, 10
als Welturheber, zweytens das Object des Willens der Weltwesen, als
ihres jenem gemäßen Endzweckes, drittens der Zustand der letztern, in
welchem sie allein der Erreichung desselben fähig sind, in praktischer Absicht selbstgemachte Ideen sind, welche aber ja nicht in theoretischer aufgestellt werden müssen, weil sie sonst aus der Theologie Theosophie, aus 15
der moralischen Teleologie Mystik und aus der Psychologie eine Pneu-
matik machen, und so Dinge, von denen wir doch etwas in praktischer
Absicht zum Erkenntniß benutzen könnten, ins Überschwengliche hin ver-
legen, wo sie für unsre Vernunft ganz unzugänglich sind und bleiben.

Die Metaphysik ist hiebey selbst nur die Idee einer Wissenschaft, als 20
Systems, welches nach Vollendung der Kritik der reinen Vernunft auf-
gebaut werden kann und soll, wozu nunmehr der Bauzeug, zusammt der
Verzeichnung vorhanden ist: ein Ganzes, was, gleich der reinen Logik,
keiner Vermehrung, weder bedürftig, noch fähig ist, welches auch be-
ständig bewohnt, und im baulichen Wesen erhalten werden muß, wenn 25
nicht Spinnen und Waldgeister, die nie ermangeln werden, hier Platz
zu suchen, sich darin einnisteln, und es für die Vernunft unbewohnbar
machen sollen.

Dieser Bau ist auch nicht weitläuftig, dürfte aber der Eleganz halber,
die gerade in ihrer Präcision, unbeschadet der Klarheit, besteht, die Ver- 30
einigung der Versuche und des Urtheiles verschiedener Künstler nöthig
haben, um sie als ewig und unwandelbar zu Stande zu bringen, und so
wäre die Aufgabe der Königlichen Academie, die Fortschritte der Metaphysik nicht blos zu zählen, sondern auch das zurückgelegte Stadium
auszumessen, in der neuern kritischen Epoche völlig aufgelöset. 35

reaching this goal by the path of speculation and theoretical knowledge was fruitless, and that science itself as full of holes as the cask of the Daniades. Only when moral laws have uncovered the supersensible in men can the reality of freedom, whose possibility reason cannot explain, be demonstrated in that practical-dogmatic doctrine.[94] Thus, reason has a justified claim to knowledge of the supersensible, but only with limitation of its use to this latter context; for then a certain organization of pure practical reason appears, where *first*, the subject of universal lawgiving, as creator of the world, *second*, the object of the will of worldly beings, as the ultimate end that conforms with that legislation, and *third*, the status of the ultimate end that alone allows it to be attained, are self-constituted ideas from a practical perspective. These must not be established theoretically, however, because that would make theology into theosophy, moral teleology into mysticism and psychology into pneumatics; thus, things that we can make some use of for knowledge in a practical context would be removed to [the realm of] the transcendent, where they are and remain altogether unapproachable by our reason.

Metaphysics itself is in this way only the idea of science as a system that can and should be errected after the completion of the *Critique of Pure Reason*, and for which the material and blueprint is at hand. It is a whole that, like pure logic, neither calls for nor permits additions. It must be constantly inhabited and maintained in a good state if one wants to keep away spiders and wood sprites, which never fail to seek refuge there, and make it uninhabitable for reason.

This edifice is not spacious, but because of its elegance, which consists just in its precision without prejudice to clarity, it requires the association of diverse artists, in order to realize it as eternal and immutable. Then the problem of the Royal Academy would be completely resolved, not merely by recording the progress of metaphysics but also by evaluating the steps taken in the new critical period.

Zweiter Entwurf

Anhang
zur Übersicht des Ganzen.

———

Wenn ein System so beschaffen ist, daß erstlich ein jedes Prinzip in demselben für sich erweislich ist, zweytens, daß, wenn man ja seiner Richtigkeit wegen besorgt wäre, es doch auch als bloße Hypothese unumgänglich auf alle übrige Prinzipien desselben als Folgerungen führt: so kann gar nichts mehr verlangt werden, um seine Wahrheit anzuerkennen.

Nun ist es mit der Metaphysik wirklich so bewandt, wenn die Vernunftkritik auf alle ihre Schritte sorgfältig Acht hat, und, wohin sie zuletzt führen, in Betrachtung zieht. Es sind nämlich zwey Angeln, um welche sie sich dreht: Erstlich die Lehre von der Idealität des Raumes und der Zeit, welche in Ansehung der theoretischen Prinzipien aufs Übersinnliche, aber für uns Unerkennbare, blos hinweiset, indessen daß sie auf ihrem Wege zu diesem Ziel, wo sie es mit der Erkenntniß a priori der Gegenstände der Sinne zu thun hat, theoretisch-dogmatisch ist; zweytens, die Lehre von der Realität des Freyheitsbegriffes, als Begriffes eines erkennbaren Übersinnlichen, wobei die Metaphysik doch nur praktisch-dogmatisch ist. Beyde Angeln aber sind gleichsam in dem Pfosten des Vernunftbegriffes von dem Unbedingten in der Totalität aller einander untergeordneter Bedingungen eingesenkt, wo der Schein weggeschafft werden soll, der eine Antinomie der reinen Vernunft, durch Verwechselung der Erscheinungen mit den Dingen an sich selbst bewirkt, und in dieser Dialektik selbst Anleitung zum Übergange vom Sinnlichen zum Übersinnlichen enthält.

———

Appendix: Overview of the Whole

In order to recognize the truth of a system, more cannot be demanded than that it be so constituted that *first*, each of its principles is in itself demonstrable and that *second*, were there scruples about its correctness, it would, taken as a mere hypothesis, lead to all remaining principles of the system as its consequences.

Now if the criticism of reason carefully examines each of its steps and considers where each finally leads, this actually is the case with metaphysics. There are two pivots on which it turns: *first*, the doctrine of the ideality of space and time, which in respect to theoretical principles merely points towards what is supersensible but unknowable by us, whereas the doctrine is theoretical and dogmatic on its way to this goal, where it is concerned with a priori cognition of the objects of sense; *second*, the doctrine of the reality of the concept of freedom as a concept of the knowable supersensible through which metaphysics is only practical-dogmatic. But both pivots are, as it were, fastened upon the post of the rational concept of the unconditioned in the totality of subordinated conditions, where the illusion that produces an antinomy of pure reason by confusion of appearance with things in themselves must be eliminated, and this dialectic itself contains guidance for the transition from the sensible to the supersensible.

Beylagen

SUPPLEMENTS

Der Anfang dieser Schrift

nach

Maßgabe der dritten Handschrift.

───────

⁵ Einleitung.

Die Aufgabe der K. Ac. d. Wiss. enthält stillschweigend zwey Fragen in sich:

I. ob die Metaphysik von jeher, bis unmittelbar nach Leibnitzens und Wolfs Zeit, überhaupt nur einen Schritt in dem, was ihren ¹⁰ eigentlichen Zweck, und den Grund ihrer Existenz ausmacht, gethan habe; denn nur wenn dieses geschehen ist, kann man nach den weitern Fortschritten fragen, die sie seit einem gewissen Zeitpunkte gemacht haben möchte. Die

IIte Frage ist: ob die vermeyntlichen Fortschritte derselben reell ¹⁵ sind.

Das, was man Metaphysik nennt (denn ich enthalte mich noch einer bestimmten Definition derselben), muß freylich, zu welcher Zeit es wolle, nachdem für sie ein Name gefunden worden, in irgend einem Besitze gewesen sein. Aber nur derjenige Besitz, den man durch Bearbeitung der- ²⁰ selben beabsichtigte, der, so ihren Zweck ausmacht, nicht der Besitz der Mittel, die man zum Behuf des letztern zusammenbrachte, ist derjenige, von dem jetzt verlangt wird, Rechnung abzulegen, wenn die Academie fragt: ob diese Wissenschaft reelle Fortschritte gemacht habe.

Die Metaphysik enthält in einem ihrer Theile (der Ontologie) Ele- ²⁵ mente der menschlichen Erkenntniß a priori, sowohl in Begriffen als Grundsätzen, und muß, ihrer Absicht nach, solche enthalten; allein der bey weitem größte Theil derselben findet seine Anwendung in den Gegen- ständen möglicher Erfahrung, z. B. der Begriff einer Ursache und der

No. I.
The Beginning of This Work
in the
Third Handwritten Draft[95]

─────

Introduction

The problem of Royal Academy of Sciences implicitly contains two questions:

I. Whether from the earliest days until immediately after *Leibniz's* and *Wolff's* time metaphysics has taken even a single step towards its proper end and towards what constitutes the reason for its existence; for only if this has occurred can one ask about the further advances that may have been made since a particular moment of time.

II. The second question is: Has metaphysics' purported progress been *real*?

After a name was found for it—whenever that may have been—what is called metaphysics (for I still refrain from providing a determinate definition) must certainly have been in possession of something. But it is only the possession that it was *intended* to work up, not possession of the means introduced on its behalf, of which an account is now requested when the Academy asks whether this science has made real progress.

One part of metaphysics (Ontology) contains—and given its purpose must contain—elements of a priori human cognition, both concepts and fundamental principles. Yet by far the greater part of these find their application in the objects of possible experience, e.g. the concept of cause and the principle of the relation of all change to it.

Grundsatz des Verhältnisses aller Veränderung zu derselben. Aber zum
Behuf der Erkenntniß solcher Erfahrungsgegenstände ist nie eine Metaphysik unternommen worden, worin jene Prinzipien mühsam auseinander-
gesetzt, und dennoch oft so unglücklich aus Gründen a priori bewiesen
werden, daß, wenn das unvermeidliche Verfahren des Verstandes nach   5
derselben, so oft wir Erfahrung anstellen, und die continuirliche Be-
stätigung durch diese letztere nicht das Beste thäte, es mit der Überzeugung
von diesem Prinzip durch Vernunftbeweise nur schlecht würde ausgesehen
haben. Man hat sich dieser Prinzipien in der Physik (wenn man darunter,
in ihrer allgemeinsten Bedeutung genommen, die Wissenschaft der Ver-   10
nunfterkenntniß aller Gegenstände möglicher Erfahrung versteht) jederzeit
so bedient, als ob sie in ihren (der Physik) Umfang mit gehöreten, ohne sie
darum, weil sie Prinzipien a priori sind, abzusondern und eine besondere
Wissenschaft für sie zu errichten, weil doch der Zweck, den man mit ihnen
hatte, nur auf Erfahrungsgegenstände ging, in Beziehung auf welche   15
sie uns auch allein verständlich gemacht werden könnten, dieses aber nicht
der eigentliche Zweck der Metaphysik war. Es wäre also in Absicht auf
diesen Gebrauch der Vernunft niemals auf eine Metaphysik, als abgesonderte Wissenschaft, gesonnen worden, wenn die Vernunft hiezu nicht
ein höheres Interesse bey sich gefunden hätte, wozu die Aufsuchung und 20
systematische Verbindung aller Elementarbegriffe und Grundsätze, die
a priori unserm Erkenntniß der Gegenstände der Erfahrung zum Grunde
liegen, nur die Zurüstung war.

Der alte Name dieser Wissenschaft μετὰ τὰ φυσικά giebt schon eine
Anzeige auf die Gattung von Erkenntniß, worauf die Absicht mit der-   25
selben gerichtet war. Man will vermittelst ihrer über alle Gegenstände
möglicher Erfahrung (trans physicam) hinausgehen, um, wo möglich, das
zu erkennen, was schlechterdings kein Gegenstand derselben seyn kann,
und die Definition der Metaphysik, nach der Absicht, die den Grund der
Bewerbung um eine dergleichen Wissenschaft enthält, würde also seyn: 30
Sie ist eine Wissenschaft, vom Erkenntnisse des Sinnlichen zu dem des
Übersinnlichen fortzuschreiten (hier nämlich verstehe ich durch das Sinnliche
nichts weiter, als das, was Gegenstand der Erfahrung seyn kann. Daß
alles Sinnliche blos Erscheinung und nicht das Object der Vorstellung an
sich selbst sey, wird nachher bewiesen werden). Weil dieses nun nicht durch 35
empirische Erkenntnißgründe geschehen kann, so wird die Metaphysik
Prinzipien a priori enthalten und, obgleich die Mathematik deren auch
hat, gleichwohl aber immer nur solche, welche auf Gegenstände möglicher
sinnlichen Anschauung gehen, mit der man aber zum Übersinnlichen

But a metaphysics wherein those principles are carefully analyzed has never been undertaken on behalf of the cognition of such objects of experience. And yet [they are] often so unsuccessfully demonstrated from a priori grounds that if the unavoidable procedure of understanding whenever we employ them in accord with experience and the continual confirmation of them by experience did not win the day, our conviction in this principle [of cause and effect] based on rational proofs would only come to no good. These principles have always been used in physics (assuming the latter is understood in its most general sense, as the science of the rational knowledge of all objects of possible experience), as if they belonged within its (physics') precincts, without separating them out and arranging a special science for them because they happen to be a priori principles, for their purpose extends only to objects of experience in relation to which alone they can be made comprehensible for us. But [to do] this was not the true goal of metaphysics. Thus, a separate science of metaphysics would never have been contemplated with respect to this use of reason had not reason found in itself a higher interest, for which the search for and systematic combination of all simple concepts and fundamental propositions that are the a priori foundation for our knowledge of objects of experience was only preparation.

The old name for this science, μετὰ τὰ φυσικά , already gives an indication of the kind of knowledge towards which it was directed. It was desired to proceed by it beyond all objects of possible experience (*trans physicam*), in order, where possible, to know what cannot possibly be such an object, and the definition of metaphysics which contains the basis for attempting such a science would thus be: It is the science of proceeding from knowledge of the sensible to that of the supersensible. (Here I understand by the sensible nothing other than what can be an object of experience. That everything sensible is merely appearance and cannot be the object of a representation in itself will be proven later.) Now since this cannot happen on the basis of empirical grounds of knowledge, metaphysics will contain a priori principles. Although mathematics also has such principles, these are nevertheless always only those that apply to objects of possible *sensible* intuition,

Dritter Entwurf

nicht hinaus kommen kann, so wird die Metaphysik doch von ihr dadurch
unterschieden, daß sie als eine philosophische Wissenschaft, die ein Inbegriff der Vernunfterkenntniß aus Begriffen a priori ist (ohne die
Construktion derselben), ausgezeichnet wird. Weil endlich zur Erweiterung
5 der Erkenntniß über die Grenze des Sinnlichen hinaus zuvor eine voll-
ständige Kenntniß aller Prinzipien a priori, die auch aufs Sinnliche angewandt werden, erfordert wird, so muß die Metaphysik, wenn man sie
nicht so wohl nach ihrem Zweck, sondern vielmehr nach den Mitteln, zu
einem Erkenntniß überhaupt durch Prinzipien a priori zu gelangen, d. i.
10 nach der bloßen Form ihres Verfahrens erklären will, als das System
aller reinen Vernunfterkenntniß der Dinge durch Begriffe definirt werden.
   Nun kann mit der größten Gewißheit dargethan werden, daß bis auf
Leibnitzens und Wolfs Zeit, diese selbst mit eingeschlossen, die Metaphysik
in Ansehung jenes ihres wesentlichen Zwecks nicht die mindeste Erwer-
15 bung gemacht hat, nicht einmal die von dem bloßen Begriffe irgend eines
übersinnlichen Objects, so daß sie zugleich die Realität dieses Begriffs
theoretisch hat beweisen können, welches der kleinst=mögliche Fortschritt
zum Übersinnlichen gewesen seyn würde; wo doch immer noch das
Erkenntniß dieses über alle mögliche Erfahrung hinaus gesetzten Ob=
20 jects gemangelt haben würde und da, wenn auch die Transcendental=
Philosophie in Ansehung ihrer Begriffe a priori, die für Erfahrungs=
gegenstände gelten, hier oder da einige Erweiterung bekommen hätte,
diese noch nicht die von der Metaphysik beabsichtigte sein würde: so kann
man mit Recht behaupten, daß diese Wissenschaft bis zu jenem Zeit=
25 punkte noch gar keine Fortschritte zu ihrer eigenen Bestimmung gethan habe.
   Wir wissen also, nach welchen Fortschritten der Metaphysik gefragt
werde, um welche es ihr eigentlich zu thun sey, und können die Erkenntniß
a priori, deren Erwägung nur zum Mittel dient, und die den Zweck dieser
Wissenschaft nicht ausmacht, diejenige nämlich, welche, obzwar a priori
30 gegründet, doch für ihre Begriffe die Gegenstände in der Erfahrung finden
kann, von der, die den Zweck ausmacht, unterscheiden, deren Object näm=
lich über alle Erfahrungsgrenze hinaus liegt, und zu der die Metaphysik,
von der erstern anhebend, nicht so wohl fortschreitet, als vielmehr, da
sie durch eine unermeßliche Kluft von ihr abgesondert ist, zu ihr über=
35 schreiten will. Aristoteles hielt sich mit seinen Kategorien fast allein
an der erstern, Plato mit seinen Ideen strebte zu der letztern Erkenntniß.
Aber nach dieser vorläufigen Erwägung der Materie, womit sich die Metaphysik beschäftigt, muß auch die Form, nach der sie verfahren soll, in Betrachtung gezogen werden.

with which one can make no transition to the supersensible, so that metaphysics is different from mathematics in that it is marked out as a philosophical science that is an epitome of rational knowledge from a priori *concepts* (without the construction of them). Finally, since the extension of knowledge *beyond* the boundaries of the sensible requires complete knowledge of all a priori principles, including those applied to the sensible, metaphysics must be defined as the system of all pure rational knowledge of things through concepts, if it is to be explained not so much according to its goal but rather in terms of its means of achieving any knowledge whatever through a priori principles, that is, through the mere form of its procedure.[96]

Now it can be shown with the greatest certainty that until, and even including Leibniz's and Wolff's time, metaphysics did not make the slightest gain in regard to its essential goal, did not even gain the mere *concept* of some supersensible object so that at the same time it could have proved theoretically the reality of this concept. This would have been the least possible progress to the supersensible. Even then *cognition* of this object that is posited beyond all possible experience would always have been lacking. And since, even if transcendental philosophy has here and there gained some ground regarding a priori concepts that are valid for objects of experience, this has not been intended for metaphysics, it can be justifiably maintained that to that time this science has made absolutely no progress towards its own vocation.

Thus, we know what kind of progress in metaphysics we have been asked about in order for it truly to be such progress. Further, we can distinguish between that knowledge whose a priori consideration serves only as a means to and never constitutes the end of this science — namely, cognition that, despite its a priori basis, can find objects in experience for its concepts — and that which constitutes its end, namely, knowledge whose objects lie beyond the bounds of any experience, to which knowledge a metaphysics that begins with the former will not so much attempt to *progress* — as to *transcend*, since it is separated from such knowledge by an immeasurable gap. With his theory of categories, *Aristotle* held almost exclusively to the first kind of knowledge, *Plato*, with his Ideas, strove for the second.[97] After this preliminary examination of the subject matter that concerns metaphysics, the form according to which it must proceed has to be taken into consideration.

Die zweyte Forderung nämlich, welche in der Aufgabe der K. Acad. stillschweigend enthalten ist, will, man solle beweisen: daß die Fortschritte, welche gethan zu haben die Metaphyfik sich rühmen mag, reell seyen. Eine harte Forderung, die allein die zahlreichen vermeyntlichen Eroberer in diesem Felde in Verlegenheit setzen muß, wenn sie solche begreifen und 5 beherzigen wollen.

Was die Realität der Elementarbegriffe aller Erkenntniß a priori betrifft, die ihre Gegenstände in der Erfahrung finden können, ingleichen die Grundsätze, durch welche diese unter jene Begriffe subsumirt werden, so kann die Erfahrung selbst zum Beweise ihrer Realität dienen, ob man 10 gleich die Möglichkeit nicht einsieht, wie sie, ohne von der Erfahrung abgeleitet zu seyn, mithin a priori, im reinen Verstande ihren Ursprung haben können: z. B. der Begriff einer Substanz und der Satz, daß in allen Veränderungen die Substanz beharre und nur die Accidenzen entstehen oder vergehen. Daß dieser Schritt der Metaphyfik reell und nicht bloß einge- 15 bildet sey, nimmt der Phyfiker ohne Bedenken an; denn er braucht ihn mit dem besten Erfolg in aller durch Erfahrung fortgehenden Naturbetrachtung, sicher, nie durch eine einzige widerlegt zu werden, nicht darum, weil ihn noch nie eine Erfahrung widerlegt hat, ob er ihn gleich so, wie er im Verstande a priori anzutreffen ist, auch nicht beweisen kann, sondern weil 20 er ein diesem unentbehrlicher Leitfaden ist, um solche Erfahrung anzustellen.

Allein das, worum es der Metaphyfik eigentlich zu thun ist, nämlich für den Begriff von dem, was über das Feld möglicher Erfahrung hinausliegt und für die Erweiterung der Erkenntniß durch einen solchen 25 Begriff, ob diese nämlich reell sey, einen Probierstein zu finden, daran möchte der waghälfige Metaphyfiker beynahe verzweifeln, wenn er nur diese Forderung versteht, die an ihn gemacht wird. Denn wenn er über seinen Begriff, durch den er Objecte bloß denken, durch keine mögliche Erfahrung aber belegen kann, fortschreitet, und dieser Gedanke nur mög- 30 lich ist, welches er dadurch erreicht, daß er ihn so faßt, daß er sich in ihm nicht selbst widerspreche; so mag er sich Gegenstände denken, wie er will, er ist sicher, daß er auf keine Erfahrung stoßen kann, die ihn widerlege, weil er sich einen Gegenstand, z. B. einen Geist, gerade mit einer solchen Bestimmung gedacht hat, mit der er schlechterdings kein Gegenstand der 35 Erfahrung seyn kann. Denn daß keine einzige Erfahrung diese seine Idee bestätigt, kann ihm nicht im mindesten Abbruch thun, weil er ein Ding nach Bestimmungen denken wollte, die es über alle Erfahrungsgrenze hinaussetzen. Also können solche Begriffe ganz leer und folglich

166

The second demand implicity contained in the problem of the Royal Academy is that it should be proved that the progress metaphysics boasts of having made is *real*. This is a hard demand that must embarass the numerous putative conquerors of this realm if they will only understand and take it to heart.

Experience itself can serve for proof of the reality of the elementary concepts of all a priori knowledge that can find their objects in experience, as well as of the fundamental principles by which experience is subsumed under those concepts, even if it is not seen how they can originate in pure understanding, and thus a priori, without being derived from experience. Examples [of these include] the concept of substance and the principle that in every change substance endures and only accidents come to be or pass away. The physicist assumes without scruple, that this step of metaphysics is real and not merely imagined, for he uses it with the best result in all observations proceeding by means of experience, certain that this [step] is not refuted by any single experience, not because experience has not yet refuted it, although experience cannot by the same token prove this concept as it is to be encountered a priori in the understanding, but rather because it is an indispensible guide for employing such experience.

That which metaphysics has uniquely to do—namely, to find a touchstone for the concept of what lies beyond possible experience and to find whether the extension of knowledge by means of such a concept is real—would nearly make the daring metaphysician despair if only he understood this demand that is placed on him. For he progresses by way of his concept—through which he can think objects but can confirm it in no experience—and this conception is only possible—which [possibility] he achieves by forming the concept so that it does not contradict itself—then he may think objects as he will, and he is certain to come up against no experience that contradicts it, for he has thought an object, e.g. a spirit, with a definition for which there can be absolutely no object of experience. For that no single experience confirms this idea of his does not deter him in the least because he wants to think a thing according to determinations that place it beyond the boundaries of all experience. Thus, such concepts can be wholly empty, and

Dritter Entwurf

die Sätze, welche Gegenstände derselben als wirklich annehmen, ganz
irrig seyn, und es ist doch kein Probierstein da, diesen Irrthum zu entdecken.

Selbst der Begriff des Übersinnlichen, an welchem die Vernunft ein
5 solches Interesse nimmt, daß darum Metaphysik, wenigstens als Versuch,
überhaupt existirt, jederzeit gewesen ist, und fernerhin sein wird; dieser
Begriff, ob er objective Realität habe, oder bloße Erdichtung sey, läßt
sich auf dem theoretischen Wege aus derselben Ursache durch keinen Probierstein direct ausmachen. Denn Widerspruch ist zwar in ihm nicht anzu-
10 treffen, aber, ob nicht alles, was ist und seyn kann, auch Gegenstand möglicher Erfahrung sey, mithin der Begriff des Übersinnlichen überhaupt
nicht völlig leer und der vermeynte Fortschritt vom Sinnlichen zum Übersinnlichen also nicht weit davon entfernt sey, für reell gehalten werden
zu dürfen, läßt sich direct durch keine Probe, die wir mit ihm anstellen
15 mögen, beweisen oder widerlegen.

Ehe aber noch die Metaphysik bis dahin gekommen ist, diesen Unterschied zu machen, hat sie Ideen, die lediglich das Übersinnliche zum Gegenstande haben können, mit Begriffen a priori, denen doch die Erfahrungsgegenstände angemessen sind, im Gemenge genommen, indem es ihr
20 gar nicht in Gedanken kam, daß der Ursprung derselben von andern reinen
Begriffen a priori verschieden seyn könne; dadurch es denn geschehen ist,
welches in der Geschichte der Verirrungen der menschlichen Vernunft
besonders merkwürdig ist, daß, da diese sich vermögend fühlt, von Dingen
der Natur und überhaupt von dem, was Gegenstand möglicher Erfahrung
25 seyn kann (nicht bloß in der Naturwissenschaft, sondern auch in der
Mathematik), einen großen Umfang von Erkenntnissen a priori zu erwerben, und die Realität dieser Fortschritte durch die That bewiesen hat, sie
gar nicht absehen kann, warum es ihr nicht noch weiter mit ihren Begriffen
a priori gelingen könne, nämlich bis zu Dingen oder Eigenschaften der-
30 selben, die nicht zu Gegenständen der Erfahrung gehören, glücklich durch-
zubringen. Sie mußte nothwendig die Begriffe aus beyden Feldern für
Begriffe von einerley Art halten, weil sie ihrem Ursprunge nach sofern
wirklich gleichartig sind, daß beyde a priori in unserm Erkenntnißvermögen
gegründet, nicht aus der Erfahrung geschöpft sind und also zu gleicher
35 Erwartung eines reellen Besitzes und Erweiterung desselben berechtigt
zu seyn scheinen.

Allein ein anderes sonderbares Phänomen mußte die auf dem Polster
ihres vermeyntlich durch Ideen über alle Grenzen möglicher Erfahrung
erweiterten Wissens schlummernde Vernunft endlich aufschrecken, und

consequently the principles that assume their objects as actual can be altogether in error, and yet there is no touchstone to discover it.

Even the concept of the supersensible — in which reason takes such an interest that metaphysics actually exists at least as an attempt, has always been, and henceforth will be, whether this concept has objective reality or is a mere fiction — cannot be directly determined in a theoretical way by a criterion (for the reasons cited above). For, to be sure, contradiction is not to be found in it. But whether or not everything that is and can be is also an object of possible experience, and thus whether the concept of the supersensible in general is not wholly empty, and whether, therefore, the purported progress from the sensible to the supersensible is not far from having to be held to be real, can neither be proved nor refuted directly by any test that we may apply to it.

But before metaphysics came to make the distinction, ideas that could only have the supersensible as their object were mixed up with a priori concepts appropriate to objects of experience, for the possibility that the origin of ideas could be different from that of other pure a priori concepts never arose. In this way, because human reason felt capable of acquiring a great range of a priori knowledge about things in nature and, generally, about what can be the object of possible experience (not only in natural science but also in mathematics), and because the reality of this progress was shown by this fact, reason was unable to foresee why it could not readily penetrate to things or properties of them that do not belong among the objects of experience, which is particularly significant in the history of the confusion of human reason. They had necessarily to take the concepts from both fields for concepts of a single kind, since they really are similar so far as the origin of both is based a priori in our faculty of knowledge and not created from experience, and thus they appear to be justified in an equal expectation of a real possession and extension of knowledge.

However, another extraordinary phenomenon must finally have startled reason slumbering on its cushion of putative knowledge extended beyond all boundaries of possible experience by means of

das ist die Entdeckung, daß zwar die Sätze a priori, die sich auf die letztere einschränken, nicht allein wohl zusammenstimmen, sondern gar ein System der Naturerkenntniß a priori ausmachen, jene dagegen, welche die Erfahrungsgrenze überschreiten, ob sie zwar eines ähnlichen Ursprungs zu seyn scheinen, theils unter sich, theils mit denen, welche auf die Natur- 5 erkenntniß gerichtet sind, in Widerstreit kommen und sich unter einander aufzureiben, hiemit aber der Vernunft im theoretischen Felde alles Zutrauen zu rauben, und einen unbegränzten Sceptizism einzuführen scheinen.

Wider dieses Unheil gibt es nun kein Mittel, als daß die reine Ver- 10 nunft selbst, d. i. das Vermögen überhaupt a priori etwas zu erkennen, einer genauen und ausführlichen Kritik unterworfen werde, und zwar so, daß die Möglichkeit einer reellen Erweiterung der Erkenntniß durch dieselbe in Ansehung des Sinnlichen und ebendieselbe, oder auch, wenn sie hier nicht möglich seyn sollte, die Begrenzung derselben in Ansehung des 15 Übersinnlichen eingesehen, und, was das letztere, als den Zweck der Metaphysik betrifft, dieser der Besitz, dessen sie fähig ist, nicht durch gerade Beweise, die so oft trüglich befunden worden, sondern durch Deduktion der Rechtsame der Vernunft zu Bestimmungen a priori gesichert werde. Mathematik und Naturwissenschaft, so fern sie reine Erkenntniß der Ver- 20 nunft enthalten, bedürfen keiner Kritik der menschlichen Vernunft überhaupt. Denn der Probierstein der Wahrheit ihrer Sätze liegt in ihnen selbst, weil ihre Begriffe nur so weit gehen, als die ihnen correspondirenden Gegenstände gegeben werden können, anstatt daß sie in der Metaphysik zu einem Gebrauche bestimmt sind, der diese Grenze überschreiten 25 und sich auf Gegenstände erstrecken soll, die gar nicht, oder wenigstens nicht in dem Maße, als der intendierte Gebrauch des Begriffs es erfordert, d. i. ihm angemessen gegeben werden können.

ideas: That is the discovery that a priori principles limited to the latter not only harmonize well together but also constitute a system of natural knowledge a priori, while those on the other hand that transcend the boundaries of experience — although they appear to have an analogous origin, partly among themselves, and partly among those directed towards knowledge of nature — come into contradiction and grate upon one another so as to rob reason of all confidence in the theoretical field and seem to introduce an unlimited skepticism.[98]

Now there is no defense against this difficulty, except when pure reason, that is, the capacity in general to know something a priori, is subjected to a precise and exhaustive critique. This must be done in order to see into the possibility of a real extension of cognition by means of critique in respect to the sensible, and into the very same with respect to the supersensible — or if [such an extension] is not to be possible here, to see into the limitation of knowledge with respect to the supersensible; and so far as the latter as the goal of metaphysics is concerned, to ascertain the possession of which it is capable — not by direct proofs, which so often are found to be deceptive, but rather by deduction of the legitimate claim of reason to a priori determinations. Mathematics and natural science, so far as they contain pure rational cognition, do not require a critique of human reason in general. For the touchstone of the truth of their propositions lies in themselves, because their concepts can extend only so far as their corresponding objects can be given, whereas in metaphysics concepts are destined to a use that transcends these boundaries and extends to objects that are incapable of being given at all, or at least cannot be given to the degree required by the intended use of the concepts, that is, as is fitting for it.

———

Abhandlung.

Die Metaphysik zeichnet sich unter allen Wissenschaften dadurch ganz besonders aus, daß sie die einzige ist, die ganz vollständig dargestellt werden kann; so daß für die Nachkommenschaft nichts übrig bleibt hinzu zu setzen
5 und sie ihrem Inhalt nach zu erweitern, ja, daß, wenn sich nicht aus der Idee derselben zugleich das absolute Ganze systematisch ergiebt, der Begriff von ihr als nicht richtig gefaßt betrachtet werden kann. Die Ursache hievon liegt darin, daß ihre Möglichkeit eine Kritik des ganzen reinen Vernunft= vermögens voraussetzt, wo, was dieses a priori in Ansehung der Gegen=
10 stände möglicher Erfahrung, oder, welches (wie in der Folge gezeigt werden wird) einerlei ist, was es in Ansehung der Prinzipien a priori der Mög= lichkeit einer Erfahrung überhaupt, mithin zum Erkenntniß des Sinn= lichen, zu leisten vermag, völlig erschöpft werden kann; was sie aber in Ansehung des Übersinnlichen, bloß durch die Natur der reinen Vernunft
15 genöthigt, vielleicht nur frägt, vielleicht aber auch erkennen mag, eben durch die Beschaffenheit und Einheit dieses reinen Erkenntnißvermögens genau angegeben werden kann und soll. Hieraus, und daß durch die Idee einer Metaphysik zugleich a priori bestimmt wird, was in ihr alles anzutref= fen seyn kann und soll, und was ihren ganzen möglichen Inhalt ausmacht,
20 wird es nun möglich zu beurtheilen, wie das in ihr erworbene Erkenntniß sich zu dem Ganzen, und der reelle Besitz zu einer Zeit, oder in einer Nation, sich zu dem in jeder andern, imgleichen zu dem Mangel der Erkenntniß, die man in ihr sucht, verhalte, und, da es in Ansehung des Bedürfnisses der reinen Vernunft keinen Nationalunterschied geben kann,
25 an dem Beyspiele dessen, was in einem Volke geschehen, verfehlt oder gelungen ist, zugleich der Mangel oder Fortschritt der Wissenschaft über= haupt zu jeder Zeit und in jedem Volke nach einem sichern Maaßstabe beurtheilt werden und so die Aufgabe als eine Frage an die Menschen= vernunft überhaupt aufgelöset werden kann.
30   Es ist also zwar bloß die Armuth und die Enge der Schranken, darin diese Wissenschaft eingeschlossen ist, welche es möglich macht, sie in einem kurzen Abrisse, und dennoch hinreichend zur Beurtheilung jedes wahren

Treatise

Metaphysics completely distinguishes itself from all other sciences in that it is the only one that can be presented in its entirety so that nothing remains for posterity to add so as to extend its content. Indeed, if the idea of metaphysics cannot systematically yield its absolute totality, its concept can be regarded as not correctly grasped. The basis of this lies in the fact that metaphysics' possibility presupposes a critique of the entire capacity of pure reason, where what this is able to accomplish a priori in respect to the objects of a possible experience or, what is the same thing (as will be shown in the sequel), what it is able to accomplish in regard to the a priori principles of the possibility of experience in general, thus to cognition of the sensible, can be fully worked out. But what it may perhaps only ask but may perhaps also know in regard to the supersensible — constrained merely by the nature and unity of this pure capacity of knowledge — can and should be precisely given just by the constitution and unity of this pure capacity of knowledge. From this, and from the fact that the idea of a metaphysics simultaneously determines a priori everything that can and must be found there and everything that constitutes its entire possible content, it becomes possible to judge how that knowledge achieved in it compares to the whole and how the real possession in one time or in one nation compares to that in every other, as well as to the lack of the knowledge that is sought in it. And since there can be no national differences with respect to the requirements of pure reason, the deficiency or progress of the science in general at all times for every race can be judged according to a secure standard from the example of what has obtained, failed, or succeeded with one people. In this way the problem can be resolved as a question concerning human reason in general.

It is thus only the poverty and narrowness of the bounds within which this science is enclosed that makes it possible to set it out completely in a short sketch and yet to judge each of its true possessions

Besitzes in ihr, ganz aufzustellen. Dagegen aber erschwert die comparativ
große Mannigfaltigkeit der Folgerungen aus wenig Prinzipien, worauf
die Kritik die reine Vernunft führt, den Versuch gar sehr, ihn in einem
so kleinen Raume, als die Königliche Academie es verlangt, dennoch vollständig aufzustellen; denn durch theilweise angestellte Untersuchung wird   5
in ihr nichts ausgerichtet, sondern die Zusammenstimmung jedes Satzes
zum Ganzen des reinen Vernunftgebrauchs ist allein dasjenige, was für
die Realität ihrer Fortschritte die Gewähr leisten kann. Eine fruchtbare,
aber doch nicht in Dunkelheit ausartende Kürze wird daher fast mehr
aufmerksame Sorgfalt in nachfolgender Abhandlung erfordern, als die   10
Schwierigkeit, der Aufgabe, welche jetzt aufgelöset werden soll, ein Gnüge
zu leisten.

Erster Abschnitt.

Von der allgemeinen Aufgabe der sich selbst
einer Kritik unterwerfenden Vernunft.   15

Diese ist in der Frage enthalten: Wie sind synthetische Urtheile
a priori möglich?

Urtheile sind nämlich analytisch, wenn ihr Prädicat nur dasjenige klar (explicite) vorstellt, was in dem Begriffe des Subjects, obzwar
dunkel (implicite), gedacht war; z. B. ein jeder Körper ist ausgedehnt.   20
Wenn man solche Urtheile identische nennen wollte, so würde man nur
Verwirrung anrichten; denn dergleichen Urtheile tragen nichts zur Deutlichkeit des Begriffs bey, wozu doch alles Urtheilen abzwecken muß, und
heißen daher leer; z. B. ein jeder Körper ist ein körperliches (mit einem
andern Wort, materielles) Wesen. Analytische Urtheile gründen sich   25
zwar auf der Identität, und können darin aufgelöset werden, aber sie
sind nicht identisch, denn sie bedürfen der Zergliederung und dienen dadurch zur Erklärung des Begriffs; da hingegen durch identische, idem per
idem, also gar nicht erklärt werden würde.

Synthetische Urtheile sind solche, welche durch ihr Prädicat über den   30
Begriff des Subjects hinausgehen, indem jenes etwas enthält, was in dem
Begriffe des letztern gar nicht gedacht war: z. B. alle Körper sind schwer.
Hier wird nun gar nicht darnach gefragt, ob das Prädicat mit dem Begriffe
des Subjects jederzeit verbunden sey oder nicht, sondern es wird nur

adequately. However, the comparatively large number of consequences derived from the few principles to which the critique leads pure reason very much complicates the attempt to set them out completely in so little space as the Royal Academy requires. Nothing will be accomplished in metaphysics by an investigation carried out piecemeal. Rather only the coordination of every principle to the whole of pure reason's employment can provide a guarantee of the reality of its progress. Thus, in what follows a fruitful brevity, which, however, does not degenerate into obscurity, will require almost more attentive care than the difficulty of adequately answering the problem that must now be solved.

FIRST SECTION

The General Problem of Reason's Subjecting Itself to a Critique

This general problem is contained in the question, "How are synthetic judgments a priori possible?" That is to say, judgments are *analytic* when their predicate only clearly (*explicite*) represents what was thought in the concept of the subject, even though obscurely (*implicite*). E.g., every body is extended. Were such judgments called identities, only confusion would be produced, for such judgments contribute nothing to the clarification of concepts, towards which all judgments must aim, and thus are called empty; for example, every body is a bodily (in other words, material) being. To be sure, analytic judgments *are* not identical because they require division and in such division serve to clarify their concept, whereas by contrast, in identical judgments, *idem per idem*, absolutely nothing is explained.

Synthetic judgments are those that by means of their predicate go beyond the concept of the subject because the predicate contains something that was not thought in the concept of the subject: e.g., all bodies are heavy. Here it will certainly not be asked whether the predicate is always *combined* with the concept of the subject or not; it will only be said that the predicate is not thought in this concept, even

gesagt, daß es in diesem Begriffe nicht mitgedacht werde, ob es gleich
nothwendig zu ihm hinzukommen muß. So ist z. B. der Satz: Eine jede
dreyseitige Figur ist dreiwinklicht (figura trilatera est triangula), ein
synthetischer Satz. Denn obgleich, wenn ich drey gerade Linien, als einen
5 Raum einschließend denke, es unmöglich ist, daß dadurch nicht zugleich
drey Winkel gemacht würden, so denke ich doch in jenem Begriffe des
Dreyseitigen gar nicht die Neigung dieser Seiten gegen einander, d. i. der
Begriff der Winkel wird in ihm wirklich nicht gedacht.

Alle analytische Urtheile sind Urtheile a priori und gelten also mit
10 strenger Allgemeinheit und absoluter Nothwendigkeit, weil sie sich gänzlich
auf den Satz des Widerspruchs gründen. Synthetische Urtheile können
aber auch Erfahrungsurtheile sein, welche uns zwar lehren, wie gewisse
Dinge beschaffen sind, niemals aber, daß sie nothwendig so seyn müssen
und nicht anders beschaffen seyn können: z. B. alle Körper sind schwer;
15 da alsdenn ihre Allgemeinheit nur comparativ ist: Alle Körper, soviel
wir deren kennen, sind schwer, welche Allgemeinheit wir die empirische,
zum Unterschiede der rationalen, welche, als a priori erkannt, eine stricte
Allgemeinheit ist, nennen könnten. Wenn es nun synthetische Sätze
a priori gäbe, so würden sie nicht auf dem Satze des Widerspruchs beruhen
20 und in Ansehung ihrer würde also die obbenannte, noch nie vorher in ihrer
Allgemeinheit aufgeworfene, noch weniger aufgelösete Frage eintreten:
Wie sind synthetische Sätze a priori möglich? Daß es aber dergleichen
wirklich gebe, und die Vernunft nicht bloß dazu diene, schon erworbene
Begriffe analytisch zu erläutern (ein sehr nothwendiges Geschäft, um sich
25 zuerst selbst wohl zu verstehen), sondern daß sie sogar vermögend sey, ihren
Besitz a priori synthetisch zu erweitern, und daß die Metaphysik zwar,
was die Mittel betrifft, deren sie sich bedient, auf den erstern, was aber
ihren Zweck anlangt, gänzlich auf den letztern beruhe, wird gegenwärtige
Abhandlung im Fortgange reichlich zeigen. Weil aber die Fortschritte,
30 welche die letztere gethan zu haben vorgiebt, noch bezweifelt werden
könnten, ob sie nämlich reell seyen oder nicht, so steht die reine Mathematik, als ein Koloß, zum Beweise der Realität durch alleinige reine
Vernunft erweiterter Erkenntniß da, trotz den Angriffen des kühnsten
Zweiflers und, ob sie gleich zur Bewährung der Rechtmäßigkeit ihrer
35 Ansprüche ganz und gar keiner Kritik des reinen Vernunftvermögens selbst
bedarf, sondern sich durch ihr eignes Factum rechtfertigt, so giebt es doch
an ihr ein sicheres Beyspiel, um wenigstens die Realität der für die Metaphysik höchstnöthigen Aufgabe: wie sind synthetische Sätze a priori
möglich? darzuthun.

though it must necessarily be added to it. Thus, for example, the proposition "Every three sided figure has three angles" (*figura trilatera est triangula*) is a synthetic proposition. Because while I think of three lines as enclosing a space, it is impossible at the same time not to think that three angles are formed. I do not think of the inclination of these sides towards one another in the concept of three sidedness, i.e., the concept of angle is not actually thought in it.

All analytic judgments are a priori and their validity is thus strictly universal and absolutely necessary for they are based entirely on the principle of contradiction. However, synthetic judgments can also be empirical judgments that teach us how certain things are constituted but never that they must necessarily be so and cannot be constituted otherwise — for example, that all bodies are heavy — where their universality is then only comparative. All bodies, so far as we know them, are heavy, which universality we may call empirical to distinguish it from what we can call rational, that is strict, universality because it is known a priori. Now if there are a priori synthetic propositions, they would not rest on the law of contradiction, and thus in respect to them the question mentioned above, which has not previously been raised in its generality, much less solved would occur: "How are synthetic judgments a priori possible?" What follows in the present treatise will amply show that there actually are some of these [synthetic a priori judgments], that reason does not serve merely to explicate already acquired concepts (a most necessary undertaking in order first to understand oneself well), but rather that reason is quite capable of synthetically expanding its a priori possession and that so far as the means that metaphysics uses is concerned it rests on the former, though so far as its purpose is concerned it rests entirely upon the latter. However, since it may still be doubted whether or not the progress that the latter has pretended to have made is real, pure mathematics stands as a colossus in proof of the reality of knowledge extended by means of pure reason alone, in spite of the attacks of the most courageous doubters. And because mathematics in no way requires confirmation of the legitimacy of its claims by a critique of the faculty of pure reason itself but is justified by itself as a fact, it provides an indubitable example that at least shows the reality of the issue that is highly important for metaphysics: "How are synthetic propositions a priori possible?"

Es bewies mehr wie alles andere Platons, eines versuchten Mathe-
matikers, philosophischen Geist, daß er über die große, den Verstand mit
so viel herrlichen und unerwarteten Prinzipien in der Geometrie be-
rührende reine Vernunft in eine solche Verwunderung versetzt werden
konnte, die ihn bis zu dem schwärmerischen Gedanken fortriß, alle diese 5
Kenntnisse nicht für neue Erwerbungen in unserm Erdenleben, sondern
für bloße Wiederaufweckung weit früherer Ideen zu halten, die nichts
geringeres, als Gemeinschaft mit dem göttlichen Verstande zum Grunde
haben könnte. Einen bloßen Mathematiker würden diese Producte seiner
Vernunft wohl vielleicht bis zur Hekatombe erfreuet, aber die Möglichkeit 10
derselben nicht in Verwunderung gesetzt haben, weil er nur über seinem
Object brütete, und darüber das Subject, so fern es einer so tiefen Erkenntniß desselben fähig ist, zu betrachten und zu bewundern keinen Anlaß
hatte. Ein bloßer Philosoph, wie Aristoteles, würde dagegen den himmelweiten Unterschied des reinen Vernunftvermögens, so fern es sich aus 15
sich selbst erweitert, von dem, welches, von empirischen Prinzipien geleitet,
durch Schlüsse zum allgemeinern fortschreitet, nicht genug bemerkt und
daher auch eine solche Bewunderung nicht gefühlt, sondern, indem er die
Metaphysik nur als eine zu höhern Stufen aufsteigende Physik ansahe,
in der Anmaßung derselben, die sogar aufs Übersinnliche hinausgeht, 20
nichts Befremdliches und Unbegreifliches gefunden haben, wozu den
Schlüssel zu finden so schwer eben seyn sollte, wie es in der That ist.

Zweyter Abschnitt.

Bestimmung der gedachten Aufgabe in Ansehung der Erkenntnißvermögen,
welche in uns die reine Vernunft ausmachen.   25

Die obige Aufgabe läßt sich nicht anders auflösen, als so: daß wir
sie vorher in Beziehung auf die Vermögen des Menschen, dadurch er der
Erweiterung seiner Erkenntniß a priori fähig ist, betrachten, und welche
dasjenige in ihm ausmachen, was man specifisch seine reine Vernunft
nennen kann. Denn, wenn unter einer reinen Vernunft eines Wesens 30
überhaupt das Vermögen, unabhängig von Erfahrung, mithin von

Nothing demonstrates Plato's philosophical spirit more than that this accomplished mathematician could be transported into such astonishment by the greatness of pure reason, which captivates the understanding with so many magnificent and unexpected principles in geometry. But he was carried away to the fantastic notion that this knowledge was not to be taken for a new acquisition of our earthly life but merely for a re-awakening of very much earlier ideas, for which the foundation could be nothing less than community with the divine understanding.[99] A mere mathematician would perhaps be pleased enough with these products of his reason to rejoice in them. However, their possibility would not have caused him astonishment because he broods only upon his object and has no occasion to reflect on and to admire the subject that is capable of such deep knowledge. By contrast, a mere philosopher, such as Aristotle, would not sufficiently have noted the immense difference between the capacity of *pure* reason, insofar as it can extend itself just by itself, and the capacity that is directed by empirical principles, which progresses by means of conclusions to more general ones; and therefore he would not have felt such astonishment. Rather, since he regarded metaphysics only as a physics that ascends to a higher level, he found nothing strange and inconceivable in reason's claim to transcend even to the supersensible, the key to which must be as difficult to find as, in fact, it is.

SECOND SECTION

Definition of the Proposed Problem with Respect to the Faculties of Knowledge in Us that Constitute Pure Reason

The foregoing problem permits no other solution than this: that before going further we consider its relation to those faculties of man by means of which he is able to extend his knowledge a priori, as well as which faculties constitute in *him* what can specifically be called *his* pure reason. For if, by the pure reason of any being in general, the

Sinnenvorstellungen, Dinge zu erkennen, verstanden wird, so wird dadurch gar nicht bestimmt, auf welche Art überhaupt in ihm (z. B. in Gott oder einem andern höhern Geiste) dergleichen Erkenntniß möglich sey, und die Aufgabe ist alsdenn unbestimmt.

5 Was dagegen den Menschen betrifft, so besteht ein jedes Erkenntniß desselben aus Begriff und Anschauung. Jedes von diesen beyden ist zwar Vorstellung, aber noch nicht Erkenntniß. Etwas sich durch Begriffe, d. i. im Allgemeinen vorstellen, heißt denken, und das Vermögen zu denken, der Verstand. Die unmittelbare Vorstellung des Einzelnen ist die 10 Anschauung. Das Erkenntniß durch Begriffe heißt discursiv, das in der Anschauung intuitiv; in der That wird zu einer Erkenntniß beydes mit einander verbunden erfordert, sie wird aber von dem benannt, worauf, als den Bestimmungsgrund desselben, ich jedesmal vorzüglich attendire. Daß beyde empirische, oder auch reine Vorstellungsarten seyn 15 können, das gehört zur specifischen Beschaffenheit des menschlichen Erkenntnißvermögens, welches wir bald näher betrachten werden. Durch die Anschauung, die einem Begriffe gemäß ist, wird der Gegenstand gegeben, ohne dieselbe wird er blos gedacht. Durch diese bloße An-schauung ohne Begriff wird der Gegenstand zwar gegeben, aber nicht 20 gedacht, durch den Begriff ohne correspondirende Anschauung wird er gedacht, aber keiner gegeben, in beyden Fällen wird also nicht erkannt. Wenn einem Begriffe die correspondirende Anschauung a priori bey-gegeben werden kann, so sagt man: dieser Begriff werde construirt; ist es nur eine empirische Anschauung, so nennt man das ein bloßes Beyspiel 25 zu dem Begriffe; die Handlung der Hinzufügung der Anschauung zum Begriffe heißt in beiden Fällen Darstellung (exhibitio) des Objects, ohne welche (sie mag nun mittelbar, oder unmittelbar geschehen) es gar kein Erkenntniß geben kann.

Die Möglichkeit eines Gedankens oder Begriffs beruht auf dem 30 Satze des Widerspruchs, z. B. der eines denkenden unkörperlichen Wesens (eines Geistes). Das Ding, wovon selbst der bloße Gedanke unmöglich ist (d. i. der Begriff sich widerspricht), ist selbst unmöglich. Das Ding aber, wovon der Begriff möglich ist, ist darum nicht ein mögliches Ding. Die erste Möglichkeit kann man die logische, die zweyte die reale Möglich- 35 keit nennen; der Beweis der letztern ist der Beweis der objectiven Realität des Begriffs, welchen man jederzeit zu fordern berechtigt ist. Er kann aber nie anders geleistet werden, als durch Darstellung des dem Begriffe correspondirenden Objects; denn sonst bleibt es immer nur ein Gedanke,

ability to know things independently of experience and thus of sensible presentations is understood, nothing at all is thereby determined about the way that such knowledge is possible in the being in general (e.g. God or some other higher spirit), and the problem will then remain indeterminate.

By contrast, so far as what concerns human beings — all cognition consists of concept and intuition. Each of these is indeed representation, but not, cognition. To represent something in general through concepts, is called *thinking*, and the capacity for thought is understanding. The immediate presentation of the particular is intuition. Knowledge by means of *concepts* is called *discursive*, by means of *intuition*, *intuitive*; in fact, knowledge requires the conjunction of the two, but each is named for the ground of determination to which I always primarily attend. That both can be either empirical or pure modes of presentation is a matter of the specific constitution of the human capacity for knowledge, which we shall soon consider more closely. An object is *given* through an intuition that conforms with a concept; without this it is only *thought*. Through intuition alone, without a concept, an object is indeed given, but not thought; through concepts, without corresponding intuition, it is thought, but none is given; in neither case is it cognized. If a corresponding intuition can be added a priori to a concept, one says that this concept is constructed. If it is only an empirical intuition, it is called only an example of the concept. In both cases, the act of adding intuition to a concept is called the exhibition (*exhibitio*) of the object, without which (whether it happens mediately or immediately) there can be no knowledge.

The possiblity of a thought or of a concept rests on the law of contradiction, e.g., that of a thinking, incorporeal being (a spirit). A thing of which even the mere thought is impossible (i.e., its concept is self-contradictory) is itself impossible. A thing whose concept is possible is not for that reason a possible thing. The first possibility may be termed logical, and the second real possibility. Proof of the latter is proof of the objective reality of the concept, something one is always justified in demanding. This can only be accomplished by a representation of the object corresponding to the concept, for otherwise it will always remain only a thought, about which, until it can be shown in an example,

welcher, ob ihm irgend ein Gegenstand correspondire, oder ob er leer sey, d. i. ob er überhaupt zum Erkenntnisse dienen könne, so lange, bis jenes in einem Beyspiele gezeigt wird, immer ungewiß bleibt. *

No. II.
Das zweyte Stadium der Metaphysik.

Ihr Stillestand im Scepticism der reinen Vernunft.

Obzwar Stillestand kein Fortschreiten, mithin eigentlich auch nicht ein zurückgelegtes Stadium heißen kann: so ist doch, wenn das Fortgehen in einer gewissen Richtung unvermeidlich ein ebenso großes Zurückgehen zur Folge hat, die Folge davon eben dieselbe, als ob man nicht von der Stelle gekommen wäre.

Raum und Zeit enthalten Verhältnisse des Bedingten zu seinen Bedingungen, z. B. die bestimmte Größe eines Raumes ist nur bedingt möglich, nämlich dadurch, daß ihn ein andrer Raum einschließt; eben so eine bestimmte Zeit dadurch, daß sie als der Theil einer noch größern Zeit vorgestellt wird, und so ist es mit allen gegebenen Dingen, als Erscheinungen, bewandt. Die Vernunft aber verlangt, das Unbedingte, und mit ihm die Totalität aller Bedingungen, zu erkennen, denn sonst hört sie nicht auf zu fragen, gerade als ob noch nichts geantwortet wäre.

Nun würde dieses für sich allein die Vernunft noch nicht irre machen; denn wie oft wird nicht nach dem Warum in der Naturlehre vergeblich gefragt, und doch die Entschuldigung mit seiner Unwissenheit gültig

* Ein gewisser Verfasser will diese Forderung durch einen Fall vereiteln, der in der That der einzige in seiner Art ist, nämlich der Begriff eines noth= wendigen Wesens, von dessen Daseyn, weil doch die letzte Ursache wenigstens ein schlechthin nothwendiges Wesen seyn müsse, wir gewiß seyn könnten, und daß also die objective Realität dieses Begriffs bewiesen werden könne, ohne doch eine ihm correspondirende Anschauung in irgend einem Beyspiele geben zu dürfen. Aber der Begriff von einem nothwendigen Wesen ist noch gar nicht der Begriff von einem auf irgend eine Weise bestimmten Dinge. Denn das Daseyn ist keine Bestimmung irgend eines Dinges, und, welche innere Prädicate einem Dinge aus dem Grunde, weil man es als ein dem Dasein nach unab= hängiges Ding annimmt, zukommen, läßt sich schlechterdings nicht aus seinem bloßen Daseyn, es mag als nothwendig oder nicht nothwendig angenommen werden, erkennen.

it will always remain uncertain whether an object corresponds to it or whether it is empty, i.e., whether it in general can serve as cognition.*

––––––––––

No. II
The Second Stage of Metaphysics

Its [Metaphysics'] Stagnation in
Pure Reason's Skepticism[101]

Although stagnation cannot be termed progress and thus properly also no stage that has been traversed, yet if moving in a certain direction inevitably results in equal backtracking, its result is exactly the same as if one had never left one's place.

Space and time contain relations of conditioned things to their conditions; e.g., the determinate size of a space is possible only as conditioned, that is, insofar as another space enlcoses it; similarly, a determinate time is presented only as part of a greater time. And the same holds for all given things as appearances. However, reason desires to know the unconditioned and, with it, the totality of all conditions; otherwise, it will not cease asking questions just as if it as yet had received no answers.

Now by itself, this would not cause reason to err; for how often are vain inquiries after the why made in natural science, and the excuse of reason's ignorance is nonetheless found valid, since ignorance is at

––––––––––

*A certain author[100] attempts to frustrate this requirement by appealing to a case that, in fact, is the only one of its kind, namely, the concept of a necessary being of whose existence we can be certain just because at least the ultimate cause must be an absolutely necessary being, and consequently, the objective reality of its concept may be proved without needing to give an intuition corresponding to it in any example. However, the concept of a necessary being is by no means the concept of a being that is in any way determinate. For existence is not a determination of any thing; and from mere existence, which may or may not be assumed to be necessary, what intrinsic predicates pertain to a thing solely because it is assumed to be a thing independent with respect to existence, may be not known at all.

gefunden, weil sie doch wenigstens beffer ist als Irrthum. Aber die
Vernunft wird dadurch an sich selbst irre, daß sie, durch die sicherſten
Grundsätze geleitet, das Unbedingte auf einer Seite gefunden zu haben
glaubt, und doch nach anderweitigen, eben so sichern Prinzipien, sich
5 selbst dahin bringt, zugleich zu glauben, daß es auf der entgegengesetzten
Seite gesucht werden müsse.

Diese Antinomie der Vernunft setzt sie nicht allein in einen Zweifel
des Mißtrauens gegen die eine sowohl als die andre dieser ihrer Be-
hauptungen, welches doch noch die Hoffnung eines so oder anders ent-
10 scheidenden Urtheiles übrig läßt, sondern in eine Verzweiflung der Vernunft an sich selbst, allen Anspruch auf Gewißheit aufzugeben, welches
man den Zustand des dogmatischen Scepticismus nennen kann.

Aber dieser Kampf der Vernunft mit sich selbst hat das Besondre
an sich, daß diese sich ihn als einen Zweykampf denkt, in welchem sie, wenn
15 sie den Angriff thut, sicher ist, den Gegner zu schlagen, so fern sie aber
sich vertheidigen soll, ebenso gewiß, geschlagen zu werden. Mit andern
Worten: sie kann sich nicht so sehr darauf verlassen, ihre Behauptung
zu beweisen, als vielmehr die des Gegners zu widerlegen, welches gar
nicht sicher ist, indem wohl alle Beyde falsch urtheilen möchten, oder
20 auch, daß wohl Beyde Recht haben möchten, wenn sie nur über den
Sinn der Frage allererst einverstanden wären.

Diese Antinomie teilt die Kämpfenden in zwey Klaſſen, davon
die eine das Unbedingte in der Zusammensetzung des Gleichartigen,
die andre in der desjenigen Mannigfaltigen sucht, was auch ungleich-
25 artig seyn kann. Jene ist mathematisch, und geht von den Theilen einer
gleichartigen Größe durch Addition zum absoluten Ganzen, oder von
dem Ganzen zu den Theilen fort, deren keiner wiederum ein Ganzes ist.
Diese ist dynamisch, und geht von den Folgen auf den obersten synthetischen Grund, der also etwas von der Folge realiter Unterschiedenes ist,
30 entweder den obersten Bestimmungsgrund der Kausalität eines Dinges
oder den des Daseyns dieses Dinges selbst.

Da sind nun die Gegensätze von der ersten Klaſſe, wie gesagt, von
zwiefacher Art. Der, so von den Theilen zum Ganzen geht: Die Welt
hat einen Anfang, und der: sie hat keinen Anfang, sind beyde
35 gleich falsch, und der, welcher von den Folgen auf die Gründe, und so
synthetisch wieder zurück geht, können, obzwar einander entgegengesetzt,
doch beyde wahr seyn, weil eine Folge mehrere Gründe haben kann,
und zwar von transscendentaler Verschiedenheit, nämlich daß der Grund
entweder Object der Sinnlichkeit oder der reinen Vernunft ist, dessen

least better than error. However, reason itself errs when, led by the most certain fundamental principles, it thinks to have found the unconditioned on one side, and yet by vastly different principles, which are just as certain, brings itself simultaneously to believe that the unconditioned must be sought on the opposite side.

This antinomy of reason not only causes mistrustful doubt of the one as well as the other of these of its contentions, but it also causes reason, in despair of itself, to surrender all of its claims to certainty, which may be called the condition of dogmatic skepticism.

However, this conflict of reason with itself has this peculiarity, that reason thinks of it as a duel, in which, if reason takes the offensive, it is certain to beat the opponent; but if it is to defend itself it is just as certain to be beaten. In other words: it cannot so much depend upon proving its contention as on refuting its opponent's. This is not at all safe, since both might well judge falsely, or indeed both might be correct, if first and foremost they only could agree on the sense of the question.

This antinomy divides the combatants into two classes, of which the one searches for the unconditioned in the combination of the homogeneous, the other in the manifold of what can also be heterogeneous. The former is mathematical, proceeding by addition of the parts of a homogeneous quantity to an absolute whole, or from a whole to the parts, none of which is a whole. The latter is dynamical and proceeds from the consequences to the ultimate synthetic foundation, which is therefore something really distinct from the consequent, either from the ultimate determining principle of the causality of a thing or that of the existence of the thing itself.

Now there are, as said, two kinds of antitheses of the first sort — the kind that proceed from the parts to the whole — "The world has a beginning," and the one, "It has no beginning," are both equally false — and the kind that proceed from consequences to their foundations, and thus regresses synthetically, where both can be true, even although they are opposed to one another, because one consequence may have several grounds, indeed grounds that are transcendentally different. That is, the ground is either an object of sensibility or of pure reason whose representation can never be given as an empirical

Vorstellung nicht in der empirischen Vorstellung gegeben werden kann; z. B.: Es ist alles Naturnothwendigkeit, und daher keine Freyheit, dem die Antithesis entgegensteht, es giebt Freyheit, und es ist nicht alles Naturnothwendigkeit, wo mithin ein sceptischer Zustand eintritt, der einen Stillestand der Vernunft hervorbringt.

Denn, was die erstern betrifft, so können, gleichwie in der Logik zwey einander contrarisch entgegengesetzte Urtheile, weil das eine mehr sagt, als zur Opposition erfordert wird, alle beyde falsch seyn, also auch in der Metaphysik. So enthält der Satz: die Welt hat keinen Anfang, den Satz: die Welt hat einen Anfang, nicht mehr oder weniger, als zur Opposition erfordert wird, und einer von beyden müßte wahr, der andre falsch seyn. Sage ich aber, sie hat keinen Anfang, sondern ist von Ewigkeit her, so sage ich mehr, als zur Opposition erforderlich ist. Denn außer dem, was die Welt nicht ist, sage ich noch, was sie ist. Nun wird die Welt, als ein absolutes Ganzes betrachtet, wie ein Noumenon gedacht, und doch nach Anfang, oder unendlicher Zeit als Phänomen. Sage ich nun diese intellectuelle Totalität der Welt aus, oder spreche ich ihr Grenzen zu als Noumenon, so ist beydes falsch. Denn mit der absoluten Totalität der Bedingungen in einer Sinnenwelt, d. i. in der Zeit, widerspreche ich mir selbst, ich mag sie als unendlich, oder als begrenzt, in einer mög= lichen Anschauung gegeben mir vorstellen.

Dagegen sie, so wie in der Logik subcontrarie einander entgegen= gesetzte Urtheile, beyde wahr sein können, weil jedes weniger sagt, als zur Opposition erfordert wird: so können in der Metaphysik zwey synthetische Urtheile, die auf Gegenstände der Sinne gehen, aber nur das Verhältniß der Folge zu den Gründen betreffen, beyde wahr seyn, weil die Reihe der Bedingungen in zweyerley verschiedener Art, nämlich als Object der Sinnlichkeit oder der bloßen Vernunft betrachtet wird. Denn die bedingten Folgen sind in der Zeit gegeben, die Gründe aber, oder die Bedingungen, denkt man sich dazu, und können mancherley sein. Sage ich also: Alle Begebenheiten in der Sinnenwelt geschehen aus Naturursachen, so lege ich Bedingungen zum Grunde, als Phänomene. Sagt der Gegner: Es geschieht nicht alles aus Naturursachen (causa phaenomen.), so würde das erstere falsch seyn müssen. Sage ich aber: Es geschieht nicht alles aus bloßen Naturursachen, sondern es kann auch zugleich aus übersinnlichen Gründen (causa noumen.) geschehen, so sage ich weniger, als zur Entgegensetzung gegen die Totalität der Bedingungen in der Sinnenwelt erfordert wird, denn ich nehme eine Ursache an, die nicht auf jene Art Bedingungen, aber auf die der Sinnen-

representation. For example, "There is only natural necessity and therefore no freedom," opposes the antithesis, "There is freedom, and not everything is [due to] natural necessity." Thus a skeptical state that produces the stagnation of reason is introduced.

Concerning the first class, in metaphysics just as in logic, where of two judgments opposed as contraries one asserts more than is required for an opposition, both can be false. Thus, the proposition, "The world has no beginning" contains neither more nor less than is necessary for opposition to the proposition "The world has a beginning," and one of them must be true, the other false. But if I say, "It has no beginning, but is eternal," I assert more than is required for opposition. Because, besides in addition to saying what the world is not, I am also saying what it is. Now the world is considered as an absolute whole, thought as a noumenon, and yet also as a phenomenon if [it is regarded either as having] a beginning or as [being] endless in time. Now if I articulate either the intellectual totality or the boundaries of the world as noumenon, both are false. For I contradict myself when I represent the totality of conditions in a sensible world, that is in time, as given to me in a possible intuition, be it as infinite or as bounded.

On the other hand, as two judgments opposed as subcontraries in logic can be true, because each says less than is required for an opposition, in metaphysics two synthetic judgments that concern only the relation of a consequence to its ground among objects of the senses can be true; for the series of conditions can be considered in two different ways, namely, as an object of sensibility or of mere reason. For the conditioned consequences are given in time, but the grounds or conditions are added to them by thought and can be of several sorts. Thus, if I say, "All events in the sensible world come about through natural causes," I set out phenomena as the fundamental conditions. If an opponent says, "Not everything comes about through natural causes (*causa phaenomen*)," the first claim would have to be false. If, however, I say, "Not everything happens through mere natural causes, but may simultaneously obtain through supersensible grounds (*causa noumen*[*on*])," I say less than is required for opposition to the totality of conditions in the sensible world. For I assume a cause that is not bound up with every sort of condition but [is bound] to those of sensible representation, and thus I do not deny conditions of that [supersensible] kind. That is, I merely suggest to myself the intelligible

vorstellung eingeschränkt ist, widerspreche also den Bedingungen dieser
Art nicht; nämlich ich stelle mir blos die intelligibele vor, davon der
Gedanke schon im Begriff eines mundi phaenom. liegt, in welchem alles
bedingt ist, also widerstreitet die Vernunft hier nicht der Totalität der
5 Bedingungen.

Dieser sceptische Stillstand, der keinen Scepticism, d. i. keine Verzichtthuung auf Gewißheit in Erweiterung unserer Vernunfterkenntniß
über die Grenze möglicher Erfahrung enthält, ist nun sehr wohlthätig;
denn ohne diese hätten wir die größeste Angelegenheit des Menschen,
10 womit die Metaphysik als ihrem Endzweck umgeht, entweder aufgeben
und unsern Vernunftgebrauch blos aufs Sinnliche einschränken, oder
den Forscher mit unhaltbaren Vorspiegelungen von Einsicht, wie so lange
geschehen ist, hinhalten müssen: wäre nicht die Kritik der reinen Vernunft
dazwischen gekommen, welche durch die Theilung der gesetzgebenden
15 Metaphysik in zwey Kammern, sowohl dem Despotism des Empirism,
als dem anarchischen Unfug der unbegrenzten Philodoxie abgeholfen hat.

No. III.
Randanmerkungen.

Sowohl die unbedingte Möglichkeit als Unmöglichkeit des Nichtseyns
20 eines Dinges sind transcendente Vorstellungen, die sich gar nicht denken
lassen, weil wir ohne Bedingung, weder etwas zu setzen, noch aufzuheben
Grund haben. Der Satz also, daß ein Ding schlechthin zufällig existire,
oder schlechthin nothwendig sey, hat beyderseits niemals einigen Grund.
Der disjunctive Satz hat also kein Object. Eben als wenn ich sagte:
25 Ein jedes Ding ist entweder x oder non x, und dieses x gar nicht kennete.

Alle Welt hat irgend eine Metaphysik zum Zwecke der Vernunft,
und sie, sammt der Moral, machen die eigentliche Philosophie aus.

Die Begriffe der Nothwendigkeit und Zufälligkeit scheinen nicht
auf die Substanz zu gehen. Auch fragt man nicht nach der Ursache des
30 Daseyns einer Substanz, weil sie das ist, was immer war und bleiben
muß, und worauf, als ein Substrat, das Wechselnde seine Verhältnisse

world, the thought of which is already contained in the concept of a *mundi phenomen*[*on*], in which everything is conditioned. Consequently, reason does not here contradict the [concept of the] totality of conditions.

This skeptical stand off, which is not skepticism — i.e., which contains no renunciation of certainty in the extension of our rational knowledge beyond the bounds of possible experience — is very salutary indeed. For without it, as men who are concerned with metaphysics as their ultimate goal, we would have had the greatest occasion either to give up and to limit our use of reason merely to the sensible, or else we would have to offer the investigator untenable illusions of insight, as has happened for so long, had the critique of pure reason not intervened, dividing legislative metaphysics into two chambers and remedying the despotism of empiricism as well as the anarchic mischief of unbounded philodoxy.

—————

No. III
Marginalia

Both a thing's unconditioned possibility and the impossibility of its non-being are transcendent representations that cannot be thought, for without a condition we have no reason for postulating or denying something. Therefore, the proposition "A thing exists altogether contingently, or it is absolutely necessary," has no basis for either alternative. Thus the disjunctive proposition has no object. Just as if I say, "Each thing is either X or non-X" and do not know this X.

—————

The whole world has some sort of metaphysics as the end of reason, and together with ethics it constitutes philosophy proper.

—————

The concepts of necessity and contingency do not appear to apply to substance. Also one does not inquire about the cause of a substance's existence, because it is what must always have been and remains, and in which, as substratum, the relations of what is changing are grounded.

gründet. Bey dem Begriffe einer Substanz hört der Begriff der Ursache auf. Sie ist selbst Ursache, aber nicht Wirkung. Wie soll auch etwas Ursache einer Substanz außer ihm seyn, so daß diese auch durch jenes seine Kraft fortdauerte? Denn da würden die Folgen der letztern blos Wirkungen der erstern seyn, und die letztere wäre also selbst kein letztes 5 Subject.

Der Satz: Alles Zufällige hat eine Ursache, sollte so lauten: Alles, was nur bedingter Weise existiren kann, hat eine Ursache.

Eben so die Nothwendigkeit des entis originarii ist nichts, als die Vorstellung seiner unbedingten Existenz. — Nothwendigkeit aber be- 10 deutet mehr, nämlich daß man auch erkennen könne, und zwar aus seinem Begriffe, daß es existire.

Das Bedürfniß der Vernunft, vom Bedingten zum Unbedingten aufzusteigen, betrifft auch die Begriffe selbst. Denn alle Dinge enthalten Realität, und zwar einen Grad derselben. Dieser wird immer als nur 15 bedingt möglich angesehen, nämlich so fern ich einen Begriff vom realissimo, wovon jener nur die Einschränkung enthält, voraussetze.

Alles Bedingte ist zufällig, und umgekehrt.

Das Urwesen, als das höchste Wesen (realissimum), kann entweder als ein solches gedacht werden, daß es alle Realität als Bestimmung in 20 sich enthalte. — Dies ist für uns nicht wirklich, denn wir kennen nicht alle Realität rein, wenigstens können wir nicht einsehen, daß sie bey ihrer großen Verschiedenheit allein in einem Wesen angetroffen werden könne. Wir werden also annehmen, daß es ens realissimum als Grund sey, und dadurch kann es als Wesen, was uns gänzlich, nach dem, was es enthält, 25 unerkennbar ist, vorgestellt werden.

Darin liegt eine vorzügliche Täuschung, daß, da man in der transscen- dentalen Theologie das unbedingt existirende Object zu kennen verlangt, weil das allein nothwendig seyn kann, man zu allererst den unbedingten Begriff von einem Object zum Grunde legt, der darin besteht, daß alle 30 Begriffe von eingeschränkten Objecten, als solchen, d. i. durch anhängende

The concept of cause ends with the concept of substance. It is itself cause, but not effect. Likewise, how can something outside of it be the cause of a substance so that the latter can even continue its efficacy by means of the former? For then the consequences of the latter would be mere effects of the former, and thus the latter would not be an ultimate subject.

———

The proposition, "Everything contingent has a cause," should read, "Everything that can exist only in a conditioned way, has a cause."

Even so, the necessity of the *entis originarii* is nothing but representation of its unconditioned existence. — Necessity means more than this, however, namely, that given its concept, it can also be known that it exists.

———

Reason's need to ascend from the conditioned to the unconditioned extends to concepts of reason as well. For all things contain reality, and indeed a [specific] degree of it. The latter is considered possible only as conditioned, that is, so far as I assume a concept of *realissimo*, of which the latter contains only the limitations.

Everything conditioned is contingent, and conversely.

———

The primordial being, as the ultimate being (*realissimum*) can be thought either [sic] as that which contains all reality in it as determination. Because we cannot know all pure reality, this is not actual for us; at least we have no insight into how, with its great diversity, it can be found alone in a single being. We will thus assume that it is the *ens realissimum* as ground, and, in that way, it can be represented as [the] being which is completely unknowable for us in terms of what it contains.

———

An illusion of the first order lies in [the fact] that since in transcendental theology one desires to know the unconditioned existing object — for it alone can be necessary — one first posits its ground to be the concept of an object that consists only in that all concepts are derived from limited objects as such, that is, by dependent negations,

Negationen oder defectus abgeleitet find, und blos der Begriff des realissimi, nämlich des Wesens, worin alle Prädicate real find, conceptus logice originarius (unbedingt) sey. Dieses hält man für einen Beweis, daß nur ein ens realissimum nothwendig sein könne, oder
5 umgekehrt, daß das absolut Nothwendige ens realissimum sey.

Man will den Beweis vermeiden, daß ens realissimum nothwendig existire, und beweiset lieber, daß, wenn ein solches existirt, es ein realissimum seyn müsse. (Nun müßte man also beweisen, daß Eines unter allem Existirenden schlechthin nothwendig existire, und das kann man auch
10 wohl.) Der Beweis aber sagt nichts weiter als: wir haben gar keinen Begriff von dem, was einem nothwendigen Wesen, als solchem, für Eigenschaften zukommen, als daß es unbedingt seiner Existenz nach existire. Was aber dazu gehöre, wissen wir nicht. Unter unserm Begriffen von Dingen ist der logisch unbedingte, aber doch durchgängig bestimmte,
15 der des realissimi. Wenn wir also diesem Begriffe auch ein Object als correspondirend annehmen dürfen, so würde es das ens realissimum seyn. Aber wir sind nicht befugt, für unsern bloßen Begriff auch ein solches Object anzunehmen.

Unter der Hypothese, daß etwas existirt, folgt: daß auch irgend etwas
20 nothwendig existirt, aber schlechtweg und ohne alle Bedingung kann doch nicht erkannt werden, daß etwas nothwendig existire, der Begriff von einem Dinge, seinen inneren Prädicaten nach, mag auch angenommen werden, wie man wolle, und es kann bewiesen werden, daß dies schlechterdings unmöglich sey. Also habe ich auf den Begriff eines Wesens ge-
25 schlossen, von dessen Möglichkeit sich Niemand einen Begriff machen kann.

Warum schließe ich aber aufs Unbedingte? Weil dieses den obersten Grund des Bedingten enthalten soll. Der Schluß ist also: 1) Wenn etwas existirt, so ist auch etwas Unbedingtes. 2) Was unbedingt existirt, existirt als schlechthin nothwendiges Wesen. Das letztere ist keine nothwendige
30 Folgerung, denn das Unbedingte kann für eine Reihe nothwendig seyn, es selber aber, und die Reihe, mag immer zufällig seyn. Dieses letztere ist nicht ein Prädicat der Dinge (wie etwa, ob sie bedingt, oder unbedingt sind), sondern betrifft die Existenz der Dinge, mit allen ihren Prädicaten, ob sie nämlich an sich nothwendig, oder nicht sey. Es ist
35 also ein bloßes Verhältniß des Objectes zu unserm Begriffe.

Ein jeder Existenzialsatz ist synthetisch, also auch der Satz: Gott existirt. Sollte er analytisch seyn, so müßte die Existenz aus dem bloßen Begriffe von einem solchen möglichen Wesen ausgewickelt werden können. Nun ist dieses auf zwiefache Weise versucht worden: 1) Es liegt in dem

and just the concept of the real (*realissimi*), namely, the being in which all predicates are real, is the *conceptus logice originarius* (unconditioned). This is taken as a proof that only one *ens realissimum* can be necessary, or vice versa, that the absolute necessity is *ens realissimum*.

One wants to avoid the proof that the *ens realissimum* necessarily exists and wants to prove instead that if such a necessary being exists it must be an *ens realissimum*. (It would have thus to be proved that among all existing beings one exists absolutely necessarily, and that can also indeed be done.) However, the proof asserts nothing more than that we have absolutely no concept of what properties pertain to a necessary being as such, except that its existence is unconditioned. However, we do not know what belongs to it. Among our concepts of things is the logically unconditioned, but yet completely determined, concept of the *realissimi*. If we allow ourselves to assume that an object corresponds to this concept, it will be the *ens realissimum*. However, we are not entitled to assume such an object for our mere concept.

Under the hypothesis that something exists, it follows that something also necessarily exists, but simply and with no condition it cannot also be known that something necessarily exists. The concept of a thing in terms of its internal predicates may be assumed as desired and it can be proven that this thing is absolutely impossible. Thus, I have concluded to the concept of a being whose possibility no one can form a concept of.

But why do I draw a conclusion to the unconditioned? Because this must contain the ultimate ground of the conditioned. The reasoning therefore is: 1) "If something exists, something is also unconditioned." 2) "What exists as unconditioned, exists as an absolutely necessary being." The latter is not a necessary conclusion, because the unconditioned can be necessary to a series, but itself and the series may always remain contingent. Contingency is not a predicate of things (as for example whether they are conditioned or unconditioned) but rather concerns the existence of things, including all their predicates, i.e., whether or not they are necessary in themselves. Thus, it is a mere relation of an object to our concept.

Every existential proposition is synthetic, including thus the proposition, "God exists." Should it be analytic, one would have to be able to unfold its existence from the mere concept of such a possible being. Now this has been attempted in two ways: 1) The existence of the most

Begriffe des allerrealesten Wesens die Existenz desselben, denn sie ist
Realität. 2) Es liegt im Begriffe eines nothwendig existirenden Wesens
der Begriff der höchsten Realität, als die einzige Art, wie die absolute
Nothwendigkeit eines Dinges (welche, wenn irgend was existirt, ange=
nommen werden muß) gedacht werden kann.   Sollte nun ein noth=   5
wendiges Wesen in seinem Begriff schon die höchste Realität einschließen,
diese aber (wie No. 1 sagt) nicht den Begriff einer absoluten Nothwendig=
keit, folglich die Begriffe sich nicht reciprociren lassen, so würde der Begriff
des realissimi conceptus latior seyn als der Begriff des necessarii, d. i.
es würden noch andre Dinge, als das realissimum, entia necessaria   10
seyn können. Nun wird aber dieser Beweis gerade dadurch geführt, daß
das ens necessarium nur auf eine einzige Art gedacht werden könne, usw.

Eigentlich ist das πρῶτον ψεῦδος darin gelegen: das necessarium
enthält in seinem Begriffe die Existenz, folglich eines Dinges, als omni=
moda determinatio, folglich läßt sich diese omnimoda determinatio   15
aus seinem Begriffe (nicht bloß schließen) ableiten, welches falsch ist,
denn es wird nur bewiesen, daß, wenn er sich aus einem Begriffe ableiten
lassen sollte, dieses der Begriff des realissimi (der allein ein Begriff
ist, welcher zugleich die durchgängige Bestimmung enthält) seyn muß.

Es heißt also: wenn wir die Existenz eines necessarii, als eines   20
solchen, sollten einsehen können, so müßten wir die Existenz eines Dinges
aus irgend einem Begriffe ableiten können, d. i. die omnimodam deter=
minationem. Dieses ist aber der Begriff eines realissimi. Also müßten
wir die Existenz eines necessarii aus dem Begriffe des realissimi ableiten
können, welches falsch ist. Wir können nicht sagen, daß ein Wesen die=   25
jenigen Eigenschaften habe, ohne welche ich sein Daseyn, als nothwendig,
nicht aus Begriffen erkennen würde, wenngleich diese Eigenschaften
nicht als constitutive Produkte des ersten Begriffes, sondern nur als
conditio sine qua non angenommen werden.

Zum Prinzip der Erkenntniß, die a priori synthetisch ist, gehört,   30
daß die Zusammensetzung das einzige a priori ist, was, wenn es nach
Raum und Zeit überhaupt geschieht, von uns gemacht werden muß.
Das Erkenntniß aber für die Erfahrung enthält den Schematism, ent=
weder den realen Schematism (transscendental), oder den Schematism
nach der Analogie (symbolisch). — Die objective Realität der Categorie   35
ist theoretisch, die der Idee ist nur praktisch. — Natur und Freyheit.

---

real being is contained in its concept, because it is reality; 2) The concept of the supreme reality is contained in the concept of a necessarily existent being, as the only manner in which the absolute necessity of a thing (which, must be assumed if anything at all exists) can be thought. Now if a necessary being must already include the supreme reality in its concept, but the latter (as No. 1 asserts) does not contain the concept of an absolute necessity, so that the concepts are not reciprocal, the concept of the *realissimi* would be *conceptus latior*, [greater] than the concept of the *necessarii*, that is there could be things other than the *realissimum* which could be *entia necessaria*. Now this proof will be managed through the fact that the *ens necessarium* can be thought in only one way, etc.

Properly speaking, the πρῶτον ψεῖδος, lies in this: that the *necessarium* contains existence in its concept, consequently the *omnimoda determinatio* may be derived (not merely concluded) from its concept. But this is false, because it has only proved that if it is to be derived from a concept, it must be the concept of the *realissimi* (which is the only concept that contains complete determination).

This is to say that, if we must be able to grasp the existence of a *necessarii*, we must be able to derive the existence of a thing from some concept, i.e., the *omnimodam determinationem*. But this is the concept of a *realissimi*. Thus we would have to be able to derive the existence of a *necessarii* from the concept of the *realissimi*, which is false. We cannot say that a being has those properties without which I would not know its existence as necessary from concepts, even although those properties were not assumed to be constitutive products of the first concept, but only to be its *conditio sine qua non*.

It belongs to the principle of a priori synthetic knowledge that composition is the only a priori principle which must be made by us if it obtains in space and time in general. Knowledge for experience contains schematism, either a real schematism (transcendental), or schematism by analogy (symbolic). — The objective reality of the category is theoretical, of the idea only practical. — Nature and freedom.

Translator's Notes

The notes that follow refer the reader to other works by Kant, where he discusses the relevant issues in greater detail. These references are to *Kant's gesammelte Schriften*, hrsg. Preussischen Akademie der Wissenschaften, (28 vols.; Berlin and Leipzig: G. Reimer and Walter de Gruyter and Co., 1901 − −) by volume and page number. References to the *Critique of Pure Reason* are to the A and B page numbers. In the following I coordinate the main works to which I refer in the notes with the best readily available English translations, in all of which one finds the Akademie edition's pagination, to which all my citations refer by volume and page number.

I. *Untersuchung uber die Deutlichkeit der Grundsätze der naturlichen Theologie und der Moral*, II, 273-302.

Ia. *Enquiry Concerning the clarity of the principles of natural theology and ethics*, in *Kant: Selected pre-Critical Writings*, trans. G.B. Kerferd and D.E. Walford, (New York, Manchester University Press, 1968), pp. 3-35. Cited as *Enquiry*.

II. *Prolegomena zu einer jeden künftigen Metaphysik, die als Wissenschaft wird auftreten konnen*, IV, 253-384.

IIa. *Prolegomena to Any Future Metaphysics that Will be Able to Come Forward as a Science*, trans. James W. Ellington, (Indianapolis: Hackett Publishing Co., 1977). Cited as *Prolegomena*.

III. *Metaphysische Anfangsgründe der Naturwissenschaft*, IV, 384-464.

IIIa. *Metaphysical Foundations of Natural Science*, trans. James Ellington, (Indianapolis: Hackett Publishing Co., 1982). Cited as *Foundations*.

IV. *Kritik der praktischen Vernunft*, V, 1-164.

Notes

IVa. *Critique of Practical Reason*, trans. Lewis White Beck, (Indianapolis: Bobbs-Merrill, 1956). Cited as *C. Prac. R.*

V. *Kritik der Urtheilskraft*, V, 165-486.

Va. *Critique of Judgment*, trans. James Creed Meredith, (Oxford: The Clarendon Press, 1964). Cited as *C. Judgment*.

VI. *Anthropologie in pragmatischer Hinsicht*, VII, 117-334.

VIa. *Anthropology from a Pragmatic Point of View*, trans. Mary J. Gregor (The Hague: Martinus Nijhoff, 1974). Cited as *Anthropology*.

VII. *Über eine Entdeckung, nach der alle neue Kritik der reinen Vernunft durch eine altere entbehrlich gemacht werden Soll*, VIII, 185-252.

VIIa. *On a Discovery According to which Any New Critique of Pure Reason Has Been Made Superfluous by an Earlier One*, in *The Kant-Eberhard Controversy* by Henry E. Allison, (Baltimore: The Johns Hopkins University Press, 1973). pp. 105-160. Cited as *Discovery*.

VIII. *Logik*, IX, 1-150.

VIIIa. *Logic*, trans. Robert S. Hartmann and Wolfgang Schwartz, (Indianapolis: Bobbs-Merrill, 1974). Cited as *Logic*.

IX. *Briefe*, X-XII.

IXa. *Kant: Philosophical Correspondence*, 1979-99, ed. and trans.

X. *Zum ewigen Frieden*, VIII, 341-386

Xa. *Perpetual Peace*, in *Perpetual Peace and Other Essays on Politics, History, and Morals*, trans. Ted Humphrey (Indianapolis: Hackett Publishing Company, 1983). Cited as *Perpetual Peace*.

1. *Preisschriften uber die Frage: Welche Fortschritte hat die metaphysik seit Leibnitzens und Wolffs Zeiten in Deutschland gemacht?* von Johann Cristoph Schwab, Karl Leonhard Reinhold und Johann Heinrich Abicht, Herausgegeben von der Konigl. Preuss. Akademie der Wissenschaften (Berlin: Friedrich Maurer, 1796). The

volume contains Schwab's, *Ausführliche Erörterung der von der Konigl. Akademie der Wissenschaften zu Berlin fur das Jahr 1791 vorgelegten Frage: "Welches sind die wirklichen Fortschritte, die die Metaphysik seit Leibnitzens und Wolffens Zeiten in Deutschland gemacht hat?,"* Reinhold's, *Versuch einer Beantwortung der von der Konigl. Ak. der Wissensch. zu Berlin aufgestellten Frage: "Was hat die Metaphysik seit Wolff und Leibnitz gewonnen?,"* and Abicht's, *Versuch einer Beantwortung der Aufgabe: "Welche Fortschritte hat die Metaphysik in Deutschland seit Leibnitz und Wolff gemacht?"* Schwab was a follower of Wolff's and contributor to Johhann August Eberhardt's *Philosophisches Archiv*, the successor to his earlier *Philosophisches Magazin*. Reinhold's and Abicht's works are defenses of Kant's views.

2. That is, pp. 259-86 are taken from the first manuscript, while pp. 286-311 are taken from the second. The first supplement, pp. 315-326, contains the third manuscript, and the second supplement, pp. 326-329, contains that portion of the first manuscript not printed in the body of the text. The third supplement contains the marginalia. One infers from Rink's comments that he is the one who labeled the manuscripts I, II, III, and that the designation he gave each was a function of its content and relative polish.

3. This is the only statement by a contemporary that I know of that supports the view that Kant's writings may have been assembled as a "patchwork." Although it is not sufficient to support the views of Adickes, Vaihinger and Kemp-Smith, one can only wonder how seriously these comments of Rink's should be taken.

4. The asterisks have been the source of considerable scholarly speculation and consternation. They occur at pages 276 (2), 277 (3,2) 280 (3), 290 (3), and 292 (3); the numbers in parentheses indicate how many asterisks occur in a grouping. Scholars have wondered if some distinction is to be drawn between groups of 2 and groups of 3 but have so far been unable to discern one.

5. Kant says of philosophy generally that it is "the mere idea of a possible science, which is never given *in concreto*," (A838/B866) A838/B866-A839/B867 is useful for understanding this entire passage. See also A845/B873.

Notes

6. Completeness (*Vollstandigkeit*) is an integral part of Kant's concept of philosophy and metaphysics. See A664/B693-A686/B694 and *Prolegomena*, IV, 331-32.

7. Kant defines "ultimate end" (*Endzweck*) as "that end that requires no other as the condition of its possiblity." *C. Judgment*, V, 434-36.

8. For Kant's views on man's natural disposition toward metaphysics see B22-24 and *Prolegomena*, IV, 327-28.

9. This is only one of several definitions that Kant gives metaphysics in the *Progress*. Each is given from a different perspective, although this is the most general. Cp. pp. 261, 316.

10. I have translated *Ubersinnlich* as supersensible throughout. The supersensible realm is that to which the formal properties of sensibility, neither those belonging to man nor to other possible cognitive agents, simply do not pertain; consequently, there can be no cognition of the supersensible realm. The supersensible realm comprises three fundamental components, God, freedom and immortality, the supersensible over us, in us, and after us. See 294-95. The non-sensible (*Nichtsinnlich*), as Kant defines it here, contrasts with the supersensible in that the former cannot have a determinate relation to the sensible, while the latter can.

11. See A246/B303-A247 and A845/B873, where Kant asserts that transcendental philosophy "considers only the understanding and reason, in a system of concepts and principles that relate to objects in general, but does not presuppose that the objets are *given* (*Ontologia*)...."

12. This reiterates the concept of a critique of pure reason that Kant presents at B24-27.

13. "To define this idea [the idea of the highest good] practically, that is, sufficiently for the maxims of our rational conduct, is [the task of] the doctrine of wisdom, which, as a science, is philosophy in the sense in which the ancients understood this word, for whom it meant instruction in the concept wherein the highest good was to be placed and in the conduct by which it was to be obtained." *C. Prac. R.,* V, 108. Beck's translation.

14. Cp. p. 263.

15. See A712/B740-A738/B766, esp. A719/B747-A720/B748 and A726/B754. On reason see A298/B355-A302/B359.

16. See *C. Judgment*, V. 293-96. This method is in accord with the first maxim of common human understanding. See also A666/B694.

17. This theme was first struck by Kant in the *Enquiry*, see II, 276-282, and became, with minor revisions one of the foundations of the critical philosophy. See note 15.

18. See BVII-XXIV.

19. In the *Critique of Pure Reason* Kant uses the term regress to designate the process whereby reason arrives at ultimate conditions that cannot be given in sensuous intuitions. See A508/B536-A515/B543. I have chosen "retreat" to translate *Ruckgang* so as to avoid confusion between this skeptical criticism of dogmatism and reason's regression to ultimate conditions.

20. See AVII-XIV. On the role of the Antinomies in Kant's thought see Bxviii-xxxvii.

21. See A6/B10-A10/B14, *Prolegomena*, V, 266-274 and *Discovery*, VIII, 228-230.

22. See B14-B18, *Prolegomena*, IV, 260-261.

23. I have chosen to translate *Erkenntnis* by "cognition" or "knowledge," depending on the context rather than by Kemp-Smith's "mode of knowledge." I have always found the latter confusing by virtue of its lack of *prima facie* meaningfulness, although it avoids some problems I have had to face. While I believe that Kant's primary use of *Erkenntnis* is to designate judgments consisting of concepts for which corresponding intuitions can be given, cognition, he also sometimes uses it in a looser sense for any judgment that is a knowledge claim, knowledge.

24. See A19/B33-A21/B35, A494/B522-A495/B523, and *Prolegomena*, IV, 318-20.

Notes

25. See B4. "Necessity and strict universality are thus sure criteria of a priori cognition, and belong inseparably together."

26. This is a complex passage because of its use of the Latin derivative *Objekt* and the more properly German *Gegenstand*, both of which are most properly and gracefully translated by "object." The distinction here is between what, given our cognitive capacitites, we are able to think an object to be in terms of its conceptual and intuitive form, and an object, consisting of both its conceptual and intuitive aspects, as it is actually given in empirical awareness. One can find this distinction in Kant's writings from the *Prolegomena* on.

27. See B160, note and *Prolegomena*, IV, 320-322.

28. The distinction between an *intellectus archetypus* and an *intellectus ectypus* was important in allowing Kant to formulate the fundamental tenets of the Critical philosophy. See the letter to Marcus Herz, 21 February 1772, *Letters*, X, 123-130, A254/B310-A260/B315 and B72.

29. See below pp. 269ff., B131-136, B139-40, B150-159, and *Anthropology*, VII, 134n.

30. The foregoing two paragraphs, and *Prolegomena*, IV, 280-294, present the doctrines of the Transcendental Aesthetic, esp. A26/B42-A30/B45 and A32/B49-B71, in accord with analytic, as opposed to synthetic, method.

31. The translations I have chosen for "*Schein*" and "*Anschein*" are almost arbitrary. But it is clear from the context that Kant intends "*Apparenz*" and "*Schein*" to be regarded as Latinate and Germanic synonyms for the same notion and that "*Anschein*" is to denote something stronger than either of them.

32. See B131-136, B139-140, B148-159, A348-351, and *Prolegmena*, IV, 333-334.

33. See *Letters*, XII, 222-25, letter to J.H. Tieftrunk, December 11, 1797. See also B154-55 and B202n.

34. See A78/B104-A79/B105.

35. See A70/B95 and A80/B105. On judgment see B94, *Prolegomena*, IV, 304-06.

36. See A81/B107-A82/B108.

37. See A137/B176., esp. A141/B181-A142.

38. For the relation between cognition (*Erkenntnis*) and experience (*Erfahrung*), see B161, A230/B282-A232/B284, *Prolegomena*, IV, 304-05.

39. But see *Prolegomena*, IV, 318-20.

40. See B1.

41. See A84/B116-A87/B119.

42. See A92/B124-B128, *Prolegomena*, IV, 297-98, 304-05, and *Logic*, IX, 113.

43. See A166/B207ff.

44. See *Prolegomena*, IV, 320-22.

45. This, of course, raises the issue concerning the specific nature of his idealism that Kant so often attempted to clarify. See A366-380, B274-279, *Prolegomena*, IV, 373-75.

46. See *Discovery*, VIII, 193-198.

47. This is the point of A24/B39 and A31-32/B47. See also A43/B60-A46/B63.

48. For this and the other ciriticisms of Leibnizian doctrine that occur in the work, especially on pp. 280-86, see A260/B316-A292/B349.

49. See *Discovery*, VIII, 198-207. Kant's references to the "metaphysician of the good old kind" likely refer not only to Leibniz and Wolff but also Eberhard and his followers.

50. This strikes one of the earliest themes of Kant's thought. See *Enquiry*, II, 275-301.

Notes

51. See *C. Judgment*, V, 351-54.

52. On analogical reasoning see *C. Judgment,* V, 461-466 and *Logic,* IX, 132.

53. See A 845/B873-A851/B879.

54. The four items that follow constitute recapitulation of Leibniz's basic doctrines as they are presented in the *Monadology.*

55. Kant errs in reporting Leibniz's position here, since the latter never used the concept of succession in his analysis of space. One may, I think, regard Kant as referring elliptically to Leibniz's analysis of time, for Kant often states that he can formulate criticisms of Leibniz's theory of time that are analogous to his criticisms of Leibniz's theory of space.

56. Kant uses precisely these same examples against Leibniz's view in his essay of 1763 *An Attempt to Introduce the Concept of Negative Quantities into Philosophy*, A-A., II, 179-188.

57. See *Foundations*, IV, 467-479.

58. See B406-432, *Prolegomena*, IV, 333-37.

59. See A298/B355-A309/B366.

60. See A408/B435-A420/B448.

61. See Avii-viii, B19-24.

62. See B110, A158/B197-A162/B202, A528/B556-A532/B560.

63. I have found no explanation for the brackets around this passage.

64. See A162/B202-A166/B207.

65. See A789/B817-A791/B819.

66. See A166/B207-A176/B218.

67. See Bvi-xiv.

68. See A503/B531-A507/B535.

69. See *Logic*, IX, 116-17.

70. See A532/B560-A557/B585, esp. A545/B573-A552/B580.

71. For this and subsequent passages concerned with the same topics, *C. Judgment*, V, 447-453 and *C. Prac. R.*, V, 107-113, 134-142.

72. See A797/B825-A819/B847, *C. Prac. R.*, V, 132-34, *C. Judgment*, V, 467-474.

73. Reading *"desselben"* to refer to *"die Freiheit."*

74. *C. Prac. R.*, V, 19-20 contains relevant definitions of knowledge of nature and practical knowledge.

75. The most concise and comprehensive discussion of the epistemic modes in this paragraph and the ones that follow is *Logic*, IX, 65-81. But see also A820/B848-A821/B859 and *C. Judgment*, V, 461-474. I have deviated from tradition in translating *Furwahrhalten* by assent, rather than holding-to-be-true, but "assent" is shorter and has, I believe, the same connotations, suggesting as it does subjective acceptance, regardless of objective truth.

76. See *Logic*, IX, 81-6, *C. Prac. R.*, V, 11.

77. The text seems to be defective here; for the reading *"Felde des Sinnlichen"* conflicts with everything else Kant says here and in other places, including the *Critique of Pure Reason*. I have therefore read *"Felde des Ubersinnlichen."*

78. See A327/B383-A328/B385, *Logic*, IX, 92-3.

79. See *Logic*, IX, 40-9 and A759/B787ff.

80. A567/B596-A642/B670, "The Ideal of Pure Reason" is relevant to this entire section.

81. Kant, of course, was puzzled by the moves he describes here in 1763, for he attacks them in two early works, *The Only Possible Basis for a Demonstration of God's Existence* and *An Attempt to Introduce the Concept of Negative Quantities into Philosophy*.

82. See *C. Judgment*, V, 392-95.

Notes

83. See A592/B620-A602/B630.

84. See A603/B632-A614/B642.

85. A218/B265-A235/B282.

86. See *C. Prac. R.,* V, 124-141, *C. Judgment,* 447-453.

87. See *C. Judgment,* V, 479f.

88. The text seems defective at this point.

89. The foregoing section may be out of place; it might better be placed after the two following sections but before the Appendix, i.e., between pp. 310 and 311.

90. This passage seems defective inasmuch as from the context one would expect Kant to be speaking of God and God's will, but the grammatical structure prevents that.

91. See B131-36, B421-23.

92. See *Discovery,* VIII, 207-210.

93. See *C. Prac. R.,* V, 121-24.

94. See *C. Prac. R.,* V, 46.

95. This is the "more polished" third draft to which Rink refers on p. 4. It covers roughly the same material as pages 259-80 in the main body of the work.

96. Compare with pp. 260-1.

97. See A313/B370-A319/B375.

98. See Kant's letter to Christian Garve, *Letters,* XⅡ, p. 258.

99. See *C. Judgment,* V, 362-66.

100. Namely, Kant himself, in *The Only Possible Basis for a Demonstration of the Existence of God,* II, 70-92.

101. Compare with pp. 286-292.